Intellectual Property
Law Fundamentals

Intellectual Property
Law Fundamentals

Michael E. Jones
Walter Toomey
M. Nancy Aiken
Michelle Bazin

CAROLINA ACADEMIC PRESS
Durham, North Carolina

Library of Congress Cataloging-in-Publication Data

Jones, Michael E., author.
Intellectual property law fundamentals / Michael E. Jones, Walter
Toomey, M. Nancy Aiken, Michelle Bazin.
   pages cm
Includes bibliographical references and index.
ISBN 978-1-61163-390-0 (alk. paper)
1. Intellectual property--United States. I. Toomey, Walter, author.
II. Aiken, M. Nancy, author. III. Bazin, Michelle, author. IV. Title.

KF2979.J66 2013
346.7304'8--dc23

2013038163

CAROLINA ACADEMIC PRESS
700 Kent Street
Durham, North Carolina 27701
Telephone (919) 489-7486
Fax (919) 493-5668
www.cap-press.com

Printed in the United States of America

Dedication

Michael gives thanks to his wife, Christine, whose love, kindness, and poetic nature make everything in life possible and worthwhile.

Walter dedicates this book to Alanna and Walter Scott Toomey, the two best parts of his life.

Nancy dedicates this book to Adam, Jack, and George, and to her parents and brother with thanks for their endless support and expertise.

Michelle acknowledges and thanks her husband, children, friends, and family for their encouragement, interest, and support and dedicates this book to those who desire and strive to learn more about Intellectual Property.

Contents

Unit 2 · Trademark Basics

Unit 3 · Domain Name Basics

Unit 4 · Geographical Indication Basics

Unit 5 · Patent Basics

Unit 6 · Trade Secret Basics

Preface

This introductory text explores the origins, sources, function, and values of the exciting world of Intellectual Property (IP). Topics covered include copyright, trademark, patent, trade secret, domain names, and geographical indication, with primary attention given to IP law in the United States and ample coverage of key international laws. The history, development, modern use, and enforcement of IP rights are explored in depth. The material is covered in plain language and presented in an easy to absorb modular format. This book is designed as a text for classroom use.

Text Outcomes: Paralegal and Legal Studies students using this text should be able to:

1. Identify and describe the basic types of protectable IP rights in the United States;
2. Differentiate between the different forms of IP and the specific common law and statutory rights secured under both United States and to a more limited degree foreign law;
3. Identify the limits of IP rights by duration and statutory interpretation of language like the "fair use" doctrine for copyrights, and constitutional boundaries under the First Amendment;
4. Understand the basic research process used to discover or locate existing protectable interests in IP in the United States;
5. Understand the basic application processes used in the United States to register certain types of IP in order to obtain greater protection, and be familiar with the scope of that greater protection;
6. Demonstrate a basic familiarity with some common government websites and online research tools used in IP legal practice;
7. Articulate causes of action to protect IP rights, and understand the common defenses to claims of infringement or unfair competition;

8. Understand the various remedies available to address IP infringement or unfair competition in the United States, including civil and criminal proceedings and monetary and non-monetary remedies;

9. Discuss the public policy and societal value considerations behind modern IP rights and their limits.

Acknowledgments

Numerous people played a vital role in shaping this text. One of the most valuable aspects of teaching at a university is the opportunity to develop meaningful collaborations with academic colleagues. To that end the authors collectively thank each other for their interaction, commitment and friendship. We were fortunate to have the support of academic administrators including the Provost Ahmed Abdelal, Dean Luis M. Falcon, and Executive Director Pauline Carroll.

Our wise and experienced editor, Beth Hall, assisted us throughout the entire writing, editing and publishing process. Her staff at Carolina Academic Press found ways to tweak the manuscript and substantially helped to improve the final product.

A former University of Massachusetts Lowell undergraduate and current law student, Ian Schaeffer, provided invaluable research and ideas especially on the copyright material. Our outside reviewers offered meaningful assistance to make the text tighter and more focused.

Comparison and Reference Chart

	Copyright	Trademark	Geographical Indications	Patent	Trade Secret
Subject Matter Protected	Works of original authorship fixed in a tangible medium of expression such as writing, music, painting, photo, literature, software, games, sculpture, sound recordings	Identifying devices, signs, or symbols, which may include words, names, emblems, designs, and logos	Identifying devices, signs, or symbols, which may include words, names, emblems, designs, and logos	Process, machine, manufacture, or composition of matter, or any new and useful improvement thereof	Undisclosed information that is valuable because it is secret, such as a formula, customer list, or business information
Requirements	Originality, expression, fixation	Identify and distinguish sources of goods or services without confusion	Identify and distinguish the geographical source of products	Novelty, nonobviousness, utility, definiteness and enablement	Reasonable effort to maintain secrecy, information not easily obtainable
Term of Protection	For works created after January 1, 1978, life of the author plus an additional 70 years. For an anonymous work, a pseudonymous work, or a work made for hire, a term of 95 years from the year of its first publication or a term of 120 years from the year of its creation, whichever expires first. For works first published prior to 1978, the term varies	20 year renewable federal terms, potentially unlimited state protection with continuous use	Protected as trademarks in the United Sates.	20 years from the effective filing date, 14 years for design patents	Potentially limitless as long as secrecy is maintained
Manner of Acquisition	Automatic; Registration with U.S. Copyright Office provides advantages	Automatic with use. Federal and state registration grants more protection	Automatic with use. Federal and state registration grants more protection	Application to the PTO	Automatic as long as secrecy is maintained
Infringement	Copying substantial portion of work; substantial similarity	Likelihood of confusion, mistake, deception, or dilution	Likelihood of confusion, mistake, deception, or dilution	Making, using, offering to sell, selling, or importing into the U.S.	Unauthorized use or disclosure of information obtained through improper means
Variations		GI, Service Marks, Certification Marks, Collective Marks, Trade Dress		Design Patent, Plant Patent	

Intellectual Property
Law Fundamentals

Chapter 1

Introduction

*"If nature has made any one thing less susceptible than all others of ex-
clusive property, it is the action of the thinking power called an idea [...]"*
—Thomas Jefferson

The quote above succinctly summarizes one of the biggest challenges faced
by legal scholars, politicians, captains of industry, local artisans, scientists, inventors, authors, and artists alike. In a world that seemingly grows smaller
each day as technology advances and increases the ease with which people
around the world can near-instantly and anonymously communicate and share
vast amounts of information, there is pressure to promote useful ideas and
creative expressions by granting and protecting exclusive property rights to
those who produce them. This task is not easy, and it requires the careful balancing of monopoly rights with the potential benefit to society as a whole from
the encouragement of useful ideas and creative expression.

Many brilliant thinkers have wrestled with the questions of whether and
how to grant exclusive property rights, for any duration, in ideas. Not all of those
thinkers have come to the conclusion that monopoly rights are necessary for
the cultivation of valuable ideas, as an expanded version of the quote above
reveals:

> "If nature has made any one thing less susceptible than all others
> of exclusive property, it is the action of the thinking power called an
> idea, which an individual may exclusively possess as long as he keeps
> it to himself; but the moment it is divulged, it forces itself into the
> possession of every one, and the receiver cannot dispossess himself of
> it. Its peculiar character, too, is that no one possesses the less, because
> every other possesses the whole of it. He who receives an idea from me,
> receives instruction himself without lessening mine; as he who lights
> his taper at mine, receives light without darkening me. That ideas
> should freely spread from one to another over the globe, for the moral
> and mutual instruction of man, and improvement of his condition,

seems to have been peculiarly and benevolently designed by nature, when she made them, like fire, expansible over all space, without lessening their density in any point, and like the air in which we breathe, move, and have our physical being, incapable of confinement or exclusive appropriation. Inventions then cannot, in nature, be a subject of property. Society may give an exclusive right to the profits arising from them, as an encouragement to men to pursue ideas which may produce utility, but this may or may not be done, according to the will and convenience of the society, without claim or complaint from any body. Accordingly, it is a fact, as far as I am informed, that England was, until we copied her, the only country on earth which ever, by a general law, gave a legal right to the exclusive use of an idea. In some other countries it is sometimes done, in a great case, and by a special and personal act, but, generally speaking, other nations have thought that these monopolies produce more embarrassment than advantage to society; and it may be observed that the nations which refuse monopolies of invention, are as fruitful as England in new and useful devices."

—Thomas Jefferson, Letter to Isaac McPherson, Monticello, August 13, 1813

The concept Jefferson references, that ideas can and should move freely as they can do so with little cost and without devaluing the idea, has been repeated many times in debates on the validity, social value, and morality of exclusive intellectual property rights. Various free-culture, open-source, and intellectual freedom organizations have voiced strong objection to laws that may be used to limit the availability of life-saving technology and medicine, to restrict access to basic software, or to hoard great artistic and literary works in the collections of wealthy individuals or institutions. Advances in computer technology that have enabled the rapid creation and transfer of virtually limitless, accurate duplications of music, movies, electronic books, and high-quality images have only fueled this debate:

"Society confronts the simple fact that when everyone can possess every intellectual work of beauty and utility—reaping all the human value of every increase of knowledge—at the same cost that any one person can possess them, it is no longer moral to exclude. If Rome possessed the power to feed everyone amply at no greater cost than that of Caesar's own table, the people would sweep Caesar violently away if anyone were left to starve. But the bourgeois system of ownership demands that knowledge and culture be rationed by the ability to pay."

—Eben Moglen, Prof. at Columbia University and Chairman of the Software Freedom Law Center

Despite these reservations, the prevailing view is that some form of exclusive property rights must be granted to those who invent and create in order to provide a financial incentive to promote the development of new ideas. The search for a compromise between monopoly and public interest has yielded a number of limitations on the duration and scope of property interests that inventors, authors, and artists receive under the law. These restrictions have largely prevented conventional monopolies from emerging, but they have hardly diminished the importance and value of intellectual property. In the United States, where the economy has shifted in large part from industrial production to cultural and technological production, intellectual property rights are more important than ever. This shift is reflected by markedly different political rhetoric than the concerned and cautious thoughts of Thomas Jefferson:

> "What's more, we're going to aggressively protect our intellectual property. Our single greatest asset is the innovation and the ingenuity and creativity of the American people. It is essential to our prosperity and it will only become more so in this century. But it's only a competitive advantage if our companies know that someone else can't just steal that idea and duplicate it with cheaper inputs and labor. There's nothing wrong with other people using our technologies, we welcome it—we just want to make sure that it's licensed, and that American businesses are getting paid appropriately."

—Barack Obama, Remarks at the Export-Import Bank's Annual Conference, March 11, 2010

At the urging of industry, the world's intellectual property laws have rapidly changed over the last several decades to provide more uniform and consistent protection of intellectual property rights internationally. The ease of doing business online has also prompted continued domestic changes to homogenize intellectual property rights throughout the states, either through federal legislation or widespread adoption of model state legislation. These changes have been positive, often reducing legal costs and clarifying expectations in legal disputes. As technological innovation continues to outpace legal innovation, however, there will be no shortage of new laws and efforts to promote and protect intellectual property.

That said, the basic core of intellectual property law in the United States has remained fairly stable even as new laws emerge to expand and protect it. That core of intellectual property law can be roughly divided into the law of copyright, trademark, patent, and trade secret. More recently in the United States, there has been greater legal recognition given to geographical indication and to the protection of domain names as a form of intellectual property as well. Each of these areas is related, and they often share common origins and overlap in some way. Successful business enterprises typically rely on many, if not all, of these areas of law to protect and promote their business assets and goodwill.

The following chapters explore the history, sources, and modern function of each of these interesting and dynamic areas of law. The academic and practical information included will provide a thorough and useful foundation for professional paralegals, students preparing for law school, and anyone interested in learning more about one of the most economically and socially important legal fields today.

Unit 1

Copyright Basics

Chapter 2

Introduction to Copyright

"The idea of copyright did not exist in ancient times, when authors frequently copied other authors at length in works of non-fiction. This practice was useful, and is the only way many authors' works have survived even in part." —Richard Stallman

Chapter Outline

Chapter Objectives

- Recognize what copyright protects.
- Understand the changes in copyright law since the first Federal Copyright Act.
- Know what becomes of old copyright.
- Explain the policy goals of copyright law.
- Identify copyright in practice.

2.1. Introduction to Copyright Law

Copyright is a form of intellectual property law that provides protection for published and unpublished *original works of authorship* fixed in a tangible medium of expression. One of the requirements for copyright protection is that the work of authorship be *original,* meaning the work must (1) be independently created by the author (as opposed to being copied from other works) and (2) exhibit a minimum degree of creativity by the author. Another requirement for copyright protection is that the work be *fixed* in a *tangible medium of expression.* This fixation requirement requires that the work of authorship be in some physical form or representation such as paper, canvas, tape, cd, disk or hard drive. Copyright law protects literary, dramatic, musical, artistic and other intellectual works, such as novels, movies, poetry, computer software, art and architecture. Copyright law protects the way things are expressed but it does not protect ideas, systems, facts or methods of operation.

2.2. A Short History of Copyright Law

Before the first copyright statute, copyright privileges and monopolies were legally available only to printers and publishers. The British Statute of Anne, enacted in England in 1710, was the first copyright statute. It opened the doors for authors to own a copyright for fourteen years. If the author survived the first fourteen years, it could be extended to twenty-eight years. Not all scholars agree whether The British Statute of Anne applied to the American Colonies. At the time, agriculture, not copyright, was a priority in the American Colonies' economy. Up until 1783, three private copyright acts were passed in America. Around that time, several authors filed petitions with the Continental Congress, the convention of delegates from the thirteen colonies serving as the governing body of the United States during the American Revolution. These authors sought to persuade the Continental Congress to protect and secure literary property. However, the Articles of Confederation did not give the Continental Congress the authority to issue copyright, so the Continental Congress passed a resolution encouraging the States to enact copyright statutes. Prior to this resolution, three states had copyright statutes in place. Following the Continental Congress' resolution, with the exception of Delaware, all of the remaining states enacted a copyright statute, ranging from two fourteen-year terms to twenty and twenty-one years, with no renewal rights. At that time Noah Webster, Jr. (cousin of the late politician Daniel Webster and whose name is synonymous with the dictionary in the United States, including the modern Merriam-Webster dictionary that was first published in 1828), had a critical role in lobbying the individual states in the 1780s to pass the first copyright laws in America.

In 1787, James Madison of Virginia and Charles Pinckney of South Carolina submitted proposals at the Constitutional Convention for Congressional power to grant copyright for a limited duration. As a result, Article I, Section 8, Clause 8, also known as the *Copyright Clause*, states that "Congress shall have the power to promote the Progress of Science and useful Arts by securing for limited Times to Authors and Inventors the exclusive Right to their respective Writings and Discoveries." The first federal *Copyright Act* adopted in the United States was passed in 1790. It granted copyright protection for a term of fourteen years from the time of recording title thereof, and if the author survived the end of the first term there was a right of renewal for another fourteen years. It provided protection to books, maps and charts. At that time, copyright registration was made in the U.S. District Court where the owner of the creative work resided. *The Philadelphia Spelling Book* by John Barry was the first copyright registration made in the United States. It was registered in the U.S. District Court of Pennsylvania on June 9, 1790. The Copyright Act of 1790 copied most of the terms from the British Statute of Anne and added its application to maps and charts.

The first general revision to the Copyright Act was made in February 1831. This revision added music to the works protected and extended the first term of copyright to twenty-eight years with an option to renew for fourteen additional years. Once again, Noah Webster, Jr. played an important role in this revision.

The second general revision to the Copyright Act was made in July 1870. This revision assigned all copyright activities, including deposit and registration to the Library of Congress, and started the indexing of the record of registrations. This legislation required all authors to deposit two (2) copies of their work in the United States with the Library of Congress. Since its inception in 1870, this requirement has supplied the Library of Congress with free books, photographs, maps, films, documents, sound recordings, computer programs, and other informational items and helped it to become the world's largest library with recent annual deposits valuing over $30 million dollars.

Despite these revisions to United States copyright law, American publishers continued to regard the work of a foreign author as unprotected *common property* creating numerous unauthorized American re-prints which could be offered to the public at very little cost. In response to this, a well-known author from England by the name of Charles Dickens and other foreign authors petitioned the United States Congress to join the international copyright union so that the pirating of foreign authors' work would discontinue in America. The United States government ignored the requests of these foreign authors. It wasn't until a famous American author, Samuel Langhorne Clemens, better known by his pen name, Mark Twain, complained that publishers were ignoring American authors' works in favor of English authors' works because the English authors' books could be reprinted for less since there weren't any royalty costs associated with such reprinting. Finally, in 1896, the United States joined the international copyright union and reciprocal copyright treaties with other nations were recognized.

The third general revision to the Copyright Act came in July 1909. This revision admitted certain classes of unpublished works to copyright registration, extended the renewal term from fourteen to twenty-eight years, and set the term of statutory protection for a work copyrighted in published form as being measured from the date of publication of the work.

The fourth general revision to the Copyright Act was made in October 1976. The principal provisions of this revision became effective on January 1, 1978. These revisions modernized existing copyright law and extended the term of protection for works created on or after January 1, 1978, to the life of the author plus fifty years.

On March 1, 1989, the United States became a member of the Berne Convention for the Protection of Literary and Artistic Works (the "*Berne Convention*"), an international treaty in copyright law. The Berne Convention consists of approximately one-hundred sixty-seven members. A Berne Convention member country must extend the same treatment to the works of nationals of other Berne Convention member countries as are enjoyed by its own nationals. Member countries of the Berne Convention are also obligated to adopt minimum standards for copyright protection. The Berne Convention is discussed in greater detail later in this copyright unit.

Major changes in copyright law came again in the 1990s. In December, 1990, Section 106A was added to the Copyright Act to include the *Visual Artists Rights Act* ("VARA"). VARA granted visual artists certain moral rights of attribution and integrity. We will evaluate VARA more extensively later in this copyright unit. In June, 1992, renewal registration became optional. Additionally, works that were copyrighted between January 1, 1964, and December 31, 1977, automatically renewed. In October, 1998, the controversial Sonny Bono Copyright Term Extension Act extended the term of copyright protection for most works to the life of the author plus seventy years after the author's death.

For a more detailed analysis of the history and notable dated in U.S. copyright law see Exhibit 2.1 at the end of this chapter. Notice that the scope, effect and term of copyright have never decreased over time.

2.3. What Becomes of Old Copyright?

When an original work of authorship isn't protected under copyright law it is said to be in the *public domain*, which means that anyone can use the work without permission from the author or its heirs.Works that fall within the public domain include:

1. Works published before 1923.
2. Works published between 1923 and 1963 that copyright protection was not renewed.
3. Works published before 1978 that lack proper copyright notice.
4. Works published between 1978 and 1989 with defective notice on the work and adequate efforts have not been made to correct the defects.
5. Works created before 1978 but not published before December 31, 2003.
6. Works prepared by a U.S. governmental officer or employee as part of its official duties.
7. Works consisting of solely facts or ideas.
8. Works deliberately placed in the public domain by the copyright owner.

Popular examples of works in the public domain include the Bible, *Moby Dick*, Shakespeare and Beethoven. Is the most recognized song in the English language, "Happy Birthday to You," in the public domain? The answer depends on whom you ask. The melody of the song comes from the song, "Good Morning to All," written and composed by sisters, Patty Hill and Mildred Hill in 1893, as a song for younger children to sing. The lyrics in "Happy Birthday to You" and its melody existed in print in 1912 without any credits or copyright notices. In 1935, The Clayton F. Summy Company registered the song for copyright registration. In 1988, Warner/Chappell Music, Inc. purchased the company that owned the copyright to "Happy Birthday to You" for $25 million. At that time, the value of the song was estimated to be $5 million. Using the 1935 copyright registration, Warner/Chappell Music, Inc. claims that copyright protection for the song in the United States does not expire until 2030. Robert Brauneis, an American law professor, has researched the song and its copyright protection and expressed his doubts that the song still has copyright protection. Most recently, a documentary filmmaker, Jennifer Nelson, brought a lawsuit against The Warner/Chappell Music, Inc. in response to their requirement that she pay them a $1,500 fee and enter into a license agreement to use the song in her documentary film.

There are several resources available to the general public that provide a wealth of public domain images, books, audio and film. The works provided through these resources are free and may be used without restrictions and permissions. Some examples of these websites are:

Smithsonian Institution Public Domain Images, http://www.flickr.com/photos/smithsonian

New York Times Public Domain Archives, http://commons.wikimedia.org/wiki/Category:Public_Domain_Images_from_the_New_York_Times

Project Gutenberg—collection public domain electronic books, http://www.gutenberg.org/wiki/Main_Page

Librivox—Public Domain of audiobooks, http://librivox.org/

Prelinger—a vast collection of advertising, educational, industrial, and amateur films, http://archive.org/details/prelinger

2.4. The Policy Goals of Copyright Law

Article I, Section 8, Clause 8 of the Constitution provides, "The Congress shall have power.... to promote the Progress of Science and useful Arts, by securing for limited Times to Authors and Inventors, the exclusive Right to their respective Writings and Discoveries." As you can see, copyright law provides an incentive for authors and artists to create works and control the reproduction of such works. Let's examine some of the policy goals of copyright law.

Economic Policy

Many scholars believe that without copyright protection, there is no incentive for an author or artist to produce or create an original work. Under this theory, the effort is to balance the protection, incentive and reward provided to the owner of copyright with the public benefit of widespread use and circulation of a copyrighted work. Let's consider music for example. Pandora radio's recent projected annual revenue was $425–432 million dollars of which

$212.9 million was returned to the copyright holders. SiriusXM radio's recent annual projected revenue in a recent year was $3.36 billion of which $268.8 million was returned to the copyright holders. Spotify's interactive streaming radio's recent projected annual revenue was $840 million, of which $588 million was returned to copyright holders. The United Kingdom, the United States, Canada, Australia, and New Zealand tend to put more of an emphasis on economic rights in copyright over the philosophical rights described below.

Moral Rights/Philosophical Policy

Some scholars link an artist's personality to the work he created. Under this theory, anyone making use of the work can affect the personality of the work. Therefore, copyright protects the author's personal integrity by preventing the distortion, destruction or misattribution of the work. Another philosophical policy goal of copyright is to protect the *labor of the man*. Under this theory, an author has the natural property right to protect what he has created through his labor. This theory is recognized more in other countries then it is in the United States. Many of the European Union and Latin American countries tend to favor this philosophical policy rather than emphasizing the economic rights.

2.5. Copyright in Practice

As we will see, copyright laws affect people and businesses in many ways. If a person or business creates an original work of authorship fixed in a tangible medium of expression, such as a novel, movie, poetry, computer software, art work or architecture, copyright protection occurs the moment the work is created in a tangible form of expression. Copyright protection informs the public of the owner of the work. As we will see, registration of the copyright with the U.S. Copyright Office is not required for an owner to obtain copyright protection, but it does help in the event of a legal dispute related to the work.

If a work has copyright protection and someone wants to use the work, they must obtain permission from the owner of the copyright. This protects the owner's work from being misused by another. The doctrine of *fair use*, which we'll evaluate in more detail later, allows copyrighted works to be used without permission from the owner. Although *fair use* is not defined in the copyright statute, there are specified favored uses such as "criticism, comment, news reporting, teaching (including making multiple copies for classroom use), scholarship or research." 17 U.S.C. § 107. For example, quoting from a book for the purpose of critiquing the work would constitute fair use and not require permission from the author of the book.

Suppose you are creating an online video and want to use another artist's work such as one of Kanye West's new songs or video footage from *The Hunger Games*. You must locate the owner, provide information of your intended use of the owner's work, and obtain permission from the owner. Keep in mind that there are plenty of resources that provide free public domain materials that do not require permission for using them. If the owner of the work cannot be found or won't give you permission to use the work, then the content should not be used in the online video unless the video falls in the *fair use* category discussed later in this copyright unit.

It is clear that copyright law serves many purposes. It provides authors of original works with exclusive rights that protect their work for a limited period of time. It also promotes creativity and learning.

Chapter Summary

Copyright is a form of intellectual property law that provides protection for published and unpublished original works of authorship fixed in a tangible medium of expression. Copyright law protects literary, dramatic, musical, artistic and other intellectual works, such as novels, movies, poetry, computer software, art, and architecture. Copyright law protects the way things are expressed but not ideas, systems, facts or methods of operation.

The first federal Copyright Act was adopted in May 1790. Since that time, the scope, effect, and term of copyright have increased with changes to the Act.

When a work of authorship is no longer or not protected under copyright it falls within the public domain. When a work is in the public domain, anyone can use the work without permission from the author or its heirs.

The policy goals of copyright law include economic and philosophical policy. Under economic policy, scholars believe that without copyright protection, there is no incentive for an author or artist to produce or create an original work. Under the philosophical policy, scholars link the artist's personality to its work and protect the "labor of the man" giving the author the natural property right to protect what was created through its labor.

Key Terms

Copyright
Original Works of Authorship
Tangible Medium of Expression
Copyright Act
Berne Convention
Visual Artists Rights Act
Public Domain

Review Questions

1. What does copyright protect?
2. Does copyright law protect ideas, systems, fact or methods of operation?
3. When was the first federal Copyright Act adopted?
4. Where were the first copyright registrations made?
5. Has copyright protection increased or decreased over time with the changes to the Copyright Act?
6. What becomes of old copyright?
7. What does it mean when a work of authorship is in the public domain?
8. What are the policy goals of copyright law?

Web Links

1. http://copyright.cornell.edu/resources/publicdomain.cfm—A detailed list of works currently in the public domain.

Discussion Exercise

1. The internet gives you the ability to copy websites, information, pictures, games, music, etc. If a work is marked as copyrighted material, do you need to get permission from the owner of the work before copying it? What if it is marked "not copyrighted"?

Exhibit 2.1. (taken from the United States Copyright Office, Circular 1a)

Notable Dates in United States Copyright

August 18, 1787
James Madison submitted to the framers of the Constitution a provision "to secure to literary authors their copyrights for a limited time."

June 23, 1789
First federal bill relating to copyrights (H.R. 10) presented to the first Congress.

May 31, 1790
First copyright law enacted under the new U.S. Constitution. Term of 14 years with privilege of renewal for term of 14 years. Books, maps, and charts protected. Copyright registration made in the U.S. District Court where the author or proprietor resided.

June 9, 1790
First copyright entry, The Philadelphia Spelling Book by John Barry, registered in the U.S. District Court of Pennsylvania.

April 29, 1802
Prints added to protected works.

February 3, 1831
First general revision of the copyright law. Music added to works protected against unauthorized printing and vending. First term of copyright extended to 28 years with privilege of renewal for term of 14 years.

August 18, 1856
Dramatic compositions added to protected works.

December 31, 1864
President Abraham Lincoln appoints Ainsworth Rand Spofford to be the sixth Librarian of Congress. Spofford served as the de facto Register of Copyrights until the position of Register was created in 1897.

March 3, 1865
Photographs and photographic negatives added to protected works.

July 8, 1870
Second general revision of the copyright law. Copyright activities, including deposit and registration, centralized in the Library of Congress. Works of art

added to protected works. Act reserved to authors the right to create certain derivative works including translations and dramatizations. Indexing of the record of registrations began.

March 3, 1891
First U.S. copyright law authorizing establishment of copyright relations with foreign countries. Records of works registered, now called the Catalog of Copyright Entries, published in book form for the first time in July 1891.

January 6, 1897
Music protected against unauthorized public performance.

February 19, 1897
Copyright Office established as a separate department of the Library of Congress. Position of Register of Copyrights created.

July 1, 1909
Effective date of third general revision of the copyright law. Admission of certain classes of unpublished works to copyright registration. Term of statutory protection for a work copyrighted in published form measured from the date of publication of the work. Renewal term extended from 14 to 28 years.

August 24, 1912
Motion pictures, previously registered as photographs, added to classes of protected works.

July 13, 1914
President Woodrow Wilson proclaimed U.S. adherence to Buenos Aires Copyright Convention of 1910, establishing convention protection between the United States and certain Latin American nations.

July 1, 1940
Effective date of transfer of jurisdiction for the registration of commercial prints and labels from the Patent Office to the Copyright Office.

July 30, 1947
Copyright law codified into positive law as title 17 of the U.S. Code.

January 1, 1953
Recording and performing rights extended to nondramatic literary works.

September 16, 1955
Effective date of the coming into force in the United States of the Universal Copyright Convention as signed at Geneva, Switzerland, on September 6, 1952. Proclaimed by President Dwight Eisenhower. Also, date of related changes in title 17 of the U.S. Code.

September 19, 1962
First of nine special acts extending terms of subsisting renewal copyrights pending congressional action on general copyright law revision.

February 15, 1972
Effective date of act extending limited copyright protection to sound recordings fixed and first published on or after this date.

March 10, 1974
United States became a member of the Convention for the Protection of Producers of Phonograms Against Unauthorized Duplication of Their Phonograms, which came into force on April 18, 1973.

July 10, 1974
United States became party to the 1971 revision of the Universal Copyright Convention as revised at Paris, France.

October 19, 1976
Fourth general revision of the copyright law signed by President Gerald Ford.

January 1, 1978
Effective date of principal provisions of the 1976 copyright law. The term of protection for works created on or after this date consists of the life of the author and 50 years after the author's death. Numerous other provisions modernized the law.

December 12, 1980
Copyright law amended regarding computer programs.

May 24, 1982
Section 506(a) amended to provide that persons who infringe copyright willfully and for purposes of commercial advantage or private financial gain shall be punished as provided in Section 2319 of title 18 of the U.S. Code, "Crimes and Criminal Procedure."

October 4, 1984
Effective date of Record Rental Amendments of 1984. Grants the owner of copyright in a sound recording the right to authorize or prohibit the rental, lease, or lending of phonorecords for direct or indirect commercial purposes.

November 8, 1984
Federal statutory protection for mask works became available under the Semiconductor Chip Protection Act, with the Copyright Office assuming administrative responsibility. Copyright Office began registration of claims to protection on January 7, 1985.

June 30, 1986
Manufacturing clause of the Copyright Act expired.

March 1, 1989
United States adhered to the Berne Convention for the Protection of Literary and Artistic Works.

November 15, 1990
Section 511 added to copyright law. Provides that states and state employees and instrumentalities are not immune under the Eleventh Amendment from suit for copyright infringement.

December 1, 1990
Effective date of the Computer Software Rental Amendments Act. Grants the owner of copyright in computer programs the exclusive right to authorize or prohibit the rental, lease, or lending of the program for direct or indirect commercial purposes.

December 1, 1990
Protection extended to architectural works. Section 106A added to copyright law by Visual Artists Rights Act. Grants to visual artists certain moral rights of attribution and integrity.

June 26, 1992
Renewal registration became optional. Works copyrighted between January 1, 1964, and December 31, 1977, automatically renewed even if registration not made.

October 28, 1992
Digital Audio Home Recording Act required serial copy management systems in digital audio recorders and imposed royalties on sale of digital audio recording devices and media. Royalties are collected, invested, and distributed among the owners of sound recording and musical compositions, certain performing artists and/or their representatives. Clarified legality of home taping of analog and digital sound recordings for private noncommercial use.

December 8, 1993
North American Free Trade Agreement Implementation Act (NAFTA) extended retroactive copyright protection to certain motion pictures first fixed in Canada or Mexico between January 1, 1978, and March 1, 1989, and published anywhere without a copyright notice; and/or to any work embodied in them; and made permanent the prohibition of sound recordings rental.

December 17, 1993
Copyright Royalty Tribunal Reform Act of 1993 eliminated the CRT and replaced it with ad hoc Copyright Arbitration Royalty Panels administered by the Librarian of Congress and the Copyright Office.

December 8, 1994
Uruguay Round Agreements Act restored copyright to certain foreign works under protection in the source country but in the public domain in the United States; repealed sunset of the Software Rental Amendments Act; and created legal measures to prohibit the unauthorized fixation and trafficking in sound recordings of live musical performances and music videos.

November 16, 1997
The No Electronic Theft Act defined "financial gain" in relation to copyright infringement and set penalties for willfully infringing a copyright either for purposes of commercial advantage or private financial gain or by reproducing or distributing, including by electronic means phonorecords of a certain value.

October 27, 1998
The Sonny Bono Copyright Term Extension Act extended the term of copyright protection for most works to the life of the author plus 70 years after the author's death.

October 28, 1998
The Digital Millennium Copyright Act provided for the implementation of the WIPO Copyright Treaty and the WIPO Performances and Phonograms Treaty; limited certain online infringement liability for Internet service providers; created an exemption permitting a temporary reproduction of a computer program made by activating a computer in the course of maintenance or repair; clarified the policy role of the Copyright Office; and created a form of protection for vessel hulls.

November 2, 2002
The Technology, Education, and Copyright Harmonization (TEACH) Act provided for the use of copyrighted works by accredited nonprofit educational institutions in distance education.

November 30, 2004
The Copyright Royalty and Distribution Reform Act phased out the Copyright Arbitration Royalty Panel system and replaced it with the Copyright Royalty Board.

April 27, 2005

The Artists' Rights and Theft Preservation Act allowed for preregistration of certain works being prepared for commercial distribution.

December 11, 2006

New Copyright Public Records Reading Room opened to the public.

July 1, 2008

Electronic registration on the Copyright Office website made available to the public.

Chapter 3

Works Subject to Copyright

*"Copyright law has got to give up its obsession with 'the copy.' The law should not regulate 'copies' or 'modern reproductions' on their own. It should instead regulate uses—like public distributions of copies of copyrighted work—that connect directly to the economic incentive copyright law was intended to foster." —*Lawrence Lessig

Chapter Outline

Chapter Objectives

- Recognize what works are subject to copyright protection.
- Differentiate works that are not subject to copyright protection.
- Identify the different categories of works of authorship.
- Understand what a compilation is.
- Know the two components of the originality requirement.
- Explain what the fixation requirement means.

- Identify works for hire.
- Identify the elements of a joint work.
- Identify the elements of a derivative work.
- Appreciate the difference between protected and non-protected material.

3.1. Works Subject to Copyright

Not all original works of authorship are protected by copyright. The work must meet certain requirements. An original work of authorship that is fixed in a tangible medium of expression is subject to copyright protection. The following three requirements must exist for the work to be eligible for copyright protection:

1. The work must be an original creation of the author.
2. The work must be fixed in a tangible medium of expression.
3. The work must exhibit creativity on the part of the author.

The following categories of materials are <u>not</u> eligible for copyright protection.

1. Works that have not been fixed in a tangible form of expression (examples include choreographic works, speeches or performances that have not been notated or recorded).
2. Titles, names, short phrases and slogans, familiar symbols or designs, mere variations of typographic ornamentation, lettering or coloring, mere listings of ingredients or contents.
3. Ideas, procedures, methods, systems, processes, concepts, principles, discoveries, or devices as distinguished from a description, explanation, or illustration.
4. Works consisting entirely of information that is common property and containing no original authorship (examples include standard calendars, height and weight charts, tape measures and rulers or lists and tables taken from public documents or other common sources).

3.2. Works of Authorship

Pursuant to 17 U.S.C. §102(a), works of authorship that are copyrightable fall into the following categories:

1. Literary works;
2. Musical works, including any accompanying words;
3. Dramatic works, including any accompany music;
4. Pantomimes and choreographic works;
5. Pictorial, graphic and sculptural works;
6. Motion pictures and other audiovisual works;
7. Sound recordings; and
8. Architectural works.

Compilations and derivative works are also copyrightable. 17 U.S.C. §103(a). Keep in mind that a work of authorship may fit more than one category. Additionally, the categories should be viewed broadly. Each category is described below.

Literary Works

Literary works are "works, other than audiovisual works, expressed in words, numbers other verbal or numerical symbols or indicia, regardless of the nature of the material objects, such as books, periodicals, manuscripts, phonorecords, film, tapes, disks or cards, in which they are embodied." 17 U.S.C. §101. Examples of literary works include fiction, nonfiction, manuscripts, poetry, contributions to collective works, compilations of data or other literary subject matter, dissertations, theses, speeches, bound or loose-leaf volumes, secure tests, pamphlets, brochures, textbooks, online works, reference works, directories, catalogs, advertising copy, single pages of text, tracts, games, automated databases, and computer programs, emails, online forums and blog posts.

Musical Works, Including Accompanying Words

The copyright statute does not define *musical works*. However, the U.S. Copyright Office describes the category of musical works to include *both* original compositions and original arrangements or other versions of earlier compositions that have new copyrightable authorship. This category covers the author of the lyrics, musical notations and the performer. Interestingly enough, the famous guitar notes in the introduction of the song "Stairway to Heaven" by the rock band Led Zeppelin is a musical work. Once musical works have been released to the public, they are subject to compulsory licensing which permits any musician to perform or record a cover version of a song without obtaining permission from the original songwriter.

Dramatic Works, Including Accompanying Music

The copyright statute does not define dramatic works. This category has been described by scholars as "any work in which performed actions, speech or incident, or all three convey theme, thoughts or character to an audience." *See Paul Goldstein, Copyright (2nd ed. 1996) at 2:110.* Examples include the television script to the award-winning series *Mad Men*, the award-winning screenplay, *Zero Dark Thirty*, and the Tony Award-winning musical play, *Kinky Boots*.

Pantomimes and Choreographic Works

The U.S. Copyright Office describes pantomimes and choreographic works as follows:

> "Choreography is the composition and arrangement of dance movements and patterns usually intended to be accompanied by music. The office notes that as distinct from choreography, pantomime is the art of imitating or acting out situations, characters, or other events. To be protected by copyright, pantomimes and choreography need not tell a story or be presented before an audience. Each work, however, must be fixed in a tangible medium of expression from which the work can be performed."

Examples of works in this category include the American Ballet Theater's production of *Swan Lake*, the Alvin Ailey American Dance Theater's production of the dance *Revelations*, or the mime performance *Ash in the Ashes*. In order to enjoy copyright protection, these works must be fixed in a permanent, tangible medium of expression such as a videotape, photograph or notation. It is interesting to note that folk dances and traditional dances cannot be protected by copyright.

Pictorial, Graphic and Sculptural Works

The category of pictorial, graphic and sculptural works includes "two dimensional and three dimensional works of fine, graphic and applied art, photographs, prints and art reproductions, maps, globes, charts, diagrams, models, and technical drawings, including architectural plans." 17 U.S.C. §101. Digital illusions are included in this category. Originality is the key requirement for obtaining protection. The quality of the artistic work is irrelevant. This means that a photo you took of a concert with your cell phone camera would receive the same protection as a great modern painting by Gerhard Richter or photograph taken by the famous photographer Cindy Sherman.

Motion Pictures and Other Audiovisual Works

The category of motion pictures and other audiovisual works includes movies, live webcasts that are being saved, video podcasts, slideshows and "works that consist of related images which are intrinsically intended to be shown by the use of machines, or devices such as projectors, viewers, or electronic equipment, together with accompanying sounds, if any, regardless of the nature of the material objects, such as films or tapes, in which the works are embodied." 17 U.S.C. §101. For example, the award-winning movie *The Girl With the Dragon Tattoo*, live webcasts from your school, video podcasts of a show or a slideshow on ice climbing are all included in this category.

Sound Recordings

Sound recordings are "works that result from the fixation of a series of musical, spoken or other sounds, but not including the sounds accompanying a motion picture or other audiovisual work, regardless of the nature of the material objects, such as disks, tapes or other phonorecords, in which they are embodied." 17 U.S.C. §101. Sound recordings are distinct from musical recordings because they include everything that can be recorded and reproduced that isn't classified as music, including speeches, audio books and sound effects. For example, the roar of the T-Rex in the movie *Jurassic Park* is a sound effect protected by copyright.

Architectural Works

Architectural works are "the design of a building as embodied in any tangible medium of expression, including a building, architectural plans or drawings. The work includes the overall form as well as the arrangement and composition of spaces and elements in the design, but does not include individual standard features." 17 U.S.C. §101. This category protects the design of a building in architectural blueprints, architectural drawings, and the buildings themselves. Copyright protection in architectural works includes the arrangement and composition of spaces and elements in the design and the form of the overall work. So, the architectural design of the World Trade Center Memorial is protected by copyright. Copyright protection is not available for the standard features that make a building habitable or the utilitarian features that make a building useful. Architectural works must contain original design elements to receive copyright protection. If the designs are there for functional purposes (i.e. to comply with housing regulations) they are not protected by copyright.

3.3. Compilations

A compilation is "a work formed by the collection and assembling of pre-existing materials or of data that are selected, coordinated or arranged in such a way that the resulting work as a whole constitutes an original work of authorship." 17 U.S.C. §101. For example, names and addresses or other data do not alone qualify for copyright protection, but the way a person selects and arranges such data may constitute an original work of authorship and be classified as a compilation that can have copyright protection. Noncopyrightable items may be part of the compilation. The compilation must be sufficiently original to have copyright protection. Some examples of compilations include a soundtrack or digital compilation album containing songs from different artists, such as *Barista's Music Blend*, crafted for fans of good music and coffee, or an anthology of stories or a compilation documentary film such as *The Civil War* produced by Ken Burns for PBS.

3.4. Originality

One of the requirements for copyright protection is that the work of authorship be *original*. There are two components to this requirement. The first is that the work be *independently created by the author* (as opposed to being copied from other works). The second is that the work exhibits a *minimum degree of creativity by the author*. The two components of this originality requirement were very well illustrated by the United States Supreme Court in *Feist Publications, Inc. v. Rural Telephone Service Co.*, 499 U.S. 340 (1991). Rural Telephone Service Co. ("Rural") was a telephone cooperative that provided service in Kansas. Rural had a statutory obligation to assemble a phone directory of all of its customers for no charge. Feist Publications, Inc. ("Feist") also assembled telephone directories of large geographical areas in Kansas. Feist sought a license from Rural to use its directory in compiling a larger telephone directory but Rural refused to grant a license to Feist. Acting without a license from Rural, Feist copied approximately 4,000 entries from the directory Rural assembled. Rural sued Feist for copyright infringement. The Supreme Court found in favor of Feist holding that Rural's phone directory was *not* copyrightable material. In its opinion, the Court noted that since Rural *did not independently create the data* incorporated in its telephone directory—the information already existed—it failed to meet the first component of originality. The Court also noted that Rural listed the names in the telephone directory in alphabetical order. This arrangement *did not meet the second component of originality* which requires a minimal degree of creativity.

3.5. Fixation

Another requirement for copyright protection is that the work be *fixed* in a tangible medium of expression. This fixation requirement requires that the work of authorship be in some physical form or representation such as paper, canvas, tape, cd, disk or hard drive. How is a work fixed in a copy? The copyright statute defines copies as "material objects, other than phonorecords, in which a work is fixed by any method now known or later developed, and from which the work can be perceived, reproduced, or otherwise communicated, either directly or with the aid of a machine or device." 17 U.S.C. §101. For example, putting paint on a canvas, print on paper, or text of documents on a hard drive satisfies this requirement.

Is the actual live telecast of the NFL Super Bowl subject to copyright protection? Yes, because it is fixed in a tangible medium of expression at the same time it is being transmitted in a broadcast form. The copyright statute states that "a work consisting of sounds, images or both that are being transmitted, is fixed for purposes of this title if a fixation of the work is being made simultaneously with its transmission." 17 U.S.C. §101. This is why you'll hear announcements during the Super Bowl containing warnings that the telecast of the game is the property of the NFL and that you cannot exploit it without the express permission of the NFL and the network that is carrying the game. What other components of the Super Bowl telecast may be individually copyrighted? Are there elements of the half-time show that are copyrighted? The music that is played during the game and half-time show is likely protected by copyright as a musical work. The choreography of the dance movements during the half-time show are likely protected by copyright as choreographic works. How about the stadium that the Super Bowl is being played in? Any original design elements in the stadium could have copyright protection as architectural works. Is the national anthem at the beginning of the game copyrighted? The National Anthem itself is not copyrighted because it is in the public domain. A performance of the National Anthem, like the one before the Super Bowl, could be copyrighted. Would the game statistics be copyrightable? Probably not, as a court has held that anyone who provides "purely factual information which any patron...could acquire from the arena without any involvement from the director, cameramen or others who contribute to the originality of the broadcast" is not liable for infringement. *National Basketball Association v. Motorola, Inc.*, 939 F. Supp. 1071, 1094 (1996).

3.6. Works for Hire

The general rule in copyright law is only the author of a work or those deriving rights from the author can claim copyright. An exception to this rule exists for *works made for hire*. If a work is made for hire, the employer or person for whom the work was prepared owns the copyright *unless* the parties have signed a written agreement stating otherwise. A work made for hire is protected by copyright for ninety-five (95) years from the date of publication or one hundred twenty (120) years from the date of creation, whichever comes first.

The copyright statute defines a *work made for hire* as (1) a work created by an employee within the scope of employment or (2) a work created by an independent contractor under a written contract specifying that the project is a work made for hire. 17 U.S.C. §101.

In *Community for Creative Non-Violence v. Reid*, 490 U.S. 730 (1989), the United States Supreme Court addressed the definition of *works made for hire*. The case involved a nonprofit group, Community for Creative Non-Violence ("CCNV") that solicited James Reid ("Reid") to create a sculpture depicting homeless people in a nativity scene. Reid donated his time in working on the sculpture. CCNV paid for the materials, made the base of the sculpture, suggested people to use as models for the sculpture and proposed changes to Reid as he worked on the sculpture. The issue of copyright was not discussed between the parties or put in writing. Once the work was completed, CCNV paid Reid and announced they were taking the sculpture on a multi-city tour. CCNV claimed they owned the work and sought possession of the sculpture, which Reid refused.

In its holding, the Supreme Court stated that it must first determine whether the work was prepared by (a) an employee or (b) an independent contractor. If the work was created by an employee (as defined under the common law of agency which is discussed more fully below), then the work will generally be considered a work made for hire. If the work was created by an independent contractor—someone who is not an employee—and the work was specially ordered or commissioned, then the work will generally be considered a work made for hire if (a) it falls within one of the following categories of works and (b) there is a written agreement specifying that the work is a work made for hire. The categories of works are:

1. A contribution to a collective work;
2. A part of a motion picture or other audiovisual work;
3. A translation;
4. A supplementary work;
5. A compilation;
6. An instructional text;
7. A test;
8. Answer material for a test; and
9. An atlas.

The Supreme Court outlined three factors that determine whether an employer-employee relationship exists. The Court failed to clarify which of the following factors must be present to establish the employment relationship in a work for hire context. The presence of all or most of the factors will characterize a work made for hire.

1. Employer has control over the work— how it is done, its location and provides the equipment.
2. The employer has control over the employee—its work schedule, method of payment, assignments and the right to hire assistants.
3. The employer's status and conduct—provides the employee with benefits, withholds tax from employee's paycheck.

The Supreme Court decided that Reid was an independent contractor because he did not fall into the category of an employee. Since Reid wasn't an employee of CCNV, the Court found that the work was not a work for hire. The case was remanded to determine the parties' rights and whether the work was a *joint work* since CCNV contributed to its design and the cost in creating the sculpture.

It is critical to understand the importance of work for hire issues. If, as part of your job, you draft a weekly newsletter, your employer, not you, owns the rights in what you've written in the newsletter. Compare this with a novel or poem you've written in your free time, unassociated with your job. In this situation, you own the rights in novel or poem. If your job requires you to create original works, be aware that the employer owns the rights in the work. Issues arise not only with employees but with freelance creators, independent photographers, screenwriters and journalists. This is one of the main reasons why it is important for the parties to enter into a written agreement that outlines each party's rights prior to creating the work.

3.7. Joint Works

A joint work is defined as "a work prepared by two or more authors who intend to merge their contributions into inseparable or interdependent parts of the whole." 17 U.S.C. §101. The authors of a joint work are considered joint copyright owners, each having equal rights to register and enforce the copyright. They key part of the statutory definition is the *intention* of the parties. Although a person may contribute a large amount of work, they may not be a joint author.

For example, in *Thomson v. Larson, 147 F.3d 195 (2d Cir. 1998)*, the author of the musical *Rent* worked with a dramaturge, Lynn Thomson, in making changes to the musical. Both Larson and Thomson worked intensively together on revisions to the work. Throughout their work together, Larson had the sole decision making authority, was consistently referred to as the author, and was referred to in all third party agreements as the sole author. Since there was no evidence that showed the parties intent for joint ownership, the court found that the work did not fall under the statutory definition of a *joint work*.

Another recent example of issues associated with a joint work involves one of the highest grossing and most expensive Broadway musical productions, *Spider-Man Turn off the Dark*, which included music from U2's Bono and the Edge. After many disagreements, the director, Julie Taymor, was fired for implementing changes to the show after it received negative reviews during its preview performances, which were full of problems and injuries. Taymor filed the lawsuit against the producers over copyright issues, claiming the producers were making money from her ideas and script and owed her over $1 million. In response to Taymor's lawsuit, the producers filed a lawsuit against Taymor claiming they fired Taymor for breach of contract and that there was no base for her claims. The litigation involved Bono, the Edge and even Marvel Entertainment. The parties finally entered into an undisclosed settlement agreement that will facilitate moving the *Spider-Man Turn Off The Dark* musical to other domestic and international locations and allow producers to make changes to the show's script, which Taymor helped write, without requiring her approval.

3.8. Derivative Works

A *derivative work* is a work based upon one or more preexisting works, such as a translation, musical arrangement, dramatization, fictionalization, motion picture version, sound recording, art reproduction, abridgment, condensation, or any other form in which a work may be recast, transformed, or adapted. A work consisting of editorial revisions, annotations, elaborations, or other modifications, which, as a whole, represent an original work of authorship, is a *derivative work*. 17 U.S.C. §101. Copyright protection is available for a derivative work if the derivative work includes original work of authorship, is sufficiently different from the original work and contains new material. Examples of derivative works include a sculpture based on a drawing, a motion picture based on a play, or a drawing based on a photograph. The movie *Fast & Furious 6*, released in 2013, is a derivative work of the original *Fast & Furious* movie about street racing. The video game *Fast & Furious: Showdown* is a derivative work that ties the events in the movie, *Fast & Furious 6*, with those of its predecessor *Fast Five*, as well as the story of other films in the franchise. The 3-D movie *Iron Man 3* is a superhero film featuring the Marvel Comics character Iron Man. It is a derivative work of the *Iron Man* Comic Books published by Marvel Comics and the original 2008 movie *Iron Man* and 2010 movie *Iron Man 2*.

3.9. Protected and Non-Protected Subject Matter

As we've seen, an original work of authorship fixed in a tangible medium of expression is subject to copyright protection. The requirements for copyright protection preclude some works from being subject to copyright protection because they don't meet the statutory requirements. If a work is not *fixed in a tangible medium of expression* it cannot be subject to copyright protection. For example, a speech or performance that has not been recorded or written is not subject to copyright protection because it lacks the *fixation* requirement. Additionally, copyright protection does not extend to an idea, procedure, method of operation, concept, principle or discovery. Ideas and inventions are covered by patent law, which is covered later in this book. The expression of ideas can be protected by copyright law. For example, if an inventor writes a paper on its invention, the written work would be protected by copyright, but the invention itself is not. The inventor could apply for patent protection for its invention. Titles, names, and short phrases are not protected by copyright law because they don't meet the requirements of the statute. This explains why some works, such as books and movies, can have the same title. Items that are in the public domain, as we saw in the previous, are also excluded from copyright protection.

Chapter Summary

An original work of authorship that is fixed in a tangible medium of expression is subject to copyright protection.

Works of authorship fall into the following categories: (1) literary works; (2) musical works; (3) dramatic works; (4) pantomimes and choreographic works; (5) pictorial, graphic and sculptural works; (6) motion pictures and other audiovisual works; (7) sound recordings; (8) architectural works.

A compilation, which is a work formed by the collection and assembling of preexisting materials or of data that are selected, coordinated or arranged in such a way that the resulting work as a whole, constitutes an original work of authorship that is copyrightable.

One of the requirements for copyright protection is that the work of authorship be original. There are two components to this originality requirement. First, the work must be independently created by the author (as opposed to being copied from other works). Second the must work exhibit a minimum degree of creativity by the author.

A work created by an employee within the scope of employment or certain works created by an independent author under a written contract specifying that the project is a work made for hire fall into the category called "works made for hire." If a work is made for hire, the employer or person for whom the work was prepared owns the copyright unless the parties have signed a written agreement stating otherwise.

A joint work is a work prepared by two or more authors who intend to merge their contributions into inseparable or interdependent parts of the whole. In determining whether a work is a joint work, one must evaluate the intention of the parties.

A derivative work is based upon one or more preexisting work. Copyright protection is available for a derivative work if the derivative work includes original work of authorship, is sufficiently different from the original work and contains new material.

Copyright protection doesn't extend to ideas, procedures, methods of operations, concepts, principles or discoveries. Items that are in the public domain are not protected by copyright.

Key Terms

Works of Authorship
Literary Works
Musical Works
Dramatic Works
Pantomimes and Choreographic Works
Pictorial, Graphic and Sculptural Works
Motion Pictures
Sound Recordings
Architectural Works
Compilations
Originality
Fixation
Works for Hire
Joint Works
Derivative Works

Review Questions

1. What are the three requirements for copyright protection?
2. What categories of materials are not available for copyright registration?
3. What are the works of authorship categories that are copyrightable?
4. What is a compilation?
5. What are the two components of the originality requirement?
6. What does the fixation requirement mean?
7. What is a work for hire?
8. Who owns the copyright in a work for hire?

9. What is a joint work?
10. What is a derivative work?
11. Name subject matter that is not copyrightable.

Web Links

1. http://www.copyright.gov/help/faq/faq-protect.html—The U.S. Copyright Office's frequently asked questions on what copyright protects.

Discussion Exercise

1. Identify which of the following are works made for hire:

    A. A software program created by a staff programmer within the scope of his or her duties at a software firm.
    B. A newspaper article written by a staff journalist for publication in the newspaper that employs the journalist (who is not a freelance writer).
    C. An illustration created by a freelance illustrator who is not an employee of the company using the illustration and there is no agreement between the parties.
    D. A sculpture created by a person who is not an employee or independently contractor of the organization that the sculpture is being made for.

Chapter 4

Formalities

"Of all the creative work produced by humans anywhere, a tiny fraction has continuing commercial value. For that tiny fraction, the copyright is a crucially important legal device." —Lawrence Lessig

Chapter Outline

Chapter Objectives

- Recognize when copyright protection commences.
- Understand the advantages of registering a copyright with the U.S. Copyright Office.
- Know the methods and procedures to register a copyright.
- Explain what recordation is and when it is utilized.
- Identify deposit requirements and exemptions from deposit.
- Distinguish between the types of notices.
- Note the length of copyright protection.

- Identify who may file for renewal and the type of works subject to renewal.
- Appreciate the doctrine of moral rights and the duration thereof.

4.1. Filing for a U.S. Copyright

As previously discussed, the moment a creative work is fixed in a tangible form of expression it is protected by copyright. Filing an application for copyright registration is a voluntary process. The advantages to registering a work with the U.S. Copyright Office include, but are not limited to, having the facts of the copyright on public record, receipt of a Certificate of Registration, and ease and ability to sue and recover damages from an infringer. Let's examine the ways to register a work with the U.S. Copyright Office.

4.2. Basic Forms

An application for copyright registration can be submitted online or by traditional paper method. Both require a completed application form, nonrefundable filing fee and nonreturnable deposit of copies of the work being registered with the U.S. Copyright Office.

4.3. Registration and Procedure— Online Application

Filing an application online through the *electronic Copyright Office* (eCO) is the preferred method to register claims for:

1. Literary works (nondramatic textual works with or without illustrations);
2. Visual arts works (pictorial, graphic, and sculptural works, which include two-dimensional and three dimensional works of fine, graphic and applied art);
3. Performing arts works (music, drama, choreography and pantomime);
4. Sound recordings (recordings of music, drama and lectures); and
5. Single serial issues (periodicals, newspapers, magazines, bulletins, newsletters, annuals, journals, and other similar works).

The online application process has three parts:

A. The creation of an online account and completing the forms provided at eCO;
B. The payment of a fee with a credit/debit card, electronic check or deposit account; and
C. Uploading or mailing copies of the work.

There are advantages to filing online through eCO. They include a lower filing fee, faster processing time, online status tracking, secure payment by credit/debit card, electronic check or deposit account, and the ability to upload deposits of the work directly into eCO as electronic files.

The U.S. Copyright Office's website located at www.copyright.gov provides access to the eCO with an option for users to click on *Electronic Copyright Office*. The Electronic Copyright Office (www.copyright.gov/eco) is very user-friendly and provides tips, answers to frequently asked questions and tutorials to help users through the electronic filing process. See *Exhibit 4.1* on this website for an electronic copyright registration tutorial provided by the United States Copyright Office.

4.4. Registration and Procedure— Paper Application

The required forms for a traditional paper application for copyright protection can be downloaded from the U.S. Copyright Office website at www.copyright.gov or requested by writing to *Library of Congress, Copyright Office–COPUBS, 101 Independence Avenue, SE, Washington, DC 20559-6304* or calling the *Forms and Publications Hotline at (202) 707-9100*.

There are different forms required depending on the type of work. The following is a list of forms for registration:

1. Form TX (literary works);
2. Form VA (visual art works);
3. Form PA (performing arts works, including motion pictures);
4. Form SR (sound recordings); and
5. Form SE (single serial issues).

Keep in mind that the applications for registration of literary works, visual art works, performing art works, sound recordings and single serial issues can be filed online *or* through the traditional paper method. Sample forms have been provided in *Exhibit 4.2* (www.copyright.gov/forms/).

The following applications <u>must</u> be completed using the traditional paper forms:

1. **Form CA.** This form is used to correct or complete facts on record of an earlier registration made with the U.S. Copyright Office that contained incorrect or incomplete facts;
2. **Form D-VH.** This form is used for the registration of an original design of a vessel hull that makes the hull attractive or distinctive in appearance to the purchasing or using public. A vessel hull includes the design of a plug or mold used to manufacture the vessel hull;
3. **Form MW.** This form is used for registration of a claim for protection in a mask work that is fixed in a semiconductor chip product, by or under the authority of the owner of the mask work. A mask work is a series of related images, fixed or encoded, having or representing the predetermined, three-dimensional pattern of metallic, insulating, or semiconductor material present or removed from the layers of a semiconductor chip product, and in which the relation of images to one another is such that each image has the pattern of the surface of one form of the semiconductor chip product;
4. **Form GATT.** This form is used for registration of a copyright claim in a work in which the U.S. copyright was restored under the 1994 Uruguay Round Agreements Act "URAA";
5. **Form RE.** This form is used for renewal of copyright claims; and
6. **Forms for all group submissions.**

To file a traditional paper application for copyright protection, the following must be mailed to the *Library of Congress, U.S. Copyright Office, 101 Independence Avenue SE, Washington, DC 20559*:

1. Fully completed (hand-written or writable form) signed and dated application form;
2. Check or money order for the filing fee; and
3. Deposit of the work.

4.5. Recordation

The statute provides that a document that transfers copyright ownership or any other document pertaining to a copyright may be recorded in the U.S. Copyright Office if the document filed for recordation bears the actual signature of the person who executed it, or if the document is accompanied by a sworn or official certification that it is a true copy of the original signed document. 17 U.S.C. § 205(a)

As we previously discussed, an owner of a copyrighted work has exclusive rights associated with the copyrighted work. The owner may also enter into agreements that authorize third parties to use their work. When an owner of a copyrighted work enters into a transaction with a third party that involves the copyrighted work, it can be recorded in the U.S. Copyright Office. Just like copyright registration, recordation is a completely voluntary process that involves filing documents with the U.S. Copyright Office to show the transfer of copyright, specific rights associated with the copyright or a transaction that pertains to a copyright. Examples include assignments, exclusive and nonexclusive licenses, sales of copyright, contracts, powers of attorney, certificates of change of corporate ownership in the copyright, wills and decrees of distribution relating to the copyright.

Although recordation is voluntary, there are several advantages to doing it. First, it provides priority between conflicting transfers. For example, if the owner of copyrighted work sells his copyright and the buyer records the transaction by filing the required documents with the Copyright Office, the buyer will be protected should the original owner sell the copyright to a different party thereafter. Second, it provides public record of the contents of the transfer or agreement. Third, it provides constructive notice to the public of the transaction or transfer of rights thus precluding them from successfully claiming that they did not have such knowledge.

The new owner must file the document evidencing the transfer of copyright with the U.S. Copyright Office to record a transfer. It should describe the work involved and the rights or transfer granted. The person granting such rights or transfer must sign the document being filed with the U.S. Copyright Office. In order to be recorded in the U.S. Copyright Office, the requisite document must:

(1) Have an original signature (or proper certification of photocopy);
(2) Be complete by its own terms;
(3) Be legible; and
(4) Be accompanied by the filing fee.

The U.S. Copyright Office provides a Document Cover Sheet to use when recording a document that transfers copyright ownership or any other document pertaining to a copyright in the U.S. Copyright Office. Although the Document Cover Sheet is optional, it facilitates the recording of the document.

4.6. Deposit

17 U.S.C. §407 requires that the owner of a copyrighted work published in the United States deposit the requisite number of copies in the U.S. Copyright Office within three months of the date of publication, unless they fall within a certain category of works that are exempt from the mandatory deposit requirements. The statute also states that the deposits are to be made available to the Library of Congress for its collections or for exchange or transfer to any other library. This mandatory deposit provision can be fulfilled if the owner of a work submits an application for registration of an original work since the registration process requires that copies of the work be deposited with the U.S. Copyright Office. There is no penalty imposed on an owner that fails to voluntarily deposit its work despite this statutory requirement. Typically, the Library of Congress or the Register of Copyrights will send a written demand for deposit of a work after its publication. If a party fails to deposit the work within three months of such demand, fines and additional expenses may be imposed.

Certain categories of works are exempt from the mandatory deposit requirement. The first exemption is for works that are published exclusively in electronic form and have no physical counterparts, such as web sites. The second exemption is applied if copies of a published work would be unduly burdensome or too expensive for the copyright owner to provide, such as a sculpture. A copyright owner that is seeking an exemption from the deposit requirement should file a request for an exemption with the Copyright Office. The request for exemption should set forth specific reasons why special relief should be granted and be signed by or on behalf of the owner of a copyright or the owner of the exclusive right of publication in the work.

4.7. Notice

For works first published on or after March 1, 1989, the copyright notice is optional for copyright protection in the United States. For works published before March 1, 1989, copyright notice is mandatory to preserve the copyright in the work.

The form of the copyright notice varies depending on the type of work. For copies of works that can be seen or read (such as books or films), also known as "visually perceptible copies" the copyright notice should contain:

1. The symbol © (letter C in a circle); the word "Copyright"; or abbreviation "Copr.";
2. The year of first publication; and
3. The name of the copyright owner or an abbreviation of such name.

For phonorecords of sound recordings, the copyright notice should contain:

1. The symbol (letter P in a circle);
2. The year of first publication of the sound recording; and
3. The name of the copyright owner of the sound recording or an abbreviation of such name.

The position of the copyright notice depends on the type of work. The following are examples of locations for the copyright notice pursuant to the guidelines of the U.S. Copyright Office:

Literary works—the front or the back of the title page.
Computer software—on the disk or cassette or in program itself.
Audiovisual works—on the screen with the credits.
Phonorecords, audiotapes and CDs—record cover or CD and tape enclosures.

4.8. Length of Protection and Renewal

The length of copyright protection for a work depends on when it was first created or published. The controversial *Sonny Bono Copyright Term Extension Act of 1988* extended the term of copyright protection. Generally, for works created after January 1, 1978, copyright protection lasts for the life of the author plus an additional seventy years. If the work is an anonymous work, pseudonymous work, or work for made for hire, the copyright lasts for ninety-five years from the date of its publication or one-hundred twenty years from the year of its creation, whichever comes first. If the work was created or published before January 1, 1978, the term varies depending on several factors. The chart on the next page shows the length of copyright protection for different works and applicable dates.

DATE AND NATURE OF WORK	LENGTH OF COPYRIGHT
Published prior to 1923	Public domain in the United States
Published 1923–1963 and no renewal	Public domain in the United States
Published 1923–1963 and effectively renewed	95 years from the date of first publication
Published 1964–1977	95 years from the date of publication
Created before 1978 but no pub./rec.	120 years from creation for unpublished works made for hire and anonymous or pseudonymous works
Created before 1978 and published 1978–2002	Copyright expires January 1, 2048
Created 1978 and later	Life of the author plus 70 years

4.9. Renewal

Works created in 1978 or later are not subject to renewal registration. For works published or registered prior to 1978, renewal is not mandatory but optional after twenty years. The advantages to renewal registration prior to the twenty-eighth year of the original term include, but are not limited to the following:

1. The renewal copyright vests in the name of the renewal applicant on the effective date of renewal registration; and
2. A renewal certificate is issued by the U.S. Copyright Office which serves as prima facie evidence of the validity of the copyright during the renewed term.

An application for renewal registration can be made by submitting Form RE (which can be obtained from the U.S. Copyright Office on their website www.copyright.gov or by written request through U.S. mail) and the correct filing fee to the U.S. Copyright Office.

The following people may claim renewal in all types of works, unless the work is included in the exceptions below.

1. The author, if living.
2. If the author is dead, the widow or widower of the author or the child or children of the author or both.
3. If there is no surviving widow, widower or child and the author left a will, the person in charge of executing or administering the author's will.

4. If there is no surviving widow, widower or child and the author didn't leave a will or the will was discharged, the author's next of kin.

The parties listed above may not file for renewal of the following types of works. Rather, renewal of the following types of works requires the copyright proprietor or owner to file.

1. Posthumous work (a work published after the author's death).
2. Periodical, cyclopedia or other composite work.
3. Work copyrightable by a corporate body otherwise than as assignee or licensee of the individual author.
4. Work copyright by an employer for whom such work was made for hire.

4.10. Duration of Moral Rights

Until 1990, the United States failed to recognize moral rights in copyright. Courts attempted to find moral rights provisions in the derivative works section of the copyright statute. This changed in 1990 when Congress amended the Copyright Act by passing the *Visual Artists Rights Act* (VARA), 17 U.S.C. §106A, which implements a moral rights system for "works of visual art." "Works of visual art" include paintings, drawings, prints or sculptures, and still photographs produced for exhibition, existing in a single copy or signed and numbered in limited editions of two hundred or less. VARA incorporates moral rights protections that are consistent with an international treaty called the Berne Convention, which will be discussed later in this chapter. Moral rights are also protected by state laws in California and New York.

VARA recognizes the moral rights of attribution and integrity. The right of attribution is the right to be identified as the author of your work and prevent the use of your name in relation to works that you didn't author. The right of integrity is the right to prevent intentional distortion, destruction or mutilation of your work. For works created on or after December 1, 1990, the moral rights conferred by VARA, attribution and integrity, are granted for the life of the author, or in the case of a joint work, until the death of the last surviving author. The moral rights granted under VARA are not transferable but can be waived in writing.

Kent Twitchell ("Twitchell") is an American muralist. He created several murals in Los Angeles, California, including a seventy-foot-tall mural of the Los Angeles pop artist, Edward Ruscha, located on the side of a building owned by the United States Department of Labor. The nineteen-year-old landmark mural was eventually painted over in 2006 without his approval. Twitchell won the largest settlement ever under VARA for $1.1 million against the U.S. government and twelve defendants. A photograph of the mural before it was painted over is set forth below.

Figure 4.1

Before: The Ed Ruscha Monument in downtown L.A. was painted over last week (photo by Robin Dunitz published in the *LA Times*).

4.11. Searching for Copyright

There are different ways to determine whether a work is under copyright protection and obtain information about the copyright. The most obvious way is to examine a copy of the work for its copyright notice, place and date of publication, author, and publisher. You can also search the U.S. Copyright Office's catalogs and other records by going to www.copyright.gov, which has copyright records in its online catalog from January 1, 1978, to the present. Copyright records prior to January 1, 1978, can be found in the *Catalog of Copyright Entries* (CCE), published by the U.S. Copyright Office. The CCE can be found in a number of libraries in the United States, including the Library of Congress. Alternatively, the U.S. Copyright Office will perform a search for you upon written request and payment of a set fee. When investigating copyrights, remember to use more than one method in order to obtain the most conclusive information.

When searching for copyright information, it's important to have detailed information about the work such as the title of the work, the name of the author, the name of the probable copyright owner, the approximate year that the work was published or registered, the type of work, the registration number or any other copyright data. A thorough search may not always be conclusive in determining the copyright status of a work. The absence of information about a work in the U.S. Copyright Office's records does not mean the work is not protected by copyright. As you may recall, copyright exists the moment original works of authorship are created and fixed in any tangible medium of expression. Copyright protection does not require formal registration with the U.S. Copyright Office, although this chapter has examined several advantages in doing so. Furthermore, even if you conclude that a work is in the public domain in the United States, it could still be protected in a foreign country. See **Exhibit 4.3** (www.copyright.gov/records/voyager_tutorial.ppt) for a Guide to Searching the Copyright Office Catalog provided by the U.S. Copyright Office.

Chapter Summary

The moment a creative work is fixed in a tangible form of expression it is protected by copyright. The voluntary process of filing for copyright protection has many advantages including having the facts of the copyright on public record, receipt of a Certificate of Registration, and ease and ability to sue and recover damages from an infringer. Copyright registration applications can be filed online or by traditional paper method, depending on the type of work being registered.

A document that transfers copyright ownership or any other document pertaining to a copyright may be recorded in the U.S. Copyright Office. The advantages to recording include providing priority between conflicting transfers and public record of the contents of the transfer or agreement.

An owner of a copyrighted work published in the United States must deposit the requisite number of copies with the U.S. Copyright Office within three months of the date of publication unless the work falls within a certain category of works that are exempt from mandatory deposit requirements such as works that are published exclusively in electronic form and have no physical counterparts or works that would be unduly burdensome or expensive for a copyright owner to provide.

For works first published on or after March 1, 1989, the copyright notice is optional for copyright protection in the United States. For works published before March 1, 1989, copyright notice is mandatory to preserve the copyright in the work. The position of the copyright notice depends on the type of work.

The length of protection for a work depends on when it was first created or published. The Sonny Bony Copyright Term Extension Act of 1988 extended the term of copyright protection. Generally for works created after January 1, 1978, copyright protection lasts for the life of the author plus an additional seventy years. If the work is an anonymous work, pseudonymous work or a work made for hire, the copyright lasts for ninety-five years from the date of its publication or one hundred twenty years from the year of its creation, whichever comes first. If the work was created or published prior to January 1, 1978, the term varies depending on several factors.

Works created in 1978 or later are not subject to renewal registration. For works published for registered prior to 1978, renewal is optional after twenty-eight years.

The Visual Artists Rights Act (VARA), 17 U.S.C. §106A, implements a moral rights system for "works of visual art." "Works of visual art" include paintings, drawings, prints or sculptures, and still photographs produced for exhibition, existing in a single copy or signed and numbered in limited editions of two hundred or less. Moral rights are also protected by state laws in California and New York. VARA recognizes the moral rights of attribution and integrity. The right of attribution is the right to be identified as the author of your work and prevent the use of your name in relation to works that you didn't author. The right of integrity is the right to prevent intentional distortion, destruction or mutilation of your work. For works created on or after December 1, 1990, the moral rights conferred by VARA, attribution and integrity, are granted for the life of the author, or in the case of a joint work, until the death of the last surviving author. The moral rights granted under VARA are not transferable but can be waived in writing.

Key Terms

Electronic Copyright Office
Recordation
Deposit
Notice
Sonny Bono Copyright Term Extension Act of 1988
Visual Artists Rights Act (VARA)

Review Questions

1. Is copyright registration a mandatory or voluntary process?
2. What are the methods to file an application for copyright registration?
3. What applications must be filed using the traditional paper method?
4. What is recordation used for?
5. Is the owner of a copyright work published in the United States required to deposit copies of the work in the U.S. Copyright Office?
6. What types of works are exempt from the mandatory deposit requirement?
7. When is copyright notice mandatory and when is it optional?
8. What is the length of copyright protection?
9. What works are subject to renewal registration and who may file for it?
10. What are moral rights and how long do they last?

Web Links

1. http://www.copyright.gov/records/—U.S. Copyright Office records search tool.

Discussion Exercise

1. Suppose you just wrote a book. Describe the ways to obtain copyright protection.

Chapter 5

Dealings in Copyright

"There is no sense in owning the copyright unless you are going to use it. I don't think anyone wants to hold all of this stuff in a vault and not let anybody have it. It's only worth something once it's popular."
—Hilary Rosen

Chapter Outline

5.1. Contracts Related to Copyright
5.2. Copyright Transfers
5.3. Open Source Options
5.4. Creative Commons

Chapter Objectives

- Understand the type of contracts related to copyright.
- Recognize the different ways copyright can be transferred.
- Explain what a copyright license does.
- Know the difference between and exclusive and non-exclusive license.
- Explain what an assignment of copyright does.
- Distinguish between a license and assignment of copyright.
- Identify who may terminate a license or assignment and how it is done.
- Note the difference between the sale of copyright and sale of a copyrighted work.
- Identify open source licenses.
- Recognize resources such as open source licenses and creative commons.

5.1. Contracts Related to Copyright

Copyright is a form of intellectual property. Just like any other property owner, the owner of copyright may transfer all or part of its rights to another. The owner of copyright may enter into contracts that give the exclusive rights that come from copyright to third parties to exercise such rights. For example, the owners of the copyright to the novel *Twilight* entered into a contract with a movie studio to make a film from the book. The owner of copyright may also license or transfer the copyright to third parties for different purposes or sell all or part of the copyright outright, such as a license to use copyrighted images from *Angry Birds* on a t-shirt or poster. This chapter will evaluate the different transactions used with copyright.

5.2. Copyright Transfers

A copyright owner can transfer all or some of its rights by conveyance, such as an assignment of rights, or as collateral under a mortgage, or the owner may bequeath them to a beneficiary through a will that would take effect upon the death of the copyright owner. Copyrights can also be transferred by operation of law. The Copyright Act requires that all transfers of copyright ownership be in writing and signed by the copyright owner or its duly authorized agent. The Copyright Act does not require any special form or words for the writing to be valid. It only requires "an instrument of conveyance, or a note or memorandum of the transfer." 17 U.S.C. §206. Courts have found certain writings insufficient to demonstrate an instrument of transfer. For example, a fax that referenced a deal but didn't specify the general terms of the deal, did not qualify as a valid writing. *See Radio Television Espanola v. New World Entertainment, 183 F.3d 922 (9th Cir. 1999).* Copyright transfers can take the form of licenses, assignments or sales.

A. Licenses

A copyright owner may enter into a license agreement with a third party when they are transferring *some* of the rights associated with a copyright. A copyright owner may grant either an exclusive or non-exclusive license to a third party. In an *exclusive license*, the copyright owner grants permission to a third party, to do something specific with the copyright such as publish, use, make or distribute copies, and that third party has the *exclusive* right to do that which is specified in the license agreement. For example, an author may enter into an *exclusive* license with a publisher to make and distribute copies of the work. The author would still retain all other rights conferred by the copyright. In this example, the author may not grant the same permission (making and distributing copies of the work) to another publisher because the author has already granted an exclusive license to do this to a publisher. Exclusive licenses require a signed writing to be valid. The writing should include, at a minimum, the following information:

A.   Parties names and contact information;
B.   Description of the item being licensed;
C.   What type of license is being granted;
D.   Time limitation or dates of license;
E.   How item is being used;
F.   Payment terms for license;
G.   Artist/Author retains all copyright (and moral rights if visual work); and
H.   What can/cannot be done to the copyrighted work.

Compare the example above with a *non-exclusive* license. In a **non-exclusive license**, a copyright owner grants permission to a third party to do something specific, but the copyright owner may still grant the same permission to another third party. The author of computer software may grant non-exclusive licenses for third parties to use it, but others are not precluded from using the software as well because the license is *non-exclusive*. *Non-exclusive* licenses do not require a signed writing to be valid; however, if there is a dispute as to the terms of the non-exclusive license, the parties can refer back to the written agreement. A grant of permission can be provided expressly or implied by the parties conduct.

B. Assignments

An assignment of copyright involves the unconditional transfer of all or portion of the copyright to a third party. With an assignment of copyright, the owner generally transfers all or a portion of its rights permanently. An assignment of copyright differs from a license in that the assignment generally involves unconditional transfers of rights whereas licenses grant permission to a third party to use the copyright with conditions. For example, if a business owner hires an independent contractor to design a business logo or website or write software for its company, the independent contractor owns the copyright and the bundle of rights that accompany copyright. Since the business owner is paying for the creation of the work, it is very prudent for them to get the copyright in the work from the independent contractor. An assignment of copyright can accomplish this by transferring the copyright in the work from the independent contractor to the business.

C. Termination of Licenses and Assignments

Copyright licenses and assignments can be terminated. Authors (or, if the authors are not alive, their surviving spouses, children or grandchildren, or executors, administrators, personal representatives or trustees) may terminate grants of copyright assignments and licenses that were made on or after January 1, 1978 when certain conditions are met. 17 U.S.C. 203. The statute requires that notices of termination be served no earlier than twenty-five years after the execution of the grant or, if the grant covers the right of publication, no earlier than thirty years after the execution of the grant or twenty-five years after publication under the grant (whichever comes first). Note, however, that termination of a grant can not be effective until thirty-five years after the execution of the grant or, if the grant covers the right of publication, no earlier than forty years after the execution of the grant or thirty-five years after publication under the grant (whichever comes first). For example, since notices of termination under 17 U.S.C. 203 may be served, at the earliest, twenty-five years after the execution of a grant made after 1977, the earliest date on which any notices provided under 17 U.S.C. 203 could be served was January 1, 2003.

D. Sale of Copyright

The owner of a work can sell its copyright outright, either before or after the work is created. Copyrights may be sold for cash or negotiable instruments, such as a check or promissory note. For example, when an artist paints an original work, the artist owns the copyright in the painting. If the artist sells the original painting, the artist still retains the copyright in the painting which allows the artists to reproduce the work. If the artist sells the original painting *and* the copyright in the painting itself, the artist is giving away the bundle of exclusive rights that accompany the copyright, such as the right to make reproductions. Sale of a copyright and transfer of the exclusive rights associated with the copyright must be made in writing.

E. Sale of Work

The sale of copyright and the bundle of exclusive rights that accompany it, as described above, is very distinct from the sale of copyrighted work alone. When a copyrighted work is sold, such as the painting in the example above, copyrights are not conveyed with the work, unless the parties specifically state the copyright in the work is being sold along with the work itself.

5.3. Open Source Options

Open source licenses allow software to be freely used, modified and shared. An author of software may use an open source license to give the public permission to use the software at no charge. The software is protected by copyright and licensed for free under an open source license. The Open Source Initiative (OSI), founded in 1998 (www.opensource.org), is an organizational movement that has created open source standards and approved various types of licenses.

5.4. Creative Commons

As you know, copyright protects an original work of authorship fixed in a tangible medium of expression. Once the work is created, it is protected by copyright and the author of such work reserves all the rights conferred through copyright. What if an author wants others to share and use its work and not be restricted by full copyright? Creative Commons, founded in 2001 (www.creativecommons.org), is a nonprofit organization that provides free copyright licenses to tell others what parts of the copyright the owner is willing to share with the public for their use. The licenses provided by Creative Commons (CC) helps authors of works keep and manage their copyright.

Chapter Summary

A copyright owner may transfer all or part of its rights to a third party. Copyrights can be transferred by licensing, assignment or sale. A license of copyright involves the transfer of some of the rights associated with copyright. An assignment of copyright involves the unconditional transfer of all or a portion of the copyright to a third party. A copyright owner can transfer its copyrighted work to a third party. The owner may also transfer the copyright itself.

Open source licenses allow software to be freely used modified and shared. An author of software may use an open source license to give the public permission to use the software at no charge.

Creative Commons is a nonprofit organization that provides free copyright licenses to tell others what parts of copyright the owner is willing to share with the public for their use.

Key Terms

Exclusive License
Non-Exclusive License
Assignment
Open Source Options
Creative Commons

Review Questions

1. May an owner of copyright enter into contracts that give the exclusive rights associated with copyright to third parties?
2. Name the types of copyright transfers?
3. What does a copyright license do?
4. What is the difference between an exclusive and non-exclusive license?
5. What does an assignment of copyright do?
6. What is the difference between a copyright license and copyright assignment?
7. How is a copyright license or assignment terminated?
8. Who may terminate a copyright license or assignment?
9. What are open source options?
10. What does Creative Commons provide?

Web Links

1. http://www.creativecommons.org—Creative Commons website and search tool.

Discussion Exercise

1. What type of transfer are the following transactions?
a. Manuel sells his painting to Maria.
b. Ivan sells Olga the copyright in his painting.
c. Jun gives permission to Li include one of Cindy's poems in a poetry book.
d. Ahmet gives *Newsweek* the exclusive right to reprint a chapter from Ahmet's book in its magazine.

Chapter 6

Exclusive Rights and Limits to Protection and Infringement

"What is worth copying is prima facie worth protecting."
—Justice Paterson in *University of London Press Ltd. v. University Tutorial Process Ltd.*, 1916

Chapter Outline

6.1. Introduction to Statutory Rights
6.2. Activities Constituting Infringement
6.3. Forms of Infringement
6.4. Primary
6.5. Secondary
6.6. Digital Millennium Copyright Act of 1998
6.7. Internet Service Providers (ISPs): Safe Harbor Rule
6.8. What Is Not Infringement?
6.9. Fair Use Doctrine
6.10. Equitable and Statutory Defenses and Licenses
6.11. First Sale Doctrine

Chapter Objectives

- Recognize the exclusive rights granted to creative authors and artists by federal statute.
- Identify common activities that might constitute infringement of a copyright.
- Understand the role of circumstantial evidence in proving infringement.

- Distinguish between direct and indirect violators of copyright law and their liability.
- Know that Congress provided a "safe harbor" for limiting liability to Internet Service Providers (ISP) under the DMCA.
- Explain the four factors found in the fair use doctrine.

6.1. Introduction to Statutory Rights

The author or owner of a copyright has limited ownership rights over any copyrighted work. *Section 106 of the Copyright Act* grants the author a bundle of *exclusive rights* to do or to authorize others to do certain things.

Section 106

(1) to reproduce the copyrighted work in copies or phonorecords (*right to make copies or reproduce*);

(2) to prepare derivative works based upon the copyrighted work (*adaptation rights*);

(3) to distribute copies or phonorecords of the copyrighted work to the public by sale or other transfer of ownership, or by rental, lease, or lending (*public distribution*);

(4) in the case of literary, musical, dramatic, and choreographic works, pantomimes, and motion pictures and other audiovisual works, to perform the copyrighted work publicly (*public performance)*;

(5) in the case of literary, musical, dramatic, and choreographic works, pantomimes, and pictorial, graphic, or sculptural works, including the individual images of a motion picture or other audiovisual work, to display the copyrighted work publicly (*display rights*); and

(6) in the case of sound recordings, to perform the copyrighted work publicly by means of a digital audio transmission (*digital performance rights*).

These exclusive rights, though, are subject to exceptions under this statute, specifically in sections 107 through 122, and any judicially imposed restrictions or limitations. The remainder of this chapter will discuss these exceptions and limitations.

The Copyright Act of 1976 gives the author or owner of a creatve work the legal right to prevent others from unauthorized use of the work. This protection, for instance, makes it unlawful to reproduce or copy any "literary, dramatic, musical or artistic work" without the permission of the owner of the copyright in that work. In other situations the law does not allow anyone to distribute, adapt or display digital music, motion pictures, television scripts, computer software, video games and the like without consent of the copyright holder. *Section 106 (4) of the Copyright Act* goes so far as to extend the protection to prevent a high school from publicly performing a copyrighted Alvin Alley choreographed dance or Tom Stoddard play without permission of the author.

6.2. Activities Constituting Infringement

The notion of what activities constitute an *infringement* is not always easy to decipher. The five basic exclusive economic *monopoly rights (reproduce, adapt, distribute, perform and display)* do not uniformly apply to each type of protected work. For example, a photograph of a wasps' nest in a pine tree is a copyrighted work so long as it is original, minimally creative and fixed on a hard drive, film, or computer disk. In what ways can this copyright be infringed? In the online world Harvard Law Professor Larry Lessig estimates 70% of young people infringe digital works. The number of ways a copyrighted photograph is subject to **unauthorized use** is nearly endless. Downloading the photograph and distributing it to friends on Instagram, digitally manipulating the original image, or using the photograph in an online commercial venture may each constitute a violation. On the other hand there is no infringement for photographing constructed architectural works located or visible from a public place without the consent of the copyright owner.

The historical changes in the rights reserved to authors under copyright laws extend beyond the simple prohibition of the act of directly reproducing original manuscripts without permission that occurred during the era of Mark Twain and Charles Dickens. Authors are entitled to write sequels. This also means an author may be protected from an unauthorized adaptation of her plotlines or key characters. Additionally, the right of adaptation also known as the right to create *derivative* works, preserves to the author the right to make a screenplay for a Hollywood movie, translate the original work into a foreign language, convert it into a audio book or video game.

The idea of the law preventing or discouraging anyone from creating new or transformative works based on viewing, listening, screening and examining the concrete expressions of others has its limits. Verbatim copying of the copyrighted works of others is somewhat rare, but does happen. The hard cases occur in determining when material in the so-called new work takes protected elements from the first, original, copyrighted work. Does it matter how much work is taken or whether it is for commercial or non-commercial purposes? Yes.

Copyright law acknowledges the rights granted are limited monopolies in terms of time and subject to statutory exceptions and exclusions.

Justice Learned Hand said it best when he wrote that "the test for infringement of a copyright is of necessity vague." One of the most distinguished legal minds of any generation had trouble determining whether someone else's work is substantially similar to the claimed copyright work or whether the new work is exempted or protected under a variety of defenses available under the law.

6.3. Forms of Infringement

A prerequisite to any claim of infringement requires the author of the work to demonstrate ownership of the right asserted and unauthorized use or misappropriation of a material amount of the copyrighted expression. Typically, a copy of the registration certificate issued by the Copyright Office is all that is needed to show ownership. In the event the author has assigned, sold or licensed the copyright then the owner not named on the registration certificate must produce a chain of title showing ownership or exclusive licensing rights. This is usually easy to prove.

The second element—*copying directly* or *copying by improper* **appropriation**—can be more problematic to prove and requires nuanced examination and analysis. On occasion someone will admit to copying and the second element is met subject to any statutory defenses we will discuss further on in this chapter. More often than not proof occurs by **circumstantial evidence**. By that we mean showing that the alleged infringer had access to the work. For instance, in the case of *Shepard Fairey vs. A.P.* the appropriation artist Shepard Fairey's created the popular Obama *"Hope"* campaign poster based on a copyrighted photograph of then Senator Obama. A freelance photographer took Obama's picture on behalf of the Associated Press (A.P.) That photograph along with a handful of other similar photographs were widely circulated on the Internet. By virtue of the discovery process lawyers for the A.P. were able to demonstrate not only did Fairey have *access* to the work, but also downloaded the images and then tried to cover his digital trail.

Keep in mind in the absence of demonstrating *access* there can be no infringement. Unlike Patent law, *copyright protects against copying.* Any creator of an original artistic expression fixed in some medium who independently arrives at a work even an identical work has not infringed. So, for instance, the 10th Circuit Court of Appeals found an architect who had no access to the designs plans of another architect could not have infringed upon the work of another even though the two homes each built looked alike. Both architects had merely taken *ideas* from the same person. A common practice among Hollywood movie studios and New York book publishers is not to open unsolicited screenplays or manuscripts. Were the studios or publishers to produce a financially successful movie or *New York Times'* best-seller book bearing similarity to the unsolicited work they would somehow have to prove they did not see or read it and, therefore, could not have based their movie or book upon it.

Besides demonstrating either *direct evidence of copying or circumstantial access to copy,* an infringement claim requires a showing of *"probative similarity"* between the two works. By this we mean whether or not one author independently created a new work or actually copied the work from another author.

6.4. Primary

Let's look at a well-publicized example of one musical work so striking in similarity to another it precludes the possibility of the second author independently penning the same musical score. In 1963, Bright Tunes Music Company released a song written by Ronnie Mack and sung by the Chiffons titled "He's So Fine." The catchy "doo-lang doo-lang doo-lang" background vocal helped make the song an instant Billboard music classic. A few years later George Harrison recorded the song "My Sweet Lord." The two songs had nearly identical melodies. In court testimony, Harrison admitted hearing "He's So Fine" before, but argued an artist of his acclaim and talent would not purposefully (directly) copyright someone else's music. The court accepted Harrison's testimony, yet found he had "subconsciously" copied the song. He was found liable for *primary* infringement and ordered to pay monetary damages.

In addition to the *proof of copying* and *probative similarity* test, courts examine how *substantially similar* the works in question are to each other. By this we mean when looking at the two works side by side is it more likely than not the alleged infringer copied the protected work? At some level the question boils down to "what was taken" and "how much is too much." The unauthorized use of a poster of a copyrighted quilt in the background of a television show was deemed an infringement even though the poster was seen for less than two minutes. Here the court rejected the argument that the amount of the copyrighted expression copied was *de minimis* or small.

When certain works have a particular value to the author then to appropriate this feature is accordingly of *qualitative* significance. In England, for example, where dramatic works are still quite popular, the law is well settled that when the plot of a copyrighted story whether found in a play or a novel "is taken bodily with or without some minor additions or subtractions for the purposes of a stage play or cinema film" there can be little doubt of *primary* infringement.

By unanimous agreement copyright infringement cases are not limited to straight duplication of another author's creative work. However, there exists no simple test to determine what taking, in terms of both *quality* and *quantity*, is unacceptable. Even copying a small, but significant, portion of an original work can constitute substantial copying.

6.5. Secondary

The Copyright Act does not expressly impose liability on anyone other than *direct* or *primary* infringers. Over time relying on tort law concepts courts have recognized that someone who contributes to another's infringement should be held accountable. Take, for instance, a local flea market where third party vendors sell counterfeit video games at discounted prices. The direct infringer is the party who illegally reproduces the copyrighted video games. The indirect or *contributing* infringers are the operators of the flea market who provide the site and facilities for a known infringing activity and financially benefit. There are limits, though, to the application of holding everyone along the distribution chain liable. The 9th Circuit Court of Appeals refused to hold Visa contributory liable for knowingly processing credit card payments where the payments were going to a website that provided access to infringing works. The ruling was based on a finding of non-material contribution by Visa because it was not actually aiding and abetting the copying, displaying or distribution of the copyrighted works.

The pre-Internet U.S. Supreme Court case of *Sony v. Universal City Studios, Inc.*, 464 U.S. 417 (1984), examined the legal issue of whether the seller of a device that can make copies of copyrighted works is liable for *indirect* infringement. Sony manufactured a Betamax videocassette recorder. Consumers would use the machine to make copies of broadcast television programs so they could watch their favorite shows at a later time. The Court held that the Betamax was "capable of commercially significant non-infringing uses"; therefore, the sale of these recording devices by Sony did *not* constitute contributory copyright infringement.

In *Metro-Goldwyn-Mayer Studios, Inc. v. Grokster, Ltd.*, 545 U.S. 913 (2005), the Supreme Court led by Justice David Souter tackled the even more complex issue of when is the distributor of a free peer-to-peer file sharing software that is capable of both lawful and unlawful use indirectly liable for acts of infringement by third parties. The "beauty" of the design of these peer-to-peer networks is it allowed for the sharing of copyrighted music and video files without the use of central servers. It was uncontested that the vast majority of users' downloads were acts of infringement. Grokster's promotional material provided clear evidence the principal purpose of its software was to allow for downloading of copyrighted electronic files. Grokster was held contributory liable for actively encouraging the acts of infringement.

Another form of indirect infringement is *vicarious* liability. It is based on the application of the tort doctrine called *respondeat superior*, which holds "superiors" responsible for the infringing acts of its "subordinates." Vicarious infringement occurs only when the "superior," frequently the employer, receives a direct financial benefit and the "superior" has the right and ability to supervise or control the direct infringer, the employee. Liability can be found even when the "superior" lacks knowledge of the infringement. A few examples will help to clarify.

A landlord and tenant arrangement can qualify as a *respondeat superior* relationship. Suppose the landlord rents space at the going market rate to a tenant. The tenant proceeds to design and activate an Internet based website in that leased space. The device created allows for free downloading and viewing of all Metropolitan Opera weekly HD broadcasts and National Football League televised games. The landlord is not vicariously liable since there was no direct profiting from the infringement and no ability to supervise the illicit activity. On the other hand, operators of entertainment venues have been held liable for permitting the exhibition of non-licensed copyrighted musical performances.

Here is an example of an employment relationship that can lead to vicarious liability. An employee who uses pirated computer software in the course of his day-to-day work activities could give rise to copyright infringement. The employer is in a position to supervise, control and stop the infringing employee from engaging in illegal activities on company grounds during work hours. The second requirement for finding *vicarious* liability is met because the employer receives a financial benefit by not having to purchase licensed software.

Collectively, these two types of indirect infringement—*contributory* and *vicarious*—are recognized as components of what the law calls *secondary* liability.

6.6. Digital Millennium Copyright Act of 1998

The prospect of findings of indirect liability for copyright infringement under *contributory* and *vicarious* theories against the emerging Internet technology community spurred Internet Service Providers (ISPs) to lobby Congress for protection. In 1998, President Bill Clinton signed into law the *Digital Millennium Copyright Act (DMCA)*. This statute amended the *Copyright Act of 1976* by providing two significant changes.

6.7. Internet Service Providers (ISPs): Safe Harbor Rule

The first is found in *section 512 of the DMCA*. It identified several different activities and conditions for limiting ISP liability for **primary** or **secondary** copyright activities. For instance, under its *"safe harbor"* provisions an ISP can avoid liability for transient routing or connecting of infringing material automatically flowing through its computers. Similarly, infringement claims are denied for permanently storing infringing material if it promptly removes the material upon request. Additionally, the "safe harbor" rule is extended to providers who merely refer or link users to an online location containing infringing material or activities. In general, ISP immunity from liability is conditioned upon expeditiously removing or disabling access to the claimed infringing material upon notification from the copyright holder. This is referred to as the "notice and take down" provisions of *section 512*.

An example of the how the "safe harbor" provision can be used occurred in a case brought by the science fiction writer Harlan Ellison against America Online (AOL). A fan of Ellison had scanned some of his short stories and uploaded them to an online user network. AOL was named in the copyright lawsuit because the content (short stories) were stored temporarily (14 days) on its servers that were accessed by its subscribers to download or read the stories. The court held that AOL was shielded from liability because it did not encourage or direct the unlawful uploading of the infringing material, it had no control over who received Harlan's copyrighted stories, and the content was on the servers for no longer than necessary to transmit or route them to users.

The second important change known as the ***anti-circumvention*** provisions are contained in *section 1201*. This controversial component of the *DMCA* makes it illegal, and sometimes even a criminal act, to attempt to devise processes, methods or devices that seek to work around technical protections that limit copying of copyrighted works. This section of the law also prohibits the production, promotion or sale of products or services designed to circumvent systems, e.g. a digital rights management system, that limits the digital copying of protected works like movies and photographs. Falsifying, altering or removing copyright information attached or accompanying a digitized copyright work is now illegal, too. Critics dislike the *anti-circumvention* aspects of the statute because for the first time the copyright law can be violated without actually infringing upon a copyright. There are a number of significant exemptions (law enforcement, security testing, nonprofit libraries, encryption research, personal privacy, and works exempted by the Library of Congress) from liability for over-riding digital management recording devices in the statute.

Two cases illustrate the challenges presented by new technologies and companies seeking to control access or prohibit the sale of substitute products under the *anti-circumvention* rules. Shortly after enactment of the *DMCA,* a company called Static Control sold replacement toner cartridges for use in Lexmark printers. Lexmark had encrypted technology in its printers that only allowed Lexmark or Lexmark licensed toner cartridges to work with its brand of printers. Static Control embedded a chip in its toner cartridges to allow Lexmark printers to "authorize" the use of the unlicensed cartridges. Initially, a lower court agreed with Lexmark that the circumvention technology (chip) Static Control incorporated into its cartridges violated section 1201. On appeal, however, the 6th Circuit Court of Appeals reversed the lower court's finding. A similar result was reached by the 8th Circuit Court of Appeals in *Chamberlain Group, Inc. v. Skylink Techs., Inc,.,*(381 F.3d 1178 (2004)) when it upheld the dismissal of a case against the manufacturer of an aftermarket universal remote control garage door opener. The logic for judicially limiting the reach of the anti-circumvention provisions was that there was no copyrighted work the encryption was protecting.

6.8. What Is Not Infringement?

Besides the limitations on the five basic exclusive rights of copyright holders, found in *section 106 of the Copyright Act,* as amended, there are a number of statutory exclusions to copyright infringement. These affirmative defenses and licenses are codified in *sections 107 through 120* of this same *Act.* While we will discuss some of the statutory defenses, e.g. statute of limitations, equitable defenses and compulsory licenses, later in the chapter, we will begin with an analysis of the most significant and influential *defense* to a claim of copyright infringement: *Fair Use.*

6.9. Fair Use Doctrine

In many ways the concept of *fair use* seems ready made for a digital world, where musicians remix and sample songs and appropriation artists effortlessly cut, paste and collage works of others. Artists from Pablo Picasso to Andy Warhol freely admit to having "borrowed" from the works of other pioneer artists. Whether it is a cubist painting by Picasso that contains distinctive features of tribal masks from the Ivory Coast or a silkscreen image of Marilyn Monroe by Warhol extracted from a copyrighted photograph of the iconic actress. At what point is the newly created work legally sufficient to stand on its own as an original? We know that just because a work is visually changed, in the case of fine art, it does not always make the work legally *transformative* for *fair use* purposes. What does all this mean?

Specific acts enumerated in the statute are automatically deemed *fair use*, and therefore not infringement: copying for the purpose of "criticism, comment, news, reporting, teaching (multiple copies for classroom use), scholarship, or research." Beyond these canonical exceptions it is an understatement to say the law is "fluid" in its interpretation of the next four factors courts must address on a case-by-case basis in any *fair use* argument.

These factors are: 1) the purpose and character of the use, including whether such use is of a commercial nature or for nonprofit, educational purposes; 2) the nature of the copyrighted work; 3) the amount and substantiality of the portion used in relation to the copyrighted work as a whole, and; 4) the effect of the use upon the potential market for, or value of, the copyrighted work. It is the task of the court to individually assess each factor weighing in favor of one party or the other, and then viewing them all together in determining whether the use qualifies for *fair use*.

In one of most defining copyright infringement decisions, the Supreme Court in *Campbell v. Acuff-Rose*, 510 U.S. 569 (1994), gave some insight on how much weight against *fair use* the commercial aspect of the alleged infringing work should be given. Writing for the majority, Justice Souter watered down a previous Supreme Court decision discussed earlier—*Sony Corp. of America v. Universal City Studios, Inc.*—that held every-money making commercial use is presumptively unfair use. Instead, Souter wrote that *context* matters and that *parody* (a "humorous" form of public comment or criticism) even *commercial parody* can be protected.

Related to the notion of how a work is used—commercial vs. non-commercial and in what manner and for what purpose—is the requirement that the new work be *transformative*. The more *transformative*; that is, the more it adds some new expression, meaning or message, the more likely the new work is deemed an independent, original, creative, non-infringing body of work. To see how legal lan-

Figure 6.1

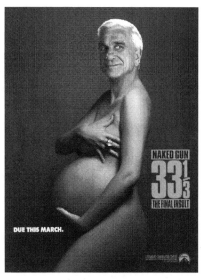

guage works in real life let's examine a pair of movie posters—one picturing an eight-month pregnant Demi Moore and the second a "pregnant" Leslie Nielson whose head was superimposed on the body of a nude double. Renowned photographer Annie Leibovitz took Moore's photograph for the *Vanity Fair* cover. Despite the fact that the lighting and poses are nearly identical the court found the *Naked Gun* parody film advertisement was both *transformative* and a form of *public comment.* Did you notice the facial distinctions: Nielson's smirking smile versus Moore's serious and pretentious expression.

The second factor—nature of the copyrighted work—concerns an inquiry as to whether the work being copied is factual or informational versus fictional or fantasy. Copying accounts of published news reporting, scholarly or scientific journals can lead to new discoveries and the exchange of debatable ideas. So factual copying of public interest material stands a greater chance of *fair use* protection than copying fictional works.

The amount and substantiality of the portion used in relation to the copyrighted work as a whole, the third consideration, requires looking largely at the *quantity* of the materials taken. For example, the creator of an initially web-based, crowd-sourced encyclopedia of *Harry Potter* terms and lexicons later published in print lost out on a *fair use* claim because of the extensive verbatim use of text from the *Harry Potter* book series. However, taking even a small amount of the work that is deemed the "the most interesting and moving parts" of the entire work can lead to a finding of copyright infringement.

The final factor examines the effect the use has on the actual and potential market for the copyright work. Consider, again, the *Naked Gun* poster. Paramount Pictures' copying of the magazine cover did not negatively impact the sales of the *Vanity Fair* magazine, which was another argument favoring *fair use.* Many courts, though, have liberally construed the meaning of "potential" market to mean whether the copyright holder intended to utilize the *derivative rights* in the work, e.g. by licensing or in the case of J.K. Rowling creating her own encyclopedia of terms and lexicons, or not, the fact that it could happen is enough to weigh heavily against *fair use.*

All four of these factors are interrelated and as the examples indicate the boundaries are not subject to rigid bright-line rules. *Fair use* is an equitable defense mixing questions of facts and law. Bad faith on the part of the infringer can also impact the final outcome.

6.10. Equitable and Statutory Defenses and Licenses

Statute of Limitations

A civil copyright claim must be filed within three years after the discovery of the infringement or after it reasonably should have been discovered. For criminal copyright claims authorized under the *DMCA* the federal government must bring suit within five years after the infringement occurred. Waiting beyond these respective time lines to file a lawsuit may lead to the infringing author arguing the *statute of limitations* was violated, and the case should be dismissed.

Equity

A number of narrowly construed equitable defenses are occasionally of avail to the alleged copyright infringer. For instance, a copyright holder who encourages, facilitates or acquiesces in the infringing activities is barred under the doctrine of *equitable estoppel* from seeking relief. An unreasonable delay in filing for infringement can conjure up the old French law defense of *laches.* Asserting the scope of a copyright extends beyond what the law recognizes, e.g. using the copyright to violate antitrust laws, may lead to the defense of *copyright misuse.*

Licenses

The general rule of requiring permission to reproduce, perform or distribute a copyrighted work from the holder of the copyright is subject to a few exceptions. These exceptions are called *compulsory licenses.* They are common in the (nondramatic) music industry. By giving notice to the copyright holder and paying the statutory fee set by the Copyright Office any person or group may record and distribute a copyrighted song. Also, it only applies to phonorecords distributed to the public. In *ABKCO Music, Inc. v. Stellar Records, Inc.,* 96 F.3d 60 (1996), the Court of Appeals held that lyrics to music are not covered under the *compulsory license* requirement because they are independently copyrighted as literary works. Harry Fox is a well-known agency that music publishers/copyright holders use to collect royalties and even issue licenses including those for cell phone ringtones, background music for movies and television, and a host of digital services. Licenses for dramatic works, e.g. operas and musicals, are *non-compulsory* and must be negotiated. Courts have the power to order a copyright holder to grant a license regardless of the type of copyrighted material. A statutory exemption also exists for the private copying of sound recordings.

The Artists' Rights Society is another organization that guards the exclusive rights of authors, in this case, creators of visual fine arts. Recently, it has sought to recover a licensing fee from James Cameron the director of the 3D version of the movie *Titanic.* Cameron publicly displayed a rendition of Picasso's famous painting *Les Demoiselles d'Avignon,* painted in 1907, without authorization. Picasso died in 1973; therefore, his exclusive copyright interests held by his heirs continue until 2043. Picasso's heirs, for the second time, asked the Artists' Rights Society to intervene.

Back in 1997 when Cameron's original *Titanic* was released, Picasso's family was upset on two counts. First, the movie depicted the loss of the painting when it was seen disappearing at sea (along with Rose's lover played by Leonardo DiCaprio). The real painting does exist, and is on public display at The Museum of Modern Art in New York City. The painting was never on the *Titanic.* Second, it infringed upon the right to publicly display the image owned by the copyright holders—the heirs. The Artists' Rights Society successfully negotiated a licensing fee.

Here are two fascinating legal questions: Is the 3D version of the original movie a derivative right; and did the parties' original licensing agreement cover the later 3D version as well or is a new licensing fee arrangement required? You should know the answer to the first part of the question—yes, it is and, therefore, a new and original creative expression was created based on the first original creative expression. The second inquiry, without knowing the terms and conditions of the licensing agreement, we cannot answer with a 100% certainty. The Artists' Rights Society has taken the position the 3D movie version was not contractually covered under the original agreement.

6.11. First Sale Doctrine

An intriguing exception to infringement claims is embedded in *Section 109 of the Copyright Act: first sale doctrine.* In short, this doctrine allows the purchaser of a legal *copy* of a copyrighted work the freedom to destroy, sell, gift or rent the copy so long as the exclusive rights of the copyright owner are not infringed. For instance, the buyer of this book may resell it to a bookstore, display it in a library, give it to a friend who plans on taking this course next semester or even toss it into a celebratory bonfire. The law distinguishes between the ownership of the copyright in the original work and the physical ownership of the medium in which the copy of the work is published.

There are exceptions to the infringement exception. The rental of computer programs and music sound recordings, but not audiobooks, is prohibited. Works of visual fine art that meet the requirements of the Visual Artists Rights Act, discussed later in the international components of copyrights chapter, may not be destroyed under the *first sale doctrine.* In a landmark 2013 decision that impacts college students, libraries and used book stores, the U.S. Supreme Court ruled against the publisher John Wiley and held that the *doctrine* applies when the legally acquired (cheaper) copyrighted works (books, in this instance) were manufactured overseas and then shipped and resold in the U.S. Previously, the freedom to resell copyrighted goods did not apply to goods that were made and first sold *outside* the U.S.

Chapter Summary

The Copyright Act giveth and taketh away. *Section 106* grants the copyright owner a bundle of exclusive rights: reproduce, prepare derivative works, distribute copies, display and publicly perform. These rights are complicated in practice and do not uniformly apply to all covered works. Keeping in mind that while ideas cannot be copyrighted one does not have to precisely duplicate a protected work to infringe.

There are two different types of infringement: primary and secondary. In the case of primary infringement the accused is charged with directly violating one or more of the exclusive rights. At some level the probative issue boils down to "what was taken" and "how much is too much." Secondary infringements have a number of components, contributory and vicarious, and require a showing of aiding and abetting others in infringing.

The introduction of the Digital Millennium Copyright Act was a statutory response to copyright concerns created by Internet digital technology. This law prohibits attempts to maneuver around processes, methods or devices that limit copying of copyrighted works. The Act also makes it wrongful to produce or market devices designed to circumvent technologies that seek to protect copyrighted works from infringement. Internet Service Providers are exempt from liability so long as they comply with the law's safe harbor provisions.

There are a number of important exclusions or defenses to copyright infringement. The Copyright Act was amended to include an allowance for public comment, criticism, teaching, and reporting. Another part of the amendment provides four factors to consider in assessing whether the use is a fair use not requiring advance permission from the copyright owner. Claims must be filed within established statute of limitations parameters to succeed. Licenses including compulsory licenses in the music industry are another means to avoid an action alleging non-permissible use. A limitation to the exclusive right of distribution known as the first sale doctrine allows the physical owner of an authorized copy of a copyrighted work to freely distribute or resell it.

Key Terms

Exclusive Rights
Derivative Rights
Monopoly Rights
Unauthorized Use
Infringement
Direct or Primary Infringers
Indirect or Secondary Infringers
Circumstantial Evidence
Appropriation
Probative Similarity
Safe Harbor

Anti-circumvention
Fair Use
Transformative
Digital Millennium Copyright Act
Statute of Limitations
Laches
Licenses
First Sale Doctrine

Review Questions

1. List the primary basic exclusive rights granted by statute to a copyright owner of a creative work.
2. When might downloading a digital photograph or song and sharing it with friends on Facebook not be considered an act of copyright infringement?
3. What are examples of derivative rights in the movie or publishing business?
4. What an artist exclaims her work is "transformative" what does she mean in copyright law terms?
5. When must a school seek a license to perform a Broadway play?
6. What steps must Internet Service Providers take to avoid liability from storing infringing material under the safe harbor rule?
7. How is it possible to violate copyright law without actually infringing upon a copyright?
8. Is a blogger who prints part of the text from a *New York Times* best-selling book for purposes of news reporting, comment or criticism violating the exclusive rights of a copyright holder?
9. Is it true that as long as one pays the statutory compulsory licensing fee set by the Copyright Office any person or band may record and distribute a publicly available song?
10. Do you think downloading a song or sound recording without compensation is the same thing as copying?

Web Links

1. Two of the leading universities for fair use research, analysis and advocacy are Harvard and Stanford. Both schools operate websites that provide rich information on copyright and fair use. See: http://www.fairuse.stanford.edu and http://www.cyber.law.harvard.edu/fairuse.

Discussion Exercise

1. Should unique and creative fashion designs be deemed copyrightable works of art? Congress is considering enacting legislation to provide up to three years of legal protection for qualifying fashion designs. If this law was enacted, then under what circumstances might stores that purposefully manufacture, distribute and sell "knock-off" designer clothing be found guilty of unlawful copyright infringement?

Chapter 7

Copyright Remedies

"There are better things in life than to copy."—Man Ray

Chapter Outline

Chapter Objectives

- Recognize Section 504 of the Copyright Act permits civil monetary damages that may bear no relation to actual damages for infringement.
- Note statutory damages are elective and actual damages and lost profits may be sought as a remedy.
- Learn money damages are legal remedies.
- Distinguish between legal and equitable remedies.
- Identify injunctions as the primary form of equitable relief.
- Understand the copyright implications digital recording devices are having on the music business.
- Appreciate jail and fines, while rare in criminal copyright cases, are available to those who purposefully infringe for commercial gain.

7.1. Civil Remedies

Introduction

Federal Courts have exclusive jurisdiction over statutory copyright infringement claims, although not over common law claims. Courts have broad authority to take reasonable actions to prevent or restrain copyright infringement. Injunctions and monetary damages are two of the most common civil remedies. In today's digital era every transfer of an mp3 music track or file-sharing action may raise issues of infringement and recovery for damages.

According to a recent study, the average teenager has downloaded 800 songs illegally. Not surprisingly, the *Recording Industry Association of America* (RIAA) acting on behalf of music companies like Sony Corp, Arista Records, Warner Music Group's Warner Bros and Atlantic labels, and Vivendi SA's Universal Music Group has brought more than 12,000 copyright infringement lawsuits against individuals accused of illegally downloading music. This is after written notice was provided to both those accused of illegally transferring an mp3 music track from a file sharing site and to the well known websites (Napster, Morpheus, Kazza and LimeWire) who contributed to the acts of infringement, as required under the *DMCA*.

7.2. Statutory Damages and Relief

Section 504 of the Copyright Act allows the aggrieved copyright holder "*statutory damages*" in an amount ranging between $750 and $150,000 for each act of infringement depending on the willfulness of the infringement. This statutory remedy is significant because it does not require any proof of actual damages suffered, it might bear no relationship to actual damages, and each illegal download can be deemed an act of infringement.

In 2012, the Supreme Court left intact a $675,000 jury award against a college student who illegally downloaded and distributed thousands of songs from the Internet. The 1st Circuit Court of Appeals rejected the student's contention that individual downloaders who do not profit from sharing songs should not be treated the same as companies whose business model is to steal copyrighted works.

There is a strong inducement to registering copyrights because statutory damages are only available if the work was registered at the time of infringement (or within three months of publication). Statutory damages are an elective *remedy* by the copyright holder. In the alternative courts may award *actual damages* and *profits*. In this instance the court must order an inquiry into just how and how much injury the infringement has caused. In those instances where the infringer is deemed "innocent," meaning unaware or had no reason to believe the actions were infringing, then the court may reduce the statutory award to no less than $200. All damages are *legal* remedies.

The daughter and executrix of a well-known deceased photographer Ruth Orkin Engel, sued the manufacturer of T-shirts for bearing reproductions of one of Engel's color photographs taken from a book. Infringement was conceded so the sole issue was how to calculate damages. More than 2500 T-shirts had been sold. The court found the extent of the actual damage was virtually impossible to ascertain. The harm to the photographer's artistic reputation from having a rarefied artistic image reproduced on the mundane medium of a T-shirt and how this willful infringement may impact future revenues of the deceased artist may become evident only over the years to come. Nonetheless, the court awarded a five-figure dollar amount in actual damages. Given the willfulness of the infringement the court could have also awarded *punitive* damages subject to constitutional limitations.

Section 502 of the Copyright Act empowers the court to "grant temporary and permanent *injunctions* on such terms as it may deem reasonable to prevent or restrain infringement of a copyright." *Injunctions* are a form of *equitable relief.* An illustration of the application of *injunctive* powers by a lower court occurred when the author of the novel *The Wind Done Gone* used the most famous scenes, plot and dialog elements, and character descriptions from the legendary Civil War book *Gone With the Wind.* The estate of Margaret Mitchell sued the author and publisher for copyright infringement. As part of the relief requested, the suit demanded the imposition of a temporary *injunction* halting the further distribution and sale of *The Wind Done Gone.* The court granted the *injunction* based on an analysis of these four factors: 1) threat of irreparable harm to *Gone With the Wind*; 2) remedies at law are inadequate: 3) balancing of the harm to the copyright holders against the harm to the author and publisher if the injunction were issued; and 4) the public interest not be disserved by granting the injunction. On appeal, the 11th Circuit Court of Appeals applied the *fair use* factors in finding *The Wind Done Gone* was a work of *parody*, and removed the temporary *injunction.*

In rare circumstances, the court may order the **impounding** and **destruction** of both the copies and the equipment (molds, masters, plates, devices, etc.) used for illicit reproduction. Do you think a court would go so far as to order the removal of a tattoo design that infringes upon, say, a visual or literary work? This may be a farfetched example, but let's have fun with the song *Motto*. Canadian rapper Drake copyrighted the lyrics to this popular digital download with voice by Lil Wayne. The most significant lyrics are "you only live once" or "*YOLO*." Let's further assume the *fair use* affirmative defense fails when a friend has a tattoo artist imprint the acronym "*YOLO*" on a visible part of the body. Might Drake seek the *equitable* remedies of enjoining the tattoo artist from further copyright infringement or seeking the destruction of any "*YOLO*" stencils? Do you think the *equitable* relief request might extend to the court ordering the removal of the tattoo? (P.S. Zac Efron got a tattoo with the word "*YOLO*.")

In 2012, the 4th Circuit Court of Appeals in Richmond, VA heard an appeal of a lower court award of $480,000 against a tattoo artist who continued to use a licensed stencil design after the expiration of the license. The *fair use* defense failed when the only change the artist made was to the color of the image. The court held the damage award was reasonable and constitutional.

7.3. Digital Sampling

The growth of digital recording devices has made it easy to "sample" a portion of a recorded song. By cutting and looping digital samples through a new recording the issue arises whether this unauthorized use is an act of infringement. In a way digital sampling of sounds is similar to collaging in the visual fine arts. Composing music or fine art through these methods is a creative endeavor. Whether it is *transformative* enough to qualify for *fair use* exclusion depends on the *quantitative* and *qualitative* importance of the sampled component to the overall copyrighted works. The answer to this question impacts the remedies available to the copyright holder.

It's well established in the music industry that unauthorized sampling infringes upon the sound recording copyright and may infringe upon the musical works held on the underlying sampled music. A $4 million jury award, later reduced, against the best-selling Notorious B.I.G album *Ready to Die* for illegal sampling included the court enjoining the sales of the album. In far reaching language, the 6th Circuit Court of Appeal ruled that Notorious B.I.G.'s *two-second* sampling was an *infringement* of the sound recording.

7.4. How Copyright Law Changed Hip Hop

The article "How Copyright Law Changed Hip Hop" reprinted from *Stay Free!* magazine tells its own story about how the industry has changed.

How Copyright Law Changed Hip Hop
An interview with Public Enemy's Chuck D and Hank Shocklee
By Kembrew McLeod | Issue #20

When Public Enemy released *It Takes a Nation of Millions to Hold Us Back*, in 1988, it was as if the album had landed from another planet. Nothing sounded like it at the time. *It Takes a Nation* came frontloaded with sirens, squeals, and squawks that augmented the chaotic, collaged backing tracks over which P.E. frontman Chuck D laid his politically and poetically radical rhymes. He rapped about white supremacy, capitalism, the music industry, black nationalism, and—in the case of "Caught, Can I Get a Witness?"—digital sampling: "CAUGHT, NOW IN COURT 'CAUSE I STOLE A BEAT / THIS IS A SAMPLING SPORT / MAIL FROM THE COURTS AND JAIL / CLAIMS I STOLE THE BEATS THAT I RAIL ... I FOUND THIS MINERAL THAT I CALL A BEAT / I PAID ZERO."

In the mid- to late 1980s, hip-hop artists had a very small window of opportunity to run wild with the newly emerging samplingtechnologies more effectively than Public Enemy, who put hundreds of sampled aural fragments into *It Takes a Nation* and stirred them up to create a new, radical sound that changed the way we hear music. But by 1991, no one paid zero for the records they sampled without getting sued. They had to pay a lot.

Stay Free! talked to the two major architects of P.E.'s sound, Chuck D and Hank Shocklee, about hip-hop, sampling, and how copyright law altered the way P.E. and other hip-hop artists made their music.

The following is a combination of two interviews conducted separately with Chuck D and Hank Shocklee.—Kembrew McLeod

＊ ＊ ＊

Stay Free!: What are the origins of sampling in hip-hop?

Chuck D: Sampling basically comes from the fact that rap music is not music. It's rap over music. So vocals were used over records in the very beginning stages of hip-hop in the 70s to the early '80s. In the late 1980s, rappers were recording over live bands who were basically emulating the sounds off of the records. Eventually, you had synthesizers and samplers, which would take sounds that would then get arranged or looped, so rappers can still do their thing over it. The arrangement of sounds taken from recordings came around 1984 to 1989.

Stay Free!: Those synthesizers and samplers were expensive back then, especially in 1984. How did hip-hop artists get them if they didn't have a lot of money?

Chuck D: Not only were they expensive, but they were limited in what they could do—they could only sample two seconds at a time. But people were able to get a hold of equipment by renting time out in studios.

Stay Free!: How did the Bomb Squad [Public Enemy's production team, led by Shocklee] use samplers and other recording technologies to put together the tracks on *It Takes a Nation of Millions.*

Hank Shocklee: The first thing we would do is the beat, the skeleton of the track. The beat would actually have bits and pieces of samples already in it, but it would only be rhythm sections. Chuck would start writing and trying different ideas to see what worked. Once he got an idea, we would look at it and see where the track was going. Then we would just start adding on whatever it needed, depending on the lyrics. I kind of architected the whole idea. The sound has a look to me, and Public Enemy was all about having a sound that had its own distinct vision. We didn't want to use anything we considered traditional R&B stuff—bass lines and melodies and chord structures and things of that nature.

Stay Free!: How did you use samplers as instruments?

Chuck D: We thought sampling was just another way of arranging sounds. Just like a musician would take the sounds off of an instrument and arrange them their own particular way. So we thought we was quite crafty with it.

Shocklee: "Don't Believe the Hype," for example—that was basically played with the turntable and transformed and then sampled. Some of the manipulation we was doing was more on the turntable, live end of it.

Stay Free!: When you were sampling from many different sources during the making of *It Takes a Nation*, were you at all worried about copyright clearance?

Shocklee: No. Nobody did. At the time, it wasn't even an issue. The only time copyright was an issue was if you actually took the entire rhythm of a song, as in looping, which a lot of people are doing today. You're going to take a track, loop the entire thing, and then that becomes the basic track for the song. They just paperclip a backbeat to it. But we were taking a horn hit here, a guitar riff there, we might take a little speech, a kicking snare from somewhere else. It was all bits and pieces.

Stay Free!: Did you have to license the samples in *It Takes a Nation of Millions* before it was released?

Shocklee: No, it was cleared afterwards. A lot of stuff was cleared afterwards. Back in the day, things was different. The copyright laws didn't really extend into sampling until the hip-hop artists started getting sued. As a matter of fact, copyright didn't start catching up with us until *Fear of a Black Planet*. That's when the copyrights and everything started becoming stricter because you had a lot of groups doing it and people were taking whole songs. It got so widespread that the record companies started policing the releases before they got out.

Stay Free!: With its hundreds of samples, is it possible to make a record like *It Takes a Nation of Millions* today? Would it be possible to clear every sample?

Shocklee: It wouldn't be impossible. It would just be very, very costly. The first thing that was starting to happen by the late 1980s was that the people were doing buyouts. You could have a buyout— meaning you could purchase the rights to sample a sound—for around $1,500. Then it started creeping up to $3,000, $3,500, $5,000, $7,500. Then they threw in this thing called rollover rates. If your rollover rate is every 100,000 units, then for every 100,000 units you sell, you have to pay an additional $7,500. A record that sells two million copies would kick that cost up twenty times. Now you're looking at one song costing you more than half of what you would make on your album.

Chuck D: Corporations found that hip-hop music was viable. It sold albums, which was the bread and butter of corporations. Since the corporations owned all the sounds, their lawyers began to search out people who illegally infringed upon their records. All the rap artists were on the big six record companies, so you might have some lawyers from Sony looking at some lawyers from BMG and some lawyers from BMG saying, "Your artist is doing this," so it was a tit for tat that usually made money for the lawyers, garnering money for the company. Very little went to the original artist or the publishing company.

Shocklee: By 1990, all the publishers and their lawyers started making moves. One big one was Bridgeport, the publishing house that owns all the George Clinton stuff. Once all the little guys started realizing you can get paid from rappers if they use your sample, it prompted the record companies to start investigating because now the people that they publish are getting paid.

Stay Free!: There's a noticeable difference in Public Enemy's sound between 1988 and 1991. Did this have to do with the lawsuits and enforcement of copyright laws at the turn of the decade?

Chuck D: Public Enemy's music was affected more than anybody's because we were taking thousands of sounds. If you separated the sounds, they wouldn't have been anything—they were unrecognizable. The sounds were all collaged together to make a sonic wall. Public Enemy was affected because it is too expensive to defend against a claim. So we had to change our whole style, the style of *It Takes a Nation* and *Fear of a Black Planet*, by 1991.

Shocklee: We were forced to start using different organic instruments, but you can't really get the right kind of compression that way. A guitar sampled off a record is going to hit differently than a guitar sampled in the studio. The guitar that's sampled off a record is going to have all the compression that they put on the recording, the equalization. It's going to hit the tape harder. It's going to slap at you. Something that's organic is almost going to have a powder effect. It hits more like a pillow than a piece of wood. So those things change your mood, the feeling you can get off of a record. If you notice that by the early 1990s, the sound has gotten a lot softer.

Chuck D: Copyright laws pretty much led people like Dr. Dre to replay the sounds that were on records, then sample musicians imitating those records. That way you could get by the master clearance, but you still had to pay a publishing note.

Shocklee: See, there's two different copyrights: publishing and master recording. The publishing copyright is of the written music, the song structure. And the master recording is the song as it is played on a particular recording. Sampling violates both of these copyrights. Whereas if I record my own version of someone else's song, I only have to pay the publishing copyright. When you violate the master recording, the money just goes to the record company.

Chuck D: Putting a hundred small fragments into a song meant that you had a hundred different people to answer to. Whereas someone like EPMD might have taken an entire loop and stuck with it, which meant that they only had to pay one artist.

Stay Free!: So is that one reason why a lot of popular hip-hop songs today just use one hook, one primary sample, instead of a collage of different sounds?

Chuck D: Exactly. There's only one person to answer to. Dr. Dre changed things when he did *The Chronic* and took something like Leon Haywood's "I Want'a Do Something Freaky to You" and revamped it in his own way but basically kept the rhythm and instrumental hook intact. It's easier to sample a groove than it is to create a whole new collage. That entire collage element is out the window.

Shocklee: We're not really privy to all the laws and everything that the record company creates within the company. From our standpoint, it was looking like the record company was spying on us, so to speak.

Chuck D: The lawyers didn't seem to differentiate between the craftiness of it and what was blatantly taken.

Stay Free!: Switching from the past to the present, on the new Public Enemy album, *Revolverlution*, you had fans remix a few old Public Enemy tracks. How did you get this idea?

Chuck D: We have a powerful online community through Rapstation.com, PublicEnemy.com, Slamjams.com, and Bringthenoise.com. My thing was just looking at the community and being able to say, "Can we actually make them involved in the creative process?" Why not see if we can connect all these bedroom and basement studios, and the ocean of producers, and expand the Bomb Squad to a worldwide concept?

Stay Free!: As you probably know, some music fans are now sampling and mashing together two or more songs and trading the results online. There's one track by Evolution Control Committee that uses a Herb Alpert instrumental as the backing track for your "By the Time I Get to Arizona." It sounds like you're rapping over a Herb Alpert and the Tijuana Brass song. How do you feel about other people remixing your tracks without permission?

Chuck D: I think my feelings are obvious. I think it's great.

7.5. Criminal Remedies

Many of you probably have seen the following cautionary language at the beginning of a Redbox movie rental:

"Warning: The unauthorized reproduction or distribution of this copyrighted work is illegal. Criminal copyright infringement, including infringement without monetary gain, is investigated by the FBI and is punishable by up to 5 years in federal prison and a fine of $250,000."

The *Copyright Act* permits the federal government to treat a copyright infringement as a criminal offense when done knowingly, willfully, intentionally and for commercial gain. The government also has to prove the reproduction or distribution including electronically means of one or more copyrighted works with a total retail value over $1000 during any 180-day period. Jail time and fines can also extend to those who aid others in purposeful infringement under the statute.

The *Family Entertainment and Copyright Act of 2005* extends criminal liability to knowingly making a copyrighted computer program, musical work, motion picture or other audiovisual work or sound recording on a computer network accessible to the public for copying. Multiple offenders can be imprisoned for up to 10 years. Willful violators of the *DMCA* are subject to fines as high as $500,000 and imprisonment for up to 5 years.

A Russian graduate student and computer programmer, Dmitri Sklyarov, was the first person indicted for trafficking and offering to the public a software program that could circumvent technological protections on copyrighted material under the *DMCA*. Sklyarov created what was known as an Advanced eBook Processor for his employer that allowed for moving eBooks from one computer to another. At a technical conference in Los Vegas he announced that the encryption software of the Amazon and Barnes & Noble eBooks was so weak it could be broken with ease. He then revealed how to crack and read the encrypted Adobe eBooks allegedly in violation of the *DMCA*. Adobe asked the federal government to investigate. Ultimately, the charges against Sklvarov were dropped in turn for his agreeing to testify against his employer, who was exonerated at trial.

Requests for remedies must be filed within existing statutory time rules to succeed. Civil requests for monetary damages or injunctive help must be filed in court within 3 years of discovering the alleged infringing activity. Criminal actions must be brought inside 5 years of when the cause of action arose.

Chapter Summary

There are broad ranges of legal and equitable remedies available in copyright infringement cases. Monetary damages are a common form of civil action in copyright infringement actions. The Copyright Act sets statutory damages by law. These civil statutory damages, however, are only available to those who register their copyrights with the U.S. Copyright Office. The alternative way to collect damages against an infringer is to sue for actual losses and to collect any profit the infringer earned. Innocent copyright infringers are treated lighter than willful violators.

Section 504 of the Copyright Act grants another form of relief to protect the exclusive rights of copyright holders. These equitable remedies are injunctions and impounding and destroying illegal copies. The interview with Public Enemy's Chuck D and Hank Shocklee describe how copyright law implicates the common practice of sampling in the music industry.

It is possible for copyright infringement to be treated as a federal crime. The government as prosecutor must demonstrate the person intentionally and with full knowledge infringed for financial purposes. Offenders are subject to substantial fines and imprisonment.

Key Terms

Statutory Damages
Recording Industry Association of America (RIAA)
Equitable Relief
Injunctions
Impounding and Destruction
Digital Sampling

Review Questions

1. Once something is posted on the Internet can it be freely distributed and shared?
2. Should the law be changed to disallow the application of statutory damages when they bear no relation to actual damages suffered by the copyright holder?

3. Is creativity thwarted when courts have broad leeway to impose damages and injunctions on common practices like mashing and sampling in the music industry?
4. Do you agree with a federal court in Florida that recently ruled statutory damages should be calculated on the basis of the number times the infringer posted the content, and not the number of times it was viewed?
5. Why is it that what you do with your iPad, guitar or pencil can land you in federal court?
6. Do you believe every unauthorized transfer of an mp3 music track from a file-sharing site should be an act of infringement?

Web Links

1. The website www.lib.uconn.edu/copyright/liability.html discusses the various liabilities and penalties for copyright infringement cases. The official government website that helps to answer questions about remedies is www.copyright.gov/help/faq/faq-infringement.html.

Discussion Exercise

1. Assume you personally video record your college's musical rendition of *Grease*. You post your unauthorized recording on a social media site readily available for viewing by your friends. Have you broken any copyright laws? Who might sue you and what remedies may they seek?

Chapter 8

Special Topics

Chapter Outline

Chapter Objectives

- Learn how content posted on social media sites has the potential to raise copyright concerns.
- Recognize social media sites use of terms of service agreements automatically serve to grant licenses to access all posted material.
- Appreciate how online devices to protect licensed software from unauthorized downloading are gaining in popularity, but in many cases raise personal privacy issues.

- Learn how relatively new technologies, digital rights management (DRM) and digital watermarking, can work to limit repetitive copying of protected media content.
- Discover new Google platforms' amazing impact on expanding search possibilities, while creating legal challenges.
- Consider whether federal prosecutors are too aggressive when they criminally charge non-commercial copyright infringers.

8.1. Introduction

The new millennium has brought about incredible leaps in technology, information, and global connections. By tapping into the Internet we have changed the way we learn, conduct business, interact with each other, and experience life. RSS feeds and blogs have supplanted print media. iTunes playlists have seared sales of old school music albums. E-readers shun purchasing bookstore hardcover books, while movies and television shows are downloaded and streamed anytime and anywhere. The creators and suppliers of information and culture have been forced to reconsider how intellectual property is managed, administered and protected in a digital world.

8.2. Social Media

In 1995, *Newsweek*—no longer published in print form—featured an article with the headline, "The Internet? Blah! Hype Alert: Why cyberspace isn't, and will never be Nirvana." The author, Clifford Stoll, wrote: "The truth is no online database will ever replace your daily newspaper, no CD-ROM can take the place of a competent teacher, and no computer will change the way government works." What was missing, according to Stoll, was human contact; " ... computers and networks isolate us from one another." Enter Mark Zuckerberg and social media. Facebook has over 1 billion registered users. Every minute five new profiles are created. Every 24 hours 1 million new Twitter accounts are born. More than 2/3 of the 6 billion people on the planet own a mobile device. At least once a day nearly 3/4 of all smart phone users access social networks through mobile apps.

Since the advent of social media sites a little more than a decade ago, social media users have increasingly uploaded personal content files for personal and shared use. Music, video, text, photographs and business logos account for a large amount of the content files that are uploaded. Facebook archives 10 times more photographs than are found at the Library of Congress. The questions from this interactive use are twofold: who owns the rights to the material uploaded and is the uploader infringing upon the copyrights or moral rights of the author?

Social media sites such as Facebook, Google+, Instagram and Twitter have lengthy *terms of service agreements* where all users of posted content are automatically granted a sub-license to access all posted material without additional permission or compensation. For example, Twitter's Terms of Service state:

> *By submitting, posting or displaying Content on or through the Services, you grant us a worldwide, non-exclusive, royalty-free license (with the right to sublicense) to use, copy, reproduce, process, adapt, modify, publish, transmit, display and distribute such Content in any and all media or distribution methods (now known or later developed).*

These open-licenses have come under criticism for attempting to take over rights' ownership of all of their users' content. These social media sites point out their inability to function without these licenses and sub-licenses. For instance, Google+'s Terms of Service state that *"in performing the required technical steps to provide the services to our users, (Google) may distribute your content over various public networks in various media,"* and may *"make changes to your content as are necessary to conform and adapt that content to the technical requirements of connecting networks, devices, services, or media."*

This is how it works. Whenever one emails a photograph to a family member, Google has to copy and modify the digital file several times, then send it to multiple servers or an Internet Service Provider (ISP), where it is cached and archived, and then finally received at the recipient's computer. The sub-license gives legal permission to Google and other sites to conduct these actions without which file transfer of the photograph is impossible.

From a technical perspective these sub-licenses readily make content available to other users; however, in many cases copyrighted material, and in some cases modified copyrighted material, is now posted on sites available for others to use without permission, attribution or royalties. The balancing act for many artists is one of trying to protect copyright photographs, music or blogs from unauthorized use while appreciating the incredible exposure to otherwise unrecognized creative works social media sites provide.

8.3. Creative Commons

An alternative licensing mechanism used by millions of authors that was discussed earlier, as a means for sharing content absent some of the concerns and restrictions of the current copyright regime, is the *Creative Commons* system. A handful of different registration options are available under this academically inspired online enterprise. In brief, authors may "gift" their works to the public or choose a "Founders Copyright" that assigns to *Creative Commons* an exclusive license for 14 or 28 years. Meanwhile, any person that uploads or downloads the work is then required to properly attribute the work to the original copyright holder.

8.4. Rights of Privacy and Publicity

Copyright protection is not always the sole issue when photos are posted online. Aaron Olson filed a lawsuit against his uncle, Randall LaBrie, for posting and tagging him in an embarrassing picture as a young child posing in front of a Christmas tree. LaBrie refused to remove the picture despite repeated requests. Olson filed charges of harassment and violation of his right to privacy. The court refused to issue an order to have the picture removed. When pictures involve those of famous people, such as, reality TV stars, professional athletes, and celebrities, the posting of their images may infringe upon their *right of publicity* especially when their images or likeness is used in a commercial setting.

In the workplace unusual copyright issues related to social media can arise. For instance, a company by the name of Ardis Health hired Ashleigh Nankivell to conduct marketing and promotional activities. She used various websites, blogs and social media to connect to potential clients. After she was terminated, she refused to hand over the passwords to every Internet site she used as part of her employment. After filing suit, the court held that all the passwords were the copyright property of Ardis Health because her hiring was considered work for hire.

8.5. Software Privacy Protection

In the early years of the Internet revolution computer software was not protected under any intellectual property laws. A 1980 amendment to the Copyright Act gave computer software the same recognition as any other original works of authorship. Certain types of *inventions* that rely on algorithms and software programming to produce useful, tangible and concrete results are patentable as well.

Avenues for software sharing and downloading began to spread exponentially via tools like USENET ("Users Network"—Conceived in 1979, USENET is an electronic bulletin board that preceded the Internet but is still used today as a newsgroup/forum tool for posting files, news, messages, etc.) and FTP (File Transfer Protocol). Every day over 200 gigabytes of data is transferred over USENET. One of the most famous original piracy cases involving software makers occurred when a 21-year-old MIT student was accused of enabling the sharing and illegal downloading of hundreds of computer games. The court held because the student was not profiting from the activity it was not an illegal infringement. In 1997, Congress quickly closed what became known as the "Lamacchia Loophole," named after the MIT student, by enacting the No Electronic Theft Act.

The *Business Software Alliance* claims more than $60 billion in licensing revenue is lost annually by businesses employing unlicensed software programs. The Software and Information Industry Alliance Association estimates that more than 75% of all the software used in China is pirated! The worldwide use of unlicensed software is around 40%.

8.6. Access Key

Several types of software piracy protection methods are available to manufacturers. The first and most widely used protection method is a verification process requiring that an access key, or serial number, be entered whenever software is installed. The number is supplied by the manufacturer to the purchaser of the software license and must match the specific internal DLL, or "Dynamic Link Library" embedded within the software. Once a single *access code* is verified, this DLL begins a domino effect, allowing all necessary functions to run based on the single verification. This method is not without drawbacks though—anyone who has experienced a ".dll error" in Windows is familiar with what happens when these links break down. Online activation is a similar method. Here the user must enter personal and purchase receipt information to the software manufacturer's website to receive verification and authorization for use. Rather than a randomly selected serial number provided at purchase, this method connects the serial number provided with the receipt and purchaser information supplied, in hopes of preventing code sharing and piracy tracking.

Hardware locking is another type of protection against piracy that marries the software sold to the specific computer it is installed in, not allowing the program to run on any other computer. Finally, Dongle locking requires a separate piece of external hardware, a USB "key" sold by the manufacturer that when combined with the software allows for authenticated use. This differs from standard serial code access because the authentication, pulled from the separate USB device, cannot be copied, shared, or hacked. Most Dongle Locked software though, will only allow one version of the software to run at a time. Specific start-up firms like SafeNew and StarForce Technologies specialize in designing encryption and copyright protection services for the business trade.

Critics claim that software manufacturers walk a fine line between protecting their product and overstepping the bounds of ownership and privacy of the purchaser. Legislation such as the Uniform Computer Transaction Information Act (UCTIA), a proposed amendment to the Uniformed Commercial Code in 2000, failed to achieve widespread passage due to the consumer outcry. Though originally thought to be 'fast-tracked' for passage, the majority of consumer activist and legal groups including the American Law Institute opposed the bill. It was perceived that instituting a standard means of regulating software sales and protection favored the software manufactures too heavily and allowed for unfair piracy control tactics, including tracking users internet surfing history and the remote cancellation of purchased software ability when piracy is suspected. What's more, critics of such legislation and protection methods claim that, despite reported losses in revenue and tax collection, many companies such as Rosetta Stone, Adobe and Microsoft actually benefit from online software piracy. The argument is those who download pirated versions of software more than likely would never have paid for the license in the first place, and yet the notoriety, goodwill and widespread use is priceless to the company in the long run as it creates a global network of compatible software. While the manufacturers claim piracy will put them out of business, these widely pirated programs, critics point out, are now the universal standard.

8.7. Digital Rights Management (DRM)

A relatively new class of technology known as Digital Rights Management (DRM) works to limit the repetitive copying capabilities of media content found in DVDs, Blue-Ray movies, compact discs and mp3s, video computer games, and eBooks. This Digital Rights Management software inherent in many media purchases differs from tradition software protection as they often function without the user's knowledge. Many are embedded within the media file and seek to track use of the file, prevent copying and sharing, and ultimately allow the retailer or manufacturer to retain control of the file after purchase.

Found in many computer and video games, one of the first DRM technologies introduced was "limited install activation." It requires authentication to occur when a software or game purchaser first installs the licensed purchase. Once the installation is perfected, further attempts at installing may be denied or limited to a set number of installations, thus prohibiting the original buyer from sharing the media content. Apple, Windows, and Electronic Arts have prominently used this preventative technology.

Sony developed a similar technology called "SecuROM." It limits the number of activations a single user has from a single purchase. SecuROM relies upon "data position measurements" to digitally recognize burned or copied CDs and DVDs to inhibit their use in media players.

A DRM program known as a "rootkit" automatically installs itself onto the user's hard drive when a CD or DVD is played. The program works by setting up a firewall within the hard drive blocking access to CD burning programs and popular file sharing sites such as Napster and Kazaa. Privacy rights activists criticized this intrusive technology because it occurred without the user's knowledge, which ultimately led to a lawsuit filed against Sony-BMG. A settlement was reached with the Federal Trade Commission that now requires clear and prominent notification on product packaging when any DRM technology exists within.

E-book providers Amazon and Barnes and Noble also employ sophisticated DRM technology to prohibit the sharing or printing or e-books. Amazon once went so far as to delete thousands of digital copies of George Orwell's *1984* and *Animal Farm* when it discovered the works had been sold on its website without proper licensing from the publisher. Amazon failed to inform customers in advance and received countless complaints. Ultimately, Amazon apologized and credited refunds. For many the larger concern was learning that Amazon had the ability to access and delete digital copies of books sold to customers. This rose the issues of what bundle of rights are customers acquiring when they purchase a digital book?

8.8. Buy vs. Rent

Consumers may think they are "buying" a digital book or movie on Amazon or a record on iTunes when they hit the "buy now" button. The reality is the "buy" is really a *rent* or a *license*. This is a major distinction between purchasing a physical book or album and the electronic version. When we purchase the physical item the law is quite clear we are free to resell it or give it away to friends. This legal right was enshrined in a 1908 U.S. Supreme Court case limiting the copyright owner's control over things like price to the *first sale* only. Unfortunately for the consumer, there is no digital version of this landmark decision. Digital sales are deemed licenses, and under the current law licenses cannot be exchanged or resold or even gifted.

8.9. Digital Marketplace

This distinction is now under severe attack thanks to a new patent recently issued to Apple for a digital marketplace. The patent application would create a system for permitting buyers to sell or gift software, and digital versions of e-books, music and even movies. This electronic bazaar is set up to allow for the *transfer* of the digital file for each media content to another rather than reproducing copies of the original file. Under Apple's system only one user could have a copy of the digital file at any one time. Amazon has developed a patented system as well that would create an electronic marketplace where digital works could be exchanged. A federal court in New York is poised to address the issue of whether an electronic "Craigslist" type of marketplace that creates a way for iTunes music to be bought and sold is a violation of copyright laws. According to experts in the field, resale of electronic educational and entertainment content would send the price of even new works crashing because no one would want to be the first buyer to pay full price when subsequent holders could buy or exchange copies for less at a digital thrift shop.

8.10. Google, Art and Copyright

Two Stanford University students, Larry Page and Sergey Brin, devised an algorithm that analyzed how websites were linked together. The compiled websites were then mathematically ranked and displayed based on each site's relevance as it related to the keywords entered. In 1998, they officially incorporated their enterprise into Google Inc. Two years later it became the sole search engine for Yahoo.

8.11. Images

A few years later Google devised a feature called "Images" that allowed users to search the entire Internet for images based on a single query. Recently, Google had indexed more than 1 billion images. Across the world digital representations of millions of photographs, paintings, logos, banner and nearly any other images imaginable now has been compiled. Any of these images can be found by typing in the keyword that then prompts the search engine to find the image based on components of the original ranking system.

Once the image is found online it is generally quite easy to save the file and then print, copy or edit the original image. Google displays *"thumbnails,"* or small preview versions, of images without the user having to navigate to the site housing the file even when these files are copyrighted and subject to restricted use by the original host. Google accomplishes this task by storing a snapshot of the image in a cache. This "Images" feature, while incredibly consumer convenient and helpful, has come under heavy criticism by copyright owners because it serves as a technical aid for would-be infringers.

Almost immediately after Google launched its "Images" platform, the men's magazine *Perfect 10* sent a notice to corporate headquarters demanding Google remove both the magazine's images (i.e. no longer store them in a cache) and the "thumbnail" versions from its search engine. Google refused, and in 2004 a lawsuit was filed alleging direct, vicarious, and contributory copyright infringement.

The lower federal court found that *Perfect 10* failed to demonstrate financial harm caused by the search engine. The court refused to require Google to direct searchers to the host site of the original image, as requested by the magazine. Initially, the court held the "thumbnails" did not qualify for non-infringing fair use. However, the Ninth Circuit Court of Appeals reversed the finding and held Google's activity did fall within the *fair use* defense. In similar cases where Google has been sued when the cached search results provide end users with copies of copyrighted works, the courts have stated Google was a passive participant in the search process. It is the end users who choose whether to view the cached images and save, print, and edit the copyrighted works so they are the potential infringers. In a sense courts have reasoned, Google has an *implied license to store the images* because the technology exists that allows the copyright holder to turn off the caching using codes and tags. The copyright holder who fails to incorporate this technology into his or her website may then lose the opportunity to claim copyright infringement.

8.12. Google Art Project

Google has not stopped its inventiveness despite continued legal challenges. In 2011, it launched "The Google Art Project." More than 30,000 high-resolution digital images of paintings, photographs and sculptures are now available for viewing creating the world's first digital museum. Google Art Project allows users all over the world to view these images in extreme clarity; many images are presented as a gigapixel image, or 1 billion pixels. For those works in the public domain and cleared by the partner museum housing the piece, the user can zoom in, explore textural properties of the work, and save a copy to their hard drive. And most in the art and legal world agree, The Google Art Project is both an amazing advance in public access to some of the greatest works ever created while also giving rise to a legal minefield that pushes the bounds of artists' rights and fair use.

Though no action has been taken against the Google Art Project to date, many are weary and choose to tread lightly on the infringement issue. "Our selection was designed to avoid disputes," says Troy Klyber, the intellectual property manager at the Art Institute of Chicago. The Institute participates in the Google Art Project, but submits only works in the public domain. Google defers to the partner museums, according to Google Art Project's terms and conditions, as these galleries retain the *display rights* of the works in their charge, and each is responsible for adhering to the applicable copyright laws in their home country. Google has also avoided any agreement with the Artists Rights Society, an organization that represents the intellectual property rights of over 50,000 artists including Picasso, Matisse and Rothko. In the wake of the 2008, $125 million settlement with the Author's Guild of America concerning a similar Google venture, a compilation of full text of books and magazines called "The Google Books Library Project," Google has chosen to leave the administrative and financial burden of obtaining Artist Rights Society permission to display the works and paying potential royalties up to the museums.

8.13. Digital Watermarking

Many artists to protect their original works have begun to employ several ways to maintain control and credit. One widespread method is *digital watermarking*. Original watermarks have been an integral aspect of the high end paper making process for years leaving a visible mark notating the owner or maker of the paper. Digital watermarks seek a similar outcome, but incorporate an untraceable and tamper-proof coding embedded into digital files. Ownership information is not separated from the original work even were editing to occur by non-licensees.

Companies like Digimarc have developed sophisticated and reliable digital coding devices allowing for not merely watermarking of copyrighted works, but can identify the time and identity the Internet Protocol address to where content was downloaded. This protective software greatly assists in somewhat locating the party responsible for infringement when content is impermissibly shared online. On the other hand critics of this technology suggest software that tracks use and surfing history may amount to an illegal invasion of privacy. Furthermore, incredibly savvy techies are clever enough to erase digital watermarking from images, audio and video files, and software. Despite these limitations, the trend among content producers and archivists including book publishers, art galleries, universities and even the Library of Congress is to move away from DRM technology and implement digital watermarking.

8.14. PRO-IP Act

One of the imperfections of the digital watermarking tracking technology is that simply because one can identify the Internet Protocol address signifying ownership of a computer by name does not mean that is the party responsible for the "theft." Capitol Records lost a copyright infringement decision because the court rejected evidence of the person's IP address as quid pro evidence of her culpability. Off-shore Bit Torrent search engines deemed "rogue" sites by the U.S. Chamber of Congress are viewed by many as major criminal commercial conspirators operating in violation of both copyright and patent rights.

In response to these concerns, President George Bush signed into law the Prioritizing Resources and Organization for Intellectual Property Act of 2008 or PRO-IP Act. The legislation offers enhanced civil (minimum of $1000 to a maximum of $200,000 per offense) fines escalating dramatically for repeat infringers. Asset forfeiture ranging from loss of computers, network hardware, and bank accounts was added to the damages section. Criminal penalties for "willful and reckless" infringers were enhanced. A new division within the Federal Bureau of Investigation (FBI) was created to work within the Computer Crime and Intellectual Property Section (CCIPS) within the Department of Justice.

Immediately, the FBI began to more aggressively investigate potential criminal infringement activities worldwide. In 2012, U.S. authorities in conjunction with New Zealand police stormed the home of Megaupload.com owner, Kim Dotcom. He was arrested and nearly $20 million in assets was seized. Prior to his arrest and the shutdown of Megaupload.com, it was the 13th most popular Internet site accounting for nearly 4% of all Internet traffic. Annually the site generated more than $175 million in revenue.

Mr. Dotcom viewed his site as a "provider of an internet-based storage platform for customers, who ranged from large businesses to individuals." Federal authorities saw it differently: the vast majority of Megaupload customers exploited its storage and bandwidth capabilities to store copyrighted documents, music files, movies, TV shows and other protected works, and all were available for universal and unlimited download. Advertising popped up only when a user performed a download function. The U.S. government charged Mr. Dotcom for acting "willfully and recklessly" under the PRO-IP Act. The indictment was dealt a tough blow in late 2012 when a New Zealand High Court judge deemed the U.S.'s seizure of property illegal under current New Zealand law. Dotcom's extradition to the U.S. was subsequently delayed and a trial is yet to be set.

President Barack Obama has consistently reiterated the government's stance, " ... we're going to aggressively protect our intellectual property." Further, he has stated, "(t)here is nothing wrong with other people using our technologies, we welcome it—we just want to make sure that it's licensed, and that American businesses are getting paid appropriately."

The passage and enforcement attempts of the PRO-IP ACT by federal authorities, in addition to Congressional steps to further ratchet up investigative authority and criminal penalties has inflamed passionate opposition. Google has submitted a petition of over 7 million signatures against any new aggressive legislative efforts. Wikipedia and YouTube have voiced serious opposition against the present law based on what they view as unlawful intimidation and censorship. Verizon, Yahoo, American Express and eBay believe the contributory liability aspects of the PRO-IP Act allowing for easily obtained injunctions levied against domains and IP address holders in advance of a trial could irreparably harm advertising revenue and shutter legitimate Internet content users.

8.15. Aaron Swartz

The 2011 indictment of one-time Internet prodigy Aaron Swartz who helped to write the code for Rich Site Summary (RSS), a means for compiling and standardizing "feed" sites like blogs, and later developed the news site Reddit, and who was found dead in 2013 by an apparent suicide, has earned widespread public outrage and criticism. The federal government alleged in its indictment that Swartz unlawfully obtained copyrighted material from the JSTOR website, an archive site housing thousands of scholarly journal articles, and from PACER, a federal court record storage site.

Swartz was not shy about airing his views on restrictive copyright laws and draconian penalties for individual offenders. "We need to take information, wherever it is stored, make our copies and share them in the world," said Swartz. "We need to take stuff that's out of copyright and add it to the archive. We need to buy secret databases and put them on the Web. We need to download scientific journals and upload them to file sharing networks." After two years of interrogation and investigation, Federal prosecutors indicted Swartz under 1984 Computer Fraud and Abuse Act, and the internet prodigy and activist faced multiple felony charges and sentences reaching as high as 35 years in federal prison. Facing an immediate criminal deadline decision to plead guilty to at least one felony charge and spend time incarcerated, it is believed Swartz chose instead to kill himself. Many observers, claim those prosecuting Swartz are complicit in his death because of the harsh intimidation tactics. In February 2013, a petition of over 50,000 signatures was filed with the White House calling for the resignation of US Attorney Carmen Ortiz, the lead prosecutor in the Swartz case.

The Swartz case has called into question the aggressive application of the criminal component of copyright law remedies against individuals. What is the appropriate treatment and punishment? Legal experts have voiced outrage at the government for treating those charged under these intellectual property protection acts in the same manner they would for violent offenders, and many have criticized the ability of the government and prosecutors like those in the Swartz case to preemptively shut down companies and intimidate and threaten individuals simply because they viewed them as an infringer, or worse, a potential piracy threat. The President of the Internet advocacy group TechFreedom, Berin Szoka, sees Swartz as an innocent victim of an "overzealous criminal justice system," as Aaron never published nor profited from the files he downloaded.

Many view Swartz's death as a clear sign of the need to amend the Computer Fraud and Abuse Act, The Pro-IP Act, and other far-reaching legislation. "Aaron's Law" was purposed in 2013 by California Congresswoman Zoe Lofgren, which would amend current law lessening the punishment of individual infringers such as Swartz, and even seeks to return infringement of this kind into the civil realm, thus putting an end to the harsh criminal punishments all together.

In the end, Aaron Swartz's unfortunate death has shined an unflattering light on the gap between the priorities of content providers and those seeking the public benefits of information freedom, and the methods and priorities of a government struggling to keep pace with an ever changing tech world. With the proposal of "Aaron's Law," the growing opposition from activist groups like TechFreedom and DemandProgress, of which Aaron was a cofounder, and an increased interest on the subject by the general public, it seems that in death, Aaron Swartz will have a lasting impact on the causes he championed in life.

Chapter Summary

New online technologies present enhanced opportunities to share and exploit content especially on social media sites, while simultaneously raising new legal considerations. Terms of service agreements by Twitter, Facebook, Instagram and other social media outlets require all users of posted material to automatically grant a license allowing access and permitting distribution of photos, video and text over various media.

In 1980, computer software garnered copyright protection giving it the same recognition as any other original works of authorship. Digital "sales" by Amazon, iTunes and others are licenses, not actual purchases. Digital resale marketplaces allowing for the *transfer* of digital content raises infringement concerns against the traditional protections of the *first sale* doctrine. The exponential growth of worldwide software piracy has encouraged the enactment of stronger laws to criminalize illegal sharing and downloading of video computer games, movies, music and other content. Apart from government efforts to stem the tide of copyright infringement activities, new classes of technology that work to limit the repetitive copying capabilities found in eBooks, mp3s, Blue-Ray movies and video games are now being inserted surreptitiously into licensed purchases of software. Some privacy activists are highly critical of the intrusive nature of this technology. The apparent suicide of Aaron Swartz, developer of Reddit, has spurned public outrage because of what some observers believe is the unjustified criminalization of Robin-Hood-like downloading of data for the public good.

Key Terms

Terms of Service Agreement
Right of Privacy and Publicity
Software Privacy Protection
Access Code
Business Software Alliance
Digital Rights Management (DRM)
Digital Marketplace
Thumbnails
Google Art Project
Digital Watermarking
PROP-IP Act
Aaron Swartz

Review Questions

1. What are the reasons for someone assigning or selling their copyrights to the online organization the Creative Commons?
2. Has society gone too far to try to prevent online piracy by criminalizing the conduct of those who tamper with DRM technology?
3. Can you explain the reasons for Facebook, Instagram, Twitter and other social media sites requiring all users to automatically grant a sub-license to access posted material?
4. How might some websites actually benefit from online software piracy?
5. How does digital rights management technology differ from traditional software protection?
6. When a person presses the "buy now" button to "purchase" a book or movie online is it really a purchase or a rent? Legally what is the difference in rights acquired?

7. Why are many media content providers moving away from DRM technology and switching to digital watermarking?

8. What arguments can you make that the Google Art Project is and is not protected by the fair use doctrine?

9. What federal statute did prosecutors use to charge Aaron Swartz with a crime when he allegedly accessed and downloaded illegally secret databases?

Web Links

1. For more on Aaron Schwartz, see http://www.slate.com/articles/technology/technology/2013/02/aaron_swartz_he_wanted_to_save_the_world_why_couldn_t_he_save_himself.

2. There are plenty of news articles about illegal file sharing, and here is one with an interesting perspective: http://www.newscientist.com/article/mg21328506.400-pirate-filesharing-goes-3d.html.

3. Information about the Google Art and Book Projects can be found at http://www.googleartproject.com/faqs/ and http://www.abajournal.com/magazine/article/its_google_but_is_it_art/.

Discussion Exercises

1. Do you believe a search engine that creates "thumbnail" reproductions of copyrighted photographs and then places them on its own website is permitted as fair use or an illegal infringement? (*See Kelly v. Arriba Soft Corp, 336 F.3d 811 (9thCir. 2003).*)

Chapter 9

International Aspects of Intellectual Property Law

"A good composer does not imitate, he steals."—Igor Stravinsky

Chapter Outline

Chapter Objectives

- Recognize it is only through multi-national copyright treaties that the rights of authors/artists are protected outside their own country.
- Learn how the Berne Convention is the most salient international copyright treaty.
- Appreciate the benefit of national treatment occurring from the U.S. joining the Berne Convention.
- Understand the Roman law tradition led to protecting authors' or artists' personal or moral rights, whereas the Anglo-Saxon law tradition led to protecting authors' or artists' economic rights.

- Grasp the broad reach of moral rights as defined by most countries belonging to the Berne Convention as opposed to the limited reach of moral rights in the U.S. under VARA.
- Know what the rights of attribution and integrity mean under U.S. law.

9.1. Brief History

The rights reserved to U.S. copyright holders granted under U.S. copyright statutes and court decisions frequently come to a screeching halt at the geographic border. The jurisdiction of U.S. law extends to its fifty states, territories and possessions unless other countries decide to recognize U.S. copyrights. The concern is reciprocal. More than 160 years ago the English author Charles Dickens condemned the U.S. for failing to protect foreign authors from literary piracy by U.S. publishers.

Originally, as was discussed in an earlier chapter, U.S. book publishers were opposed to any bilateral or international reciprocal copyright agreements because they believed their economic success hinged on the sale of inexpensive reprints of British works. Ironically, over time, many U.S. authors rallied around Dickens' plea for protection from infringement. The reason was their books were not selling well because readers would rather pay a quarter to read Dickens than a dollar to read the copyrighted works of U.S. authors Cooper or Hawthorne.

Legislation enacted in the U.S. known as the *International Copyright Act of 1891* made reciprocal copyright protection available to published works by foreign authors. In a rather sneaky Congressional move, the Act required all foreign books, photographs and lithographs that sought U.S. copyright protection to have the works printed or manufactured in the U.S.!

9.2. Universal Copyright Convention

Believe it or not, other than an occasion multi-national copyright treaty with a few nations in the Western Hemisphere, it was not until 1955 for the U.S. to finally join a global multilateral copyright treaty. This treaty—*Universal Copyright Convention*—is still one of two main copyright treaties. All countries who sign onto this treaty, and there are more than 120 nations that have done so, agree to recognize the copyrights of authors from other signatory countries in the same way it recognizes the copyrights of its own nationals. This reciprocal status afforded authors is called "*national treatment.*"

9.3. Berne Convention

The second, and most significant, copyright treaty the U.S. has signed is the *Berne Convention for the Protection of Literary and Artistic Works* (hereinafter the **Berne Convention**). Originally drafted in 1886, it, too, establishes minimum international protections that must be granted copyright holders and is the principal subject for the remainder of this chapter. One hundred seventy countries currently have signed onto this multinational treaty.

The author of this chapter recently returned from a trip to Cuba, where he learned about the variances between U.S. and Cuban copyright law. The Director of the Cuban government agency charged with protecting the rights of visual artists (ADAVIS) began the conversation by describing the root differences between the two systems of law. Latin American and continental European countries derive their law from codes or edicts and legal principles dating back to the Roman Empire. When these governments grant copyright protection for authors and artists it is based on the notion that they are basic *inalienable, natural, human or moral rights*. These rights are *personal* to the *creator* of the works. They cannot be taken away. They cannot be bought or sold.

Contrast this view of copyrights with why the U.S. and the United Kingdom (U.K.) recognize copyrights. For authors and artists in these Anglo-Saxon countries, where judicial precedents have the same force of law as statutes, copyrights are an *economic* monopoly grant that is provided to stimulate innovation and creativity. The *Berne Convention* is based on the **Roman law** model, not Anglo-American legal traditions. Consequently, there was a long-standing reluctance by the U.S. to join the *Berne Convention* because of its emphasis on what the French refer to as "droit moral" (*moral rights*). For similar reasons the U.K. resisted fully joining the *Berne Convention* until 1988 when by an Act of Parliament it revised its copyright laws to bring it into accord.

9.4. Moral Rights

In 1989, thirteen years after the enactment of the 1976 Copyright Act, the U.S. officially became a signatory nation to the *Berne Convention* subject to not specifically recognizing *moral rights*. Before examining how the U.S. swiveled around this basic mandate let us look more closely at what *moral rights* mean. This discussion is a further articulation of the basic aspects of moral rights covered in an earlier copyright unit.

The notion of moral rights includes the legal right 1) to be identified as the author of the work or disclaim authorship also called the *right of attribution* or as the French refer to it droit de paternite; 2) to protest or object to the distortion, mutilation, or any other modification of the work that might be injurious to the author's reputation or honor (this is referred to as the *right of integrity* or droit d'integrite); and 3) to decide the circumstances by which a work may be published, the *right of disclosure* or droit de divulgation.

Signatory countries to the *Berne Convention* are free to expand these rights. Some countries have provided for the right to collect royalties after an artist sells a work and where the new owner makes a profit on the resale (droit de suite). Even the state of California under Civil Code Sections 986-989 has a similar grant entitling artists to 5% of the resale of a work of fine art. This royalty right lasts for the life of the artist plus twenty years. Can you image the resale royalties for a painter like Picasso who might have sold a sketch or drawing for a few dollars in his youth and at auction years later the same work of art might sell for in excess of a million dollars! The French even provide a right for authors to reply to criticism, e.g. when a literary critic unfavorably reviews a writer's novel.

Shortly after the U.S. joined the *Berne Convention,* Congress ratified the *General Agreement on Tariffs and Trade* (GATT) treaty. By law all signatory countries to GATT must also adhere to the *Berne Convention,* except for the *moral rights* provision.

9.5. National Treatment

What copyright benefits are derived from signing onto the *Berne Convention*? Foremost all countries agree to afford the same treatment to an author from another country as it does to authors in its own country. National treatment results in the law of where protection is sought as being the applicable law as opposed to courts having to learn and apply foreign law. At a minimum copyright protection extends to the life of the author plus fifty years. In an earlier chapter we discussed the legislation that extended the U.S. time period to the life of the author and seventy years, which is perfectly legal under the *Convention*. The formalities of requiring registration, notice or deposit within the Library of Congress for protection is no longer required, although there are plenty of reasons why authors in the U.S. should still consider following these rules. The no formal filing or notice requirement is part of the Roman law tradition.

A copyright infringer in the U.S. loses the ability to claim she didn't know her act constituted infringement when the author follows the U.S. statutory filing requirements. Courts tend to award higher damages, including the prospects of statutory damages, when a person willfully and knowingly engages in copyright infringement. Copyright notice is still a significant protection tool. One author refers to it as similar to posting a "No Trespass" sign telling the world you claim authorship in this work and don't tread on my work without permission. The recommendation here is to continue to adhere to the three notice elements by adding to the work: year of first publication (date), name of the copyright owner (author), and copyright symbol (©) all together in close proximity. The *Universal Copyright Convention* requires a statement in the form of "All rights reserved." This reservation of rights language . is frequently added to the front or back of title pages of books especially those sold throughout the world. The best advice for authors to guarantee the fullest international copyright protection is to give notice by identifying the name of the author, date of first publication, copyright symbol (©) and add "All rights reserved."

The *Berne Convention* does not demand uniformity of what can and cannot be copyrighted. The vast majority of signatories to the *Convention* extend protection to literary works, film, photography, sculptures, drawing, and paintings. Sound recordings are not covered under the *Berne Convention* or the *Universal Copyright Convention*. Members of GATT have agreed to treat software programs as literary works under the *Berne Convention* scheme.

9.6. Visual Artists Rights Act

The U.S. was obligated to recognize some form of *moral rights* or protection of an author's right to attribution and integrity independent of economic rights upon joining the *Berne Convention*. Unsuccessfully in its arguments that its patchwork quilt of federal trademark and copyright statutes, acknowledgement of the right of publicity, and protections against defamation were equivalent to *moral rights*; in 1990, Congress passed the **Visual Artists Rights Act** (VARA). The right of disclosure was left out of the final bill's passage.

9.7. Limited Works

It is important to recognize that VARA provides very limited protection for a narrow set of copyrightable works—visual arts. By statutory definition the term visual arts means *"works of art"* or paintings, drawings, prints, sculptures, and photographs (if the photograph was "produced for exhibition purposes only"). Any other type of works subject to copyright, such as, musical, literary, dramatic, and audiovisual works along with software programs, motion pictures, newspapers, sound recordings, electronic information services and databases are excluded. Mass produced posters, maps, globes, charts, diagrams, models, applied art or works with functional aspects also are not included. Nor do these rights apply to any advertising, merchandising or packaging materials. Any works for hire are excluded, too. Therefore, an employee who paints a portrait of the company president as part of his job requirement has neither a moral right in the painting nor the original copyright because the employer is viewed as the author of the art work.

9.8. Attribution and Integrity Rights

Section 106A of the Copyright Act (VARA amended the *Copyright Act*) limits the "work of visual art" that enjoys rights of attribution and integrity to no more than 200 copies, and the author must sign (name of author or identifying mark of the author like a symbol) and consecutively number each painting, drawing, print, photograph (for exhibition) or sculpture for full protection. Unlike the time period for copyrights, *moral rights last only for the life of the author.* Even prize winning news photographs are not covered under VARA because they are not created for exhibition purposes. The *fair use* provisions found in *Section 107 of the Copyright Act* are available as a *defense to moral rights'* claims.

> Sect. 106A. Rights of certain authors to attribution and integrity
> (a) Rights of attribution and integrity.
> Subject to section 107 and independent of the exclusive rights provided in section 106 [17 USCS Sect. 106], the author of a work of visual art—
> (1) shall have the right—
> (A) to claim authorship of that work, and
> (B) to prevent the use of his or her name as the author of any work of visual art which he or she did not create;
> (2) shall have the right to prevent the use of his or her name as the author of the work of visual art in the event of a distortion, mutilation, or other modification of the work which would be prejudicial to his or her honor or reputation; and
> (3) subject to the limitations set forth in section 113(d)[17 USCS Sect. 113(d)], shall have the right—

(A) to prevent any intentional distortion, mutilation, or other modification of that work which would be prejudicial to his or her honor or reputation, and any intentional distortion, mutilation, or modification of that work is a violation of that right, and

(B) to prevent any destruction of a work of recognized stature, and any intentional or grossly negligent destruction of that work is a violation of that right.

(b) Scope and exercise of rights.

Only the author of a work of visual art has the rights conferred by subsection (a) in that work, whether or not the author is the copyright owner. The authors of a joint work of visual art are coowners of the rights conferred by subsection (a) in that work.

(c) Exceptions.

(1) The modification of a work of visual art which is a result of the passage of time or the inherent nature of the materials is not a distortion, mutilation, or other modification described in subsection (a)(3)(A).

(2) The modification of a work of visual art which is the result of conservation, or of the public presentation, including lighting and placement, of the work is not a destruction, distortion, mutilation, or other modification described in subsection (a)(3) unless the modification is caused by gross negligence.

(3) The rights described in paragraphs (1) and (2) of subsection (a) shall not apply to any reproduction, depiction, portrayal, or other use of a work in, upon, or in any connection with any item described in subparagraph (A) or (B) of the definition of "work of visual art" in section 101 [17 USCS Sect. 101], and any such reproduction, depiction, portrayal, or other use of a work is not a destruction, distortion, mutilation, or other modification described in paragraph (3) of subsection (a).

(d) Duration of Rights.

(1) With respect to works of visual art created on or after the effective date set forth in section 610(a) of the Visual Artists Rights Act of 1990 [note to this section], the rights conferred by subsection (a) shall endure for a term consisting of the life of the author.

(2) With respect to works of visual art created before the effective date set forth in section 610(a) of the Visual Artists Rights Act of 1990 [note to this section], but title to which has not, as of such effective date, been transferred from the author, the rights conferred by subsection (a) shall be coextensive with, and shall expire at the same time as, the rights conferred by section 106 [17 USCS Sect. 106].

(3) In the case of a joint work prepared by two or more authors, the rights conferred by subsection (a) shall endure for a term consisting of the life of the last surviving author.

(4) All terms of the rights conferred by subsection (a) run to the end of the calendar year in which they would otherwise expire.

(e) Transfer and waiver.

(1) The rights conferred by subsection (a) may not be transferred, but those rights may be waived if the author expressly agrees to such waiver in a written instrument signed by the author. Such instrument shall specifically identify the work, and uses of that work, to which the waiver applies, and the waiver shall apply only to the work and uses so identified. In the case of a joint work prepared by two or more authors, a waiver of rights under this paragraph made by one such author waives such rights for all such authors.

(2) Ownership of the rights conferred by subsection (a) with respect to a work of visual art is distinct from ownership of any copy of that work, or of a copyright or any exclusive right under a copyright in that work. Transfer of ownership of any copy of a work of visual art, or of a copyright or any exclusive right under a copyright, shall not constitute a waiver of the rights conferred by subsection (a). Except as may otherwise be agreed by the author in a written instrument signed by the author, a waiver of the rights conferred by subsection (a) with respect to a work of visual art shall not constitute a transfer of ownership of any copy of that work, or of ownership of a copyright or of any exclusive right under a copyright in that work.

What does VARA really mean for visual artists? The strongest *moral right* granted under VARA is the right to prevent the distortion, mutilation or other modification of an artist's work that may harm her honor or reputation. Let us take an example of a U.S. art collector who purchased a limited edition, numbered, signed, mono print by the renowned Latin American artist Wilfredo Lam. Assume in 2014 a collector purchased the 9th print of the 10 print series created by Lam. The collector cannot destroy the work without permission from the artist so long as the work was created prior to the enactment of VARA, December 1, 1990, and the artist is still alive. Lam died in 1982 in Paris so the collector may lawfully modify or destroy the print. VARA does not permit the transferability of the rights of attribution and integrity so even had Lam attempted to transfer these rights to his children who are living it is ineffective.

Over the twenty-plus years VARA has been enshrined in U.S. copyright law there have been fewer than two-dozen reported cases raising the issue of *moral rights.* In 2006, a First Circuit Federal Appeals' Court held that VARA does not apply to "site-specific" artwork that is integrated into the surrounding landscape. More recently, a New Jersey artist challenged this interpretation of VARA. In 1994, the visual artist created a sculpture for a Holocaust Memorial located on the banks of a river near the state capital of Pennsylvania. A decaying element near the base of the original sculpture made from rust-colored "barbed wire" was replaced with stainless steel. The local Jewish Federation performed the restoration. The artist maintained the alteration was an unauthorized modification under VARA. In 2011, the parties reached an amicable resolution. The sculpture will be retrofitted in a fashion that upholds the artist's original intent at minimal costs to the Jewish Foundation.

One of the reasons there may be so few VARA cases is the sheer expense of filing and defending lawsuits. It has been reported that the cost to litigate a typical *moral rights* case ranges from $200,000 to $250,000. Another factor is that there is so little precedent to guide everyone involved making outcomes vulnerable to uncertainty. Cases settled out of court offer no judicial value in determining what the law protects under the U.S. Anglo-Saxon legal system. Criminal penalties are not available to a VARA lawsuit. Otherwise the remedies for a Section 106A violation are the same as the civil remedies for a copyright infringement.

9.9. Waivers

VARA does permit written, express and signed space *waivers*. So requesting from the visual artist for consideration a waiver specifically identifying the singular or limited edition work of art and its use is a way for a purchaser to avoid the prospects of litigation under VARA. Keep in mind that moral rights are independent of copyrights, which are independent of ownership of the physical work of art.

The *World Intellectual Property Organization* (WIPO) helps to administer and foster the *Berne Convention*. Unlike GATT it is a United Nations organ that can serve as a forum for the discussion of international copyright concerns.

Chapter Summary

One of the first major changes to the 1976 Copyright Act occurred in 1989 when the United States acceded or joined the Berne Convention. This major international treaty eliminated the requirement for U.S. authors or artists to register, notice or deposit with the Library of Congress works to gain copyright protection.

In Europe and many other countries with a Roman law tradition authors are granted three basic moral rights: right of attribution, right of integrity, right of disclosure under the Berne Convention. It is also extends copyright protection for the life of the author/artist plus 50 years. Initially, the U.S. balked at adding these personality rights to her traditional economic rights. However, in 1990, the U.S amended its copyright law again to incorporate two features of European moral rights—attribution and integrity. These rights are independent of the other rights granted under copyright law. They apply to certain visual works of art produced in a single copy or limited edition of 200 copies or fewer signed and numbered. Four years later the U.S enacted the GATT as law; and this treaty requires all members to adhere to the Berne Convention (except the moral rights provision).

Key Terms

Universal Copyright Convention
Berne Convention
Roman Law
Moral Rights
Right of Attribution
Right of Integrity
Right of Disclosure
General Agreement on Tariffs and Trade (GATT)
National Treatment
Visual Artists Rights Act (VARA)
Works of Art under VARA
Waivers
World Intellectual Property Organization (WIPO)

Review Questions

1. What does the term "national treatment" mean under the Berne Convention?
2. Explain how the concept and application of "moral rights" differs between Europe and the U.S.
3. What protection do moral rights provide some visual artists in the U.S.?
4. Is the fair use doctrine available as a defense in moral rights claims?

5. Identify the limited works of visual arts protected under VARA.
6. Is the following statement true or false: Moral rights cannot be transferred but they can be waived.

Web Links

1. Harvard Law School has a web link for artists' rights at http://www.law.harvard.edu/faculty/martin/art_law/image_rights.htm
2. A list of signatory countries to the Berne Convention is found at http://www.copyrightaid.co.uk/copyright_information/berne_convention_signtories

Discussion Exercise

1. Assume last year a film director downloaded a U.S. copyrighted song, modified the sound track and then used the revised version in a film distributed in Chile, Columbia, Uruguay and Spain. The copyright owner was not credited as the author or artist. Were any moral rights violated?

Unit 2

Trademark Basics

Chapter 10

Introduction to Trademark Law

"A great trademark is appropriate, dynamic, distinctive, memorable and unique."—Primo Angeli

Chapter Outline

Chapter Objectives

- Understand the basic idea of what a trademark is and how it might be used.
- Become familiar with common trademark examples.
- Learn the basic history behind trademark use and protection.
- Understand early common law protection for trademarks.
- Learn the purpose of trademark law and the basic public policy behind it.

A *trademark* is essentially a sign or other device that is used to identify the source of a product or service and distinguish it from similar products or services. A trademark is typically a word (such as the name Nike®) or design of some kind (the Nike® "swoosh"), but trademarks are not limited to these conventional types. Less common trademark embodiments include color (the red sole of Christian Louboutin® shoes or yellow WIFFLE® bats), sound (the NBC chimes), fragrance (Smead® peppermint scented office products), shape (the spiral of Fritos® Flavor Twists®), overall appearance of a product or packaging (the blue box of Tiffany & Co.®), and a service provider's uniform (such as the Dallas Cowboys Cheerleaders' uniforms). In all of these examples, the underlying purpose is the same. These trademarks inform consumers about the origin of the product or service, and convey information about the quality and characteristics of those goods and services that have come to be associated with each mark.

10.1. A Short History of Trademark Law

Trademark law is primarily concerned with protecting the reputations and business of legitimate product and service providers, and protecting consumers from imitation products. This concern is hardly new, and it isn't surprising to find similar concepts far back in history. It isn't clear when trademarks were first used, but there are historical examples of weapons and jewelry bearing marks indicating their maker at least as far back as Roman times, and probably earlier. The Löwenbräu brewery in Munich claims to have used the same lion design trademark since 1383, and it was registered in 1886. These marks served as advertising for the craftsmen who produced products, and as an indicator of quality for consumers, just as modern trademarks do today.

Before statutes were passed to better define, recognize, and protect trademarks, the common law offered some protection under the law of torts. Specifically, the common law of torts provided causes of action for *"passing off"* and a variant of that called *"reverse passing off."* While important even today when dealing with unregistered trademarks, passing off was the only effective cause of action for pre-statutory trademark holders who became victims of trademark infringement. Actions for fraud, although relevant under the circumstances, would only be available to consumers who were actually deceived and harmed by such infringement, and not to the trademark holders themselves.

The tort of passing off was committed when a person misrepresented his or her goods or services as being the goods or services of the trademark holder, or otherwise untruthfully held out his or her goods or services as having some association with the trademark holder. This would often be done by a competing merchant to benefit from the good reputation earned by the trademark holder and to take sales from customers who associated quality with the trademark in question. In some cases, the passing off was accomplished by copying a trademark directly, which was *trademark infringement*. In other cases, passing off was accomplished by imitating the appearance, shape, or other distinguishing features of a product without actually copying the trademark itself. This is called *unfair competition*, and it is only actionable when the public comes to associate the non-trademark appearance, shape or other distinguishing features of a product with one specific source: the trademark holder. This public association between non-trademark distinguishing features and a specific source is called *"secondary meaning."*

Reverse passing off was a variation on passing off where the person committing the tort would falsely represent the trademark holder's products or services as his own products or services. In a typical passing off case, the person committing the tort falsely represents that his products or services are actually products or services of the trademark holder, in order to benefit from the goodwill and reputation of the trademark holder and thereby sell his own products or services. In reverse passing off cases, the intent is to claim responsibility for the trademark holder's products or services, in order to appear to be a more established, successful, reputable enterprise with quality products or services. This allows the person committing the tort to benefit again from the goodwill of the trademark holder by building consumer confidence in his own products or services. Reverse passing off can be accomplished through direct trademark infringement or through unfair competition.

While trademark holders could not bring actions for fraud as consumers could, the courts treated actions for passing off in a similar manner to actions for fraud. In early passing off cases, courts required the trademark holder to prove that the defendant intended to defraud consumers. This requirement put trademark holders in a tough spot in cases where the defendant's infringement could have been inadvertent, especially in cases of unfair competition where the trademark itself was not copied but similar packaging was used. Fortunately for trademark holders, the law slowly changed to focus less on the subjective intent of the defendant and more on whether or not consumers were actually confused by the alleged passing off. This trend is reflected in the modern *Restatement (Third) of Unfair Competition (1995)*, which states in section four that the tort of passing off is not dependent solely on the defendant's subjective intent, but on whether "the actor makes a representation likely to deceive or mislead prospective purchasers by causing the mistaken belief that the actor's business is the business of the other, or that the actor is the agent, affiliate, or associate of the other, or that the goods or services that the actor markets are produced, sponsored, or approved by the other."

In the United States, the first federal trademark statute was passed in 1870. This Act was found to be unconstitutional in *The Trademark Cases* in 1879, and Congress began working on a series of new laws that would continue to change and reflect different priorities and concerns over time. The *Trademark Act of 1905* improved federal law by allowing the registration of trademarks used in interstate commerce, but it excluded descriptive marks and trade dress in all cases. The *1920 Act* extended protection to descriptive marks that had acquired secondary meaning in the marketplace. The *Lanham Trademark Act of 1946* provides the bulk of modern federal trademark legislation, and we will review its provisions later in this chapter.

10.2. The Policy Goals of Trademark Law

The purpose of trademark law has been stated succinctly by the United States Supreme Court:

> [T]rademark law, by preventing others from copying a source-identifying mark, "reduce[s] the customer's costs of shopping and making purchase decisions," for it quickly and easily assures a potential customer that this item—the item with this mark—is made by the same producer as other similarly marked items that he or she liked (or disliked) in the past. At the same time, the law helps assure a producer that it (and not an imitating competitor) will reap the financial, reputation-related rewards associated with a desirable product. *Qualitex Co. v. Jacobson Prods. Co. Inc.*, 514 U.S. 159, 163-64 (1995).

In addition to these basic principles, there is a strong policy goal in trademark law to protect only those trademarks that are actively used in business and that are currently associated in the minds of consumers with one specific source of goods and services. If a trademark ceases to be used in business, or if the public ceases to consider a trademark to be an indicator of one specific source of goods or services, then the trademark will no longer be protected. This idea is similar to limitations on protection for patents and trade secrets. The law of intellectual property generally is designed to provide protection for a limited duration or under certain limited circumstances in order to prevent stagnant monopolies and provide freedom of creativity and innovation to the public while still protecting those legitimate business people and innovators who invest the requisite time, money, and effort to advance the scientific, artistic, and economic interests of the general population.

Chapter Summary

Although the formal level of legal recognition and protection has changed over time, the idea behind trademark law is very old. There is value to society in allowing providers of goods and services to distinguish their goods and services from others, both from an economic perspective and from a consumer protection perspective. As the use of trademarks has become more sophisticated and more important to trade, the law has evolved to keep pace.

Key Terms

Trademark
Passing Off
Reverse Passing Off
Trademark Infringement
Unfair Competition
Secondary Meaning
The Lanham Trademark Act of 1946

Review Questions

1. List one example each of a trademark embodied by a word, a device or design, a color, a sound, a fragrance, a shape, trade dress, and a uniform.
2. What is passing off?
3. What is reverse passing off?
4. Why does it make sense to protect trademarks from a consumer's point of view?
5. Is a trademark better protected from passing off if the law requires a plaintiff to show the intent of the defendant to pass off, or the likelihood of consumers to be confused?

Web Links

1. http://www.lib.utexas.edu/engin/trademark/timeline/tmindex.html—A short and interesting history of the development of trademark use from pre-history to modern times.

Discussion Exercise

1. Should color alone ever be allowed as a trademark? There are only so many colors that can reasonably be distinguished easily from one another when used on similar and competing products. Should one business entity be able to claim a monopoly on a common color and thereby prevent all competitors or manufacturers of similar products from using that color? See *Qualitex Co. v. Jacobson Products Co., Inc.*, 514 U.S. 159 (1995), for a discussion and the United States Supreme Court decision on the issue.

Chapter 11

What Can Be Protected By Trademark?

"Make it a life-rule to give your best to whatever passes through your hands. Let superiority be your trademark."—Orison Swett Marden

Chapter Outline

Chapter Objectives

- Learn the basic types of trademarks that are commonly used in the United States.
- Learn the symbols used to denote types of marks.
- Understand the basic requirements for trademark protection.
- Become familiar with the types of expression that are commonly used as trademarks.
- Become familiar with examples of each type of trademark expression.

11.1. Types of Trademarks

Trademark protection may apply to any type of device that indicates the source of goods or services in the marketplace. In addition to traditional trademarks, protection may also apply to a *"service mark,"* a *"certification mark,"* a "*collective mark,*" or to "*trade dress.*" Each of these applications may be used or represented differently. Unregistered trademarks are typically represented with a superscript "TM" after the mark. By way of example, the unregistered trademark "Example" would be written as "Example™." A trademark that has been registered with the United States Patent and Trademark Office ("PTO") would be written as "Example®," with a superscript "R" in a circle.

A *service mark* is a type of trademark that is used to identify a service provider, instead of a provider of goods. An unregistered service mark is written as "ExampleSM," with a superscript "SM". A registered service mark is written as "Example®," in the same way as a normal trademark with a superscript "R" in a circle. As some industries, such as personal service industries, do not produce tangible products suitable for branding with a conventional trademark, service marks are usually used on service vehicles, on business cards, or in other advertising or promotional materials. While all trademarks require evidence of use in commerce, which is typically done by displaying the trademark on goods, service marks can satisfy the evidence requirement through evidence of their use on vehicles, uniforms, or advertising materials.

A *certification mark* is a type of trademark held by an organization or governmental entity that may indicate that a particular product is certified by that organization or entity to meet some particular standard or set of standards. A certification mark might indicate that a product meets particular safety requirements, that it passed some specific testing procedure, that is meets requirements for certain uses, that it was produced in accordance with certain manufacturing standards, that it was manufactured in a certain location or with certain materials, or that a product has any other qualities or characteristics that are required or deemed desirable. Generally, organizations that hold certification marks charge a fee for their certification services and for their certification labels. The companies purchasing those services and labels hope to recoup their expenses by increasing sales through increased consumer confidence inspired by the use of well-known certification marks.

Common certification marks in the United States include the marks of Underwriters Laboratories and Energy Star, both of which are shown below. Underwriters Laboratories permits its certification mark to be displayed on electrical and safety equipment that has been certified and that is subject to a follow-up certification agreement with Underwriters Laboratories. The Energy Star certification mark may be displayed on a wide variety of products that meet specific energy efficiency criteria, such as computers, appliances, office equipment, lighting, and even buildings. The specifications required for use on each type of product vary, and are typically set by either the Environmental Protection Agency or the Department of Energy.

Figure 11.1

A *collective mark* is a trademark that is held by an organization or association with members who may use the mark. Collective marks may be used to identify products with particular characteristics of quality, origin, or other desirable attributes. Like certification marks, collective marks are trademarks that do not identify the source of the product upon which the mark is displayed. The main difference between collective marks and certification marks is that a collective mark can only be used by a member of the organization that holds the collective mark, while certification marks may generally be used by anyone who meets the specifications set by the certification mark holder and pays whatever fee may be required.

Trade dress refers to the overall appearance of a product or its packaging. It may be protected as a trademark when it acquires a secondary meaning in the minds of the public that indicates the source of the product, as a conventional trademark does. Trade dress protection draws from the common law of unfair competition and its goal is to protect consumers from imitation products that use the same or similar product appearance to trick consumers into mistakenly believing the imitation product is either genuine or associated with or produced by the producer of the genuine goods. Although the common law provides some protection for trade dress, there is statutory protection as well. The *Lanham Act* states:

> "Any person who, on or in connection with any goods or services, or any container for goods, uses in commerce any word, term, name, symbol, or device, or any combination thereof, or any false designation of origin, false or misleading description of fact, or false or misleading representation of fact, which
>
> (A) is likely to cause confusion, or to cause mistake, or to deceive [...] as to the origin, sponsorship, or approval of his or her goods, services, or commercial activities by another person, or
>
> (B) in commercial advertising or promotion, misrepresents the nature, characteristics, qualities, or geographic origin of his or her or another person's goods, services, or commercial activities,

shall be liable in a civil action by any person who believes that he or she is likely to be damaged by such an act."
Lanham Act 15 U.S.C. § 1125.

11.2. What Can Be Trademarked?

Generally speaking, any device or expression may be trademarked as long as it indicates the source of the product or service it is used with, and it is not a functional component of those goods or services. A trademark *device* may be a word, a phrase, a symbol or design, a color or combination of colors, a sound, a fragrance, the overall appearance of a product or packaging, a texture, or potentially any other form of expression. Examples of many of these devices were mentioned previously, and include words (such as the name Nike®), designs (the Nike® "swoosh"), colors (the red sole of Christian Louboutin® shoes or yellow WIFFLE® bats), sounds (the NBC chimes), fragrances (Smead® peppermint scented office products), shapes (the spiral of Fritos® Flavor Twists®), overall appearance of a product or packaging (the blue box of Tiffany & Co.®), and a service provider's uniforms (such as those of the Dallas Cowboys Cheerleaders).

The logic behind the prohibition on functional trademarks is intended to prevent inventors from using trademark protection to avoid the limits of patent protection. If an inventor was able to trademark the functional design of a new invention, rather than obtain a patent with a limited lifespan, that trademark could last indefinitely. Such indefinite protection from competition would invite monopolies and undermine the compromise system put in place by patent law. However, an inventor of a non-functional ornamental design may obtain both a design patent and trademark protection, if that ornamental design acquires a secondary meaning in the marketplace indicating the source of the goods or services with which it is used. In other words, if the subject matter of an ornamental design patent is also used as trade dress, it may lawfully be protected by both a patent and an indefinite-duration trademark.

Similarly, a design may be protected by both a trademark and a copyright. If a design is an original work of authorship fixed in a tangible form, and it is used on goods in commerce as an identifier of the specific source of those goods, it may be eligible for copyright protection and trademark protection. In fact, if that same design is novel and nonobvious, it might be eligible for simultaneous protection with a design patent as well.

Chapter Summary

Trademark law provides protection to a variety of marks that are used as trademarks. While the most common of these is the traditional trademark, service marks, certification marks, collective marks, and protected trade dress also serve important and distinct functions in business. While most marks used as trademarks incorporate some form of language or wording, this is not a requirement. Many valuable and protected trademarks use other forms of expression, such as design, color, sound, fragrance, shape, overall appearance, or some combination of these things.

Key Terms

Service Mark
Certification Mark
Collective Mark
Trade Dress
Device

Review Questions

1. Give one example each of a traditional trademark, a service mark, a certification mark, a collective mark, and trade dress.
2. List one example each of a trademark embodied by a word, a device or design, a color, a sound, a fragrance, a shape, trade dress, and a uniform.
3. Can a perfume's scent be protected by trademark? Why or why not?

Web Links

1. http://www.marketwire.com/press-release/the-trademarked-sounds-sights-and-smells-of-summer-1803145.htm—A Marketwire Incorporated article about the commentary by attorney Michael Spink of Brinks Hofer Gilson & Lione on unusual trademarks.
2. http://www.erikpelton.com/2010/09/27/marching-ducks-goats-on-a-roof-sound-of-a-lightsaber-and-other-unusual-trademarks/—Website of Erik

M. Pelton & Associates, PLLC with a blog entry discussing and linking to a variety of unusual trademarks.

Discussion Exercise

1. What might some practical problems be with registering fragrance-based trademarks? The next chapter offers some answers to this question.

Chapter 12

Acquiring Rights

"Rights that do not flow from duty well performed are not worth having."—Mahatma Gandhi

Chapter Outline

Chapter Objectives

- Learn how trademark rights are acquired under the common law.
- Learn basic differences in how trademark rights are acquired under federal law.
- Examine the requirement of "use in trade" or "use in commerce" for trademark protection under both common law and federal law systems.
- Understand the concept of the "spectrum of distinctiveness," which is used to determine the strength of trademarks and their eligibility for protection.
- Learn the differences between marks that are arbitrary, fanciful, suggestive, descriptive, and generic and what each classification means for protection as a trademark.
- Understand how a descriptive mark may become a trademark through the accumulation of secondary meaning in the marketplace.

- Understand what it means when a trademark is functional and why functionality may bar trademark protection.
- Learn the public policy considerations behind the bar against functional trademarks.

12.1. What Rights Does a Trademark Holder Have?

The specific legal rights a trademark holder has depend on a number of factors, including whether the trademark is registered and whether others have the legal right to use the same trademark. Generally speaking, a trademark holder has the right to use his trademark to identify and distinguish his goods and services in the marketplace, to use that trademark to identify the source of his goods and services, and to exclude others from using his trademark or from using marks that would be confusingly similar to his trademark.

12.2. Common Law

Under the common law, the first to use a particular trademark in connection with the sale of goods or services, and who continues to do so, has an automatically acquired right to prevent competitors from using the same or confusingly similar trademarks. This right may be enforced regardless of an infringer's intent to infringe, even in cases where the infringer had no actual notice that the trademark in question was being used at all. This right will last as long as the trademark holder continues to use the trademark without abandoning it and without it becoming generic. This right may be enforced in any geographic area where the trademark holder was the first to use the trademark in the sale of goods or services and has continuously done so. No registration is required in order to acquire or enforce common law trademark rights, although registration with the state or federal government may be beneficial.

12.3. The Lanham Act

The *Lanham Act* recognizes and protects trademark rights existing under the common law. The *Lanham Act* does not supersede existing common law rights, but it does have additional requirements for trademark holders seeking its additional benefits and protections. Due to the fact that the *Lanham Act* is not the exclusive source of trademark rights, a trademark holder who loses rights under the *Lanham Act* for any reason still retains common law trademark rights. The requirements for federally registering a trademark and the associated benefits beyond those afforded by the common law are discussed later in this chapter.

12.4. Use in Commerce

Under the common law, actual use of the trademark in commerce is required to acquire trademark protection. This must be genuine use of the trademark in the sale of goods or services, and not merely a token transaction or the adoption of a mark for future use. The geographical scope of protection under the common law is also dependent on actual use of the mark in any given geographical market. If the mark is not actually used in commerce in a given location, then no protection is granted for that mark in that location. Use in commerce may be evidenced by preparations to sell, even if no actual sales have yet occurred. An example would be the use of a trademark in advertisements in a new market, combined with the intent to continue to use the trademark in that market, even though no actual sales have yet occurred in that market.

Given these requirements, it is possible that two competing merchants might adopt and use the same trademark in different geographic markets and both will have common law rights to their trademark. When this happens in geographical locations that are distant from each other, the competing merchants simply have their own rights in their own distinct geographical markets. When their markets overlap, the trademark rights belong to the senior user in the contested market. To determine the geographical area where the senior user has established priority of use, courts will consider the area where the mark is actually used, the area where the user has established a business presence, and the user's natural "*zone of expansion.*"

With regard to actual use, courts will determine whether a senior user has established actual use of the trademark in the usual course of business. This is often done by examining the senior user's sales records in the territory in question. The greater the volume and value of sales in the territory are, the greater the likelihood is that the court will determine that the requirement of actual use is met. With regard to business presence, courts will examine not only the locations of business operations, but the extent and range of advertising in the territory in question, as well as the number of customers who order from that territory. The more well-known the trademark is in the subject territory, the more likely the court will be to determine that the senior user has established a business presence in that territory. With regard to the senior user's zone of expansion, courts will consider the potential of the senior user for expansion. This analysis is typically based on the size and resources of the business, the business' history and rate of past expansion, current plans to expand, the level of advertising in new markets, and the level of trademark awareness in those new markets.

While most trademark holders will establish priority in new markets through some combination of actual use, business presence, and the zone of expansion, any of the three on its own can be sufficient to establish priority in a contested market. For these reasons trademark holders without federal registration must be careful to plan ahead and monitor any competitive use of rival trademark holders. Courts will evaluate each of the three pathways to priority to reject any token efforts made simply to claim priority in a contested market, but strategic advertising and sales promotion in key markets for expansion can still be critical for business growth.

While these requirements are nearly identical under federal law, there are some distinctions. Actual use in "commerce," as opposed to use in "trade," is required for federal registration. Commerce is used to highlight the limitations on Congress to regulate commerce, which boils down to anything that "substantially affects" interstate commerce. Therefore, any trade that is purely intra-state and that has no "substantial effect" on interstate commerce, if such trade could exist under the current interpretation of the Commerce Clause, cannot form the basis for priority under federal law. Federal law also rejects any token use in commerce for the purpose of establishing priority, and requires more than mere advertising of goods in a territory.

Federal law does offer some additional ways to establish use in commerce for the purposes of priority. Regarding goods, they may either be sold or transported in a contested territory. Either action, if done with the awareness of the public and not in secret or as a purely intra-company measure, can establish use in commerce. Regarding services, the use of a service mark in either the sale or advertising of services in a contested market may constitute use in commerce so long as the service mark holder is engaged in commerce in connection with the services.

12.5. The Spectrum of Distinctiveness

Distinctiveness is critical to a trademark. If a mark is not capable of adequately distinguishing goods or services with which it is used from other, similar goods or services from another source, then that mark is not eligible for trademark protection. Distinctiveness may either be inherent or it may be acquired through use. *Inherently distinctive* marks may be *arbitrary* (such as Apple® computers), *fanciful* (such as Kodak® film), or *suggestive* (such as Greyhound® bussing service). Marks that are merely *descriptive* are not eligible for trademark protection, though they may become eligible if they acquire a secondary meaning in the marketplace that links the mark to a specific source of goods or services, thereby providing the required distinctiveness. Examples of this type of mark include McDonald's® and KOOL menthol cigarettes.

Courts have evaluated the ability of particular trademarks to distinguish the origin of the goods or services they are used with by using a *"spectrum of distinctiveness."* This concept applies under both the common law and under federal law. On this spectrum, the strongest trademarks are arbitrary or fanciful. The next strongest marks are suggestive, and the weakest are descriptive. Marks that are arbitrary, fanciful, or suggestive are considered to be inherently distinctive, and they do not need to show any secondary meaning in the market to be protectable as trademarks. Descriptive marks must show secondary meaning to be eligible for protection. *Generic marks* are marks using general or descriptive terms that are incapable of acquiring secondary meaning, and are therefore never eligible for trademark protection.

Classification of marks into these categories on the spectrum of distinctiveness will help determine when a mark is entitled to protection as a trademark. This is usually a straightforward process, but courts have noted the various ways in which the process may be complicated by the difference in meaning of words applied to one type of product versus another, or the difference in meaning of words over time, or in different markets, or with specific segments of the population. By way of example, the hypothetical trademark "Mint" would be arbitrary and eligible for trademark protection as applied to a line of sunglasses. However, the same mark would be descriptive as applied to mint flavored chewing gum, and generic as applied to mint plants. Creative people will sometimes attempt to convert a generic term into a protectable trademark by changing the spelling of a generic or descriptive term to make it seem arbitrary. Courts are generally unimpressed by this approach, and they will typically reject variations in spelling that are pronounced the same way as descriptive or generic terms. Using the term "Mynt" to sell mint plants is unlikely to result in a protectable trademark.

Fanciful marks are composed of made-up terms. They have no preexisting meaning or definition, and they are therefore considered to be the strongest trademarks from a legal perspective. The only context within which a consumer may be exposed to such a term would be during exposure to the trademark itself. Confusion with other marks or descriptive or generic terms is therefore very unlikely. Well-known examples of fanciful marks include Kodak® and Xerox®. Fanciful marks are considered inherently distinctive and therefore they do not require any showing of secondary meaning in the marketplace.

Arbitrary marks are typically composed of common words that are seemingly chosen arbitrarily for their trademark use. The trademark holder may select the words used because of those words' positive association in the minds of consumers, but the words chosen do not have any descriptive association with the products or services the trademark is applied to. When used in this manner, arbitrary marks are considered to be inherently distinctive. One problem with arbitrary marks is that the mark may be arbitrary as applied to one industry, and considered to be descriptive or even generic in another industry. "Apple" is a classic example of an arbitrary mark as applied to computers. However, if the same mark is used in apple farming, it would be a generic term.

Suggestive marks also make great trademarks, but there is danger in adopting a potential trademark that is too descriptive. A suggestive mark must have some element of descriptiveness in order to be suggestive, but it cannot be overly descriptive or it will be treated as a descriptive mark and require the establishment of a secondary meaning in order to be eligible for trademark protection. Suggestive marks that are not overly descriptive are considered inherently distinctive, and therefore no showing of secondary meaning is required to obtain trademark protection.

The challenge with suggestive marks, therefore, is determining whether they are truly suggestive or overly descriptive. "A term is suggestive if it requires imagination, thought and perception to reach a conclusion as to the nature of goods. A term is descriptive if it forthwith conveys an immediate idea of the ingredients, qualities or characteristics of the goods."[1] Many courts have relied upon a six-factor test to distinguish between suggestive and descriptive marks. These factors are as follows:

First, a court will consider how much imagination is required by a consumer trying to draw a direct message from the mark about the quality, ingredients or characteristics of the product or service.

Second, a court will consider whether the mark directly conveys a real and unequivocal idea of some characteristic, function, quality or ingredient of the product or service to a reasonably informed potential buyer.

---

1. *Blinded Veterans Ass'n v. Blinded American Veterans Found.*, 872 F.2d 1035, 1040 (D.C. Cir. 1989).

Third, a court will consider whether the mark so closely tells something about the product or service that other sellers of like products would be likely to want to use the term in connection with their goods.

Fourth, a court will consider whether other sellers are actually using the mark or terms in the mark to describe their products.

Fifth, a court will consider whether the mark is just as likely or more likely to bring to mind something unrelated to the product or service as it is to be descriptive.

Sixth, a court will consider how the mark fits into the basic concept that descriptive marks cannot pinpoint one source by identifying and distinguishing only one seller.

Another useful approach is to ask whether a consumer who is exposed to the mark without knowing what product it is attached to would be unable to correctly guess the product, but would understand the suggestive connection to the product once the product is revealed. If the consumer can guess the product correctly, then the mark is likely to be too descriptive.

12.6. Secondary Meaning

A descriptive mark is not distinctive on its own, and therefore cannot be a proper trademark without acquiring some secondary meaning in the marketplace. Secondary meaning is acquired through use of the mark when the public coms to recognize the mark as referring to a specific source of goods or services, instead of merely being descriptive of those goods or services. The key is to determine whether the public, when exposed to the mark, thinks primarily of the product or the source of the product. If the public thinks primarily of the product, then the mark is still too descriptive. In order to establish the existence of secondary meaning, courts will consider survey evidence, consumer testimony, the exclusivity of use of the mark, the extent of advertising with the mark, sales volume and value, and other factors that evidence the value of the mark as a source indicator, as opposed to a merely descriptive term.

12.7. Non-Functionality

As previously discussed, the functional or utilitarian elements of a product may not be the subject of trademark protection, as allowing potentially-perpetual trademark protection to a functional component of a product would effectively bypass the time limitations imposed on monopolies by patent law. Something that could properly be the subject of a utility patent generally cannot properly be a trademark. Regarding the determination of what might constitute a functional component, the Supreme Court has stated:

> Discussing trademarks, we have said in general terms, a product feature is functional, and cannot serve as a trademark, if it is essential to the use or purpose of the article or if it affects the cost or quality of the article. Expanding upon the meaning of this phrase, we have observed that a functional feature is one the exclusive use of which would put competitors at a significant non-reputation-related disadvantage. The Court of Appeals in the instant case seemed to interpret this language to mean that a necessary test for functionality is whether the particular product configuration is a competitive necessity. This was incorrect as a comprehensive definition. As explained in *Qualitex, supra,* and *Inwood, supra,* a feature is also functional when it is essential to the use or purpose of the device or when it affects the cost or quality of the device. The *Qualitex* decision did not purport to displace this traditional rule. Instead, it quoted the rule as *Inwood* had set it forth. It is proper to inquire into a significant non-reputation-related disadvantage in cases of aesthetic functionality, the question involved in *Qualitex*. Where the design is functional under the *Inwood* formulation there is no need to proceed further to consider if there is a competitive necessity for the feature. In *Qualitex*, by contrast, aesthetic functionality was the central question, there having been no indication that the green-gold color of the laundry press pad had any bearing on the use or purpose of the product or its cost or quality.[2]

Stated differently, there is a two-part test to determine whether a component is functional or not. First, it must be determined whether the design of the component is essential to the use or purpose of the article or if it affects the cost or quality of the article. This is the more obvious utilitarian inquiry, and it prevents the use of trademark protection to establish a monopoly on a useful design. If the answer to this question is yes, then the component cannot be trademarked and there is no need to go on to the second part of the inquiry. If the answer is no, then it must be determined whether the component is one that, if only the trademark holder was given the exclusive use of it, would put competitors at a significant non-reputation-related disadvantage. This asks whether the use of the component is a competitive necessity, or if there are al-

---

2. *TrafFix Devices, Inc. v. Mktg. Displays, Inc.*, 532 U.S. 23 (2001).

ternatives available that do not require duplication of the trademark holder's design. If the answer to this second question is yes, then the component cannot be trademarked. This prevents the use of trade dress to perpetuate rights that might properly be protectable with a utility patent.

When evaluating this "*aesthetic functionality*," it is important to note the distinction between "*de facto functional features*" and "*de jure functional features.*" A feature of a device may be de facto functional if it serves any purpose. For example, a bottle of any design typically holds fluid and therefore has a function, regardless of how artistic or arbitrary the bottle's design may be. This will ordinarily not prevent trademark protection. However, de jure functional features are those that are specifically designed in a particular way because they work better that way. De jure functional features are not arbitrary or artistic, but utilitarian. These functional features will prevent trademark protection.

A good example of this is the famous contoured bottle of Coca-Cola®, depicted below in one of its two design patents, which expired in due course and led the company to register the design as a trademark. Obviously a glass bottle is functional, and the company required its bottle to perform the functional task of containing its soft drink. However, the company held a design competition in 1915 to create a new glass bottle that would distinguish it from its competitors and be "a bottle which a person could recognize even if they felt it in the dark, and so shaped that, even if broken, a person could tell at a glance what it was."[3] This goal of creating a distinct and recognizable bottle led to an arbitrary and artistic design that was not a functional feature, although the bottle itself, in essence, was still a functional bottle. This is an example of de facto functionality, which would not, and did not, defeat trademark protection. If this design had instead been developed and chosen because, for example, it was stronger and resisted breakage better during shipping, or because it kept the beverage inside cooler for longer, then it may well have been considered a de jure functional feature and its design would not be eligible for trademark protection.

Chapter Summary

Trademark rights may be acquired automatically by use of a mark in trade or commerce, but the mark used must be eligible for protection in the first place. Some types of marks are better suited as trademarks under the law, and

---

3. "Inventory: Earl R. Dean Collection," Vigo County Public Library.

Figure 12.1

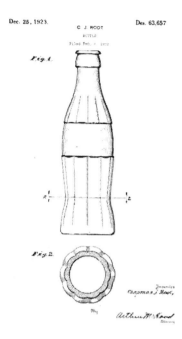

those will be more easily protected. Some trademarks are inherently distinctive, while others must acquire distinctiveness over time through use and consumer recognition before they may be protected as trademarks. Generally, functional marks may not be trademarks. However, while some aspects of a trademark may be functional by their nature, thy may still be eligible for protection if they have arbitrary or artistic elements that are not functional and that serve to distinguish the mark from others.

Key Terms

De Facto Functional Features
De Jure Functional Features
Aesthetic Functionality
Zone of Expansion
Spectrum of Distinctiveness
Inherently Distinctive
Arbitrary Marks

Fanciful Marks
Suggestive Marks
Descriptive Marks
Generic Marks

Review Questions

1. What is the spectrum of distinctiveness? What is it used for?
2. If a mark is not inherently distinctive, can it still be protected as a trademark?
3. Give one example each of an arbitrary mark, a fanciful mark, a suggestive mark, a descriptive mark, and a generic mark.
4. Which of the types of marks listed above may be eligible for trademark protection?
5. What is a de facto functional element of a mark? Give an example.
6. What is a de jure functional element of a mark? Give an example.

Web Links

1. http://www.law.cornell.edu/uscode/text/15/chapter-22—Cornell University Law School's Legal Information Institute page on the Lanham Act.

Discussion Exercise

1. Should scented candle manufacturers be able to trademark the names of their scented candles? What if they are descriptive? If a candle has an abstract name, like "Midnight Moondance," it doesn't seem to pose a problem. What if the name of the scent is "Home Sweet Home"? What about "Strawberries-n-Cream," or "Sugar Cookie"? Those seem much more descriptive. What about "Christmas Eve"? Are these names too descriptive to be proper trademarks? For an interesting discussion of this topic see http://www.candlecauldron.com/trademarks.html.

Chapter 13

Federal Registration of Trademarks

"The bureaucracy is expanding to meet the needs of the expanding bureaucracy." —Oscar Wilde

Chapter Outline

Chapter Objectives

- Learn the purpose and function of the United States Patent and Trademark Office as it relates to trademark law.
- Understand the basics of the trademark registration process.
- Understand problems that may prevent a successful trademark registration.
- Learn the duration of federal trademark registration and renewal requirements.

13.1. United States Patent and Trademark Office

The United States Patent and Trademark Office (PTO) is a federal agency operating under the United States Department of Commerce that issues patents and trademarks. The PTO has a staff of trademark examining attorneys who examine applications for trademark registration. Approved trademarks are either registered in the Principal Register or the Supplemental Register, depending on their level of distinctiveness. Trademarks must be inherently distinctive, or have acquired distinction through secondary meaning in the marketplace, in order to be registered in the Principal Register.

The Lanham Act established the Principal Register as the primary register of trademarks that are recognized as such by federal law and formally registered by the PTO. Trademarks in the Principal Register are eligible for greater protection than what is available under the common law, though the common law protections still apply. Some of these additional protections include a presumption of trademark validity in infringement actions, nationwide constructive use and constructive notice, the potential for incontestable status, the availability of federal infringement actions, Customs and Border Protection enforcement assistance, and the availability of awards of multiple damages and attorney's fees in successful infringement actions.

The presumption of validity of the trademark in infringement actions shifts the burden of proof to the defendant with regard to trademark validity. An infringement plaintiff with an unregistered mark must establish that his mark is valid as part of his case. A plaintiff with a registered mark may rely on the federal registration in the Principal Register as sufficient proof of validity, and the defendant must then try to prove that the registration was defective or that the mark has since become unenforceable. This makes it easier for the plaintiff to protect its trademarks in court.

The benefit of constructive use allows a successful registration in the Principal Register to satisfy the legal requirement of actual use of the mark nationwide for priority purposes with respect to the goods or services for which the mark is registered as of the date the application for registration was filed. This means that, unless another party is currently using the same mark or has already filed an application to register the same mark, the mark will be protected nationwide despite the fact that it may not have been used nationwide. This is obviously beneficial to any trademark holder who wishes to expand his business over time, without concern over later encountering a competing business using the same trademark in another part of the country. The benefit of constructive notice prevents any future party from using the registered trademark and claiming, even in good faith, that it used the trademark without knowledge of its registration. Prior to the Lanham Act providing this benefit, it was possible for a party to lawfully use a registered trademark in good faith as long as that party had no actual knowledge of its registration and as long as that party was the first to use the mark in that particular region.

Customs and Border Protection assistance is available to trademark holders whose trademarks are registered in the Principal Register. This assistance usually comes in the form of active prevention of importation of infringing goods. Another major benefit of federal registration in the Principal Register is the possibility of incontestable status. Incontestable status is available to trademarks that have been in continuous use in commerce for at least five consecutive years from the date of registration in the Principal Register, and it provides conclusive proof of the validity of the registered mark, ownership of the mark, and exclusive right to use of the mark in commerce with respect to the goods and services for which is was registered. Incontestable status limits the ways that a trademark may be cancelled, and limits the defenses available to an alleged infringer.

The Supplemental Register is a secondary registry of trademarks established by the Lanham Act to allow trademarks that don't qualify for federal registration in the Principal Registry to be federally registered anyway in order to qualify for registration in other countries. The Paris Convention for the Protection of Industrial Property requires domestic registration of trademarks in order to obtain foreign registration. Many countries have less restrictive requirements for trademark registration than the United States, and registration in the Supplemental Register allows the pursuit of trademark registration in those countries. A mark must be capable of distinguishing goods or services in order to be registered in the Supplemental Register, even if it does not actually do so. The Lanham Act permits registration on the Supplemental Register of "any trademark, symbol, slogan, phrase, surname, geographical name, numeral, device, any matter that as a whole is not functional, or any combination of any of the foregoing, but such mark must be capable of distinguishing the applicant's goods or services." This allows holders of descriptive marks, who may be waiting to acquire sufficient secondary meaning in the marketplace to obtain registration in the Principal Registry, to put other potential users of the same mark or of confusingly similar marks on notice that such a mark is already in use in commerce. Registration in the Supplemental Register may be sufficient grounds to deny registration of confusingly similar marks in either the Principal Register or the Supplemental Register. Registration in the Supplemental Register has no effect on any common law rights the owner of the mark may have.

13.2. Application Process

The Lanham Act allows applications for registration in the Principal Register based on either actual use of a mark or intent to use that mark. An application based on actual use of the mark must contain the date of the first use of the mark in commerce, the goods or services with which the mark is used, a drawing or detailed description of the mark, and a specimen of the mark. If the mark is a descriptive mark, then evidence of distinctiveness acquired through secondary meaning must also be submitted. Applications for collective marks or certification marks must submit sufficient information for the PTO to verify that the marks are eligible for those types of registration. If a PTO trademark examining attorney accepts the mark for registration, it will be published by the PTO in the Official Gazette of the PTO for public review. If nobody files an opposition within thirty days, a certificate of registration will issue. If the examining attorney rejects the application, the applicant can appeal that rejection to the Trademark Trial and Appeals Board.

An application based on intent to use a mark must meet basically the same requirements as an application based on actual use must meet, but without the need to submit the date of first use or an actual specimen of the mark. An intent to use applicant must submit a statement setting forth a bona fide intent to use the mark in commerce, and the fact that the applicant is not aware of anyone else entitled to use the mark or a confusingly similar mark in commerce. If the application is not rejected, then the mark will be published in the Official Gazette for opposition. If no opposition is received within thirty days, or if any opposition is resolved in the favor of the applicant, then a Notice of Allowance is issued to the applicant. The applicant then has six months to file a verified statement that the mark is being used in commerce, providing the date of first use, and describing the goods and services with which the mark is being used. The applicant must also provide specimens if requested by the PTO.

If an applicant cannot file the verified statement of use within six months, he may request a six-month extension. He may request additional six-month extensions for good cause, up to a total of twenty-four months. Good cause for these additional extensions may be satisfied by virtually any effort to prepare for commercial use of the mark, such as research and development of goods to be sold, promotional or business networking activities, establishing the business, waiting for licenses or approvals, etc. Each requested extension must be made in writing and submitted before the expiration of the prior deadline.

Once the application has been completed, with all required statements and evidence of actual use of the mark, the PTO will examine the application and either reject it or issue a certificate of registration. If a certificate of registration is issued, its effective date will be the date the intent to use application was first filed. If the application is rejected, that decision may be appealed to the Trademark Trial and Appeals Board.

13.3. Performing a Trademark Search

While it is certainly not required, many people choose to hire an experienced attorney to perform a trademark search prior to submitting their application. Working with an attorney makes the process much easier, and will probably increase the chances of having an application approved by avoiding common application mistakes and ensuring that the application is complete and comprehensive. The obvious downside to working with a skilled attorney is the expense of legal fees in addition to the required filing fees. The PTO makes efforts to make the complicated application process more understandable to the general public, and the website links at the end of this section contain a vast amount of information and resources that break down and explain the trademark search process and the entire application process.

The PTO has an online trademark search system called the Trademark Electronic Search System (TESS), which is free to use. A link to this system is included in the links section below, and it is worth exploring. While this is the most common way to perform an initial trademark search prior to applying for registration, it is also possible to conduct a trademark search at a Patent and Trademark Resource Center. These centers are libraries in each state chosen by the PTO to house patent and trademark records and databases to help provide greater access to these materials by the public. Generally, these centers have computers available to access TESS, and they may also have trained personnel available to provide basic search assistance.

TESS contains the federal records of active and inactive trademark registrations and applications. It is important to review TESS materials to help ensure that there are no pre-existing marks in the database that are the same as, or confusingly similar to, a mark being submitted for registration. If there is such a pre-existing mark, that may be grounds for rejection of the application as a likelihood of confusion will exist. One weakness of the federal database system is that many trademark holders do not choose to register with the PTO, and so their trademarks will not be found in a TESS search. Private trademark search databases exist that may include state trademark registrations and common law trademark databases. These resources are not typically available for free, and the PTO does not maintain its own database of state trademarks or common law trademarks.

When conducting a trademark search, it is important to look at the registered use of the mark as well as the mark itself. While two marks may be very similar, they may both be valid and eligible for registration if they are both registered for use on different types of goods or services. The same exact trademark may be used and registered by different owners if, for example, one owner uses the mark on bags of potatoes for sale and the other uses the mark in connection with mortgage services. Obviously, this may not be a desirable situation for either owner, but it illustrates why a trademark search must include both the wording or design and the use of the mark.

The United States follows the trademark classification system established by the Nice Agreement Concerning the International Classification of Goods and Services for the Purposes of the Registration of Marks. This system is organized by the World Intellectual Property Organization and it is currently used by eighty-three countries. The system assigns a classification to each registered trademark that is intended to assist others in searching for preexisting marks and their uses. There are currently forty-five different classes of goods and services, set forth below, which can be viewed in greater detail and with the addition of explanatory and clarifying notes by following the link provided in the links section below.

CLASS 1
Chemicals used in industry, science and photography, as well as in agriculture, horticulture and forestry; unprocessed artificial resins, unprocessed plastics; manures; fire extinguishing compositions; tempering and soldering preparations; chemical substances for preserving foodstuffs; tanning substances; adhesives used in industry.

CLASS 2
Paints, varnishes, lacquers; preservatives against rust and against deterioration of wood; colorants; mordants; raw natural resins; metals in foil and powder form for painters, decorators, printers and artists.

CLASS 3
Bleaching preparations and other substances for laundry use; cleaning, polishing, scouring and abrasive preparations; soaps; perfumery, essential oils, cosmetics, hair lotions; dentifrices.

CLASS 4

Industrial oils and greases; lubricants; dust absorbing, wetting and binding compositions; fuels (including motor spirit) and illuminants; candles and wicks for lighting.

CLASS 5

Pharmaceutical and veterinary preparations; sanitary preparations for medical purposes; dietetic food and substances adapted for medical or veterinary use, food for babies; dietary supplements for humans and animals; plasters, materials for dressings; material for stopping teeth, dental wax; disinfectants; preparations for destroying vermin; fungicides, herbicides.

CLASS 6

Common metals and their alloys; metal building materials; transportable buildings of metal; materials of metal for railway tracks; non-electric cables and wires of common metal; ironmongery, small items of metal hardware; pipes and tubes of metal; safes; goods of common metal not included in other classes; ores.

CLASS 7

Machines and machine tools; motors and engines (except for land vehicles); machine coupling and transmission components (except for land vehicles); agricultural implements other than hand-operated; incubators for eggs; automatic vending machines.

CLASS 8

Hand tools and implements (hand-operated); cutlery; side arms; razors.

CLASS 9

Scientific, nautical, surveying, photographic, cinematographic, optical, weighing, measuring, signalling, checking (supervision), life-saving and teaching apparatus and instruments; apparatus and instruments for conducting, switching, transforming, accumulating, regulating or controlling electricity; apparatus for recording, transmission or reproduction of sound or images; magnetic data carriers, recording discs; compact discs, DVDs and other digital recording media; mechanisms for coin-operated apparatus; cash registers, calculating machines, data processing equipment, computers; computer software; fire-extinguishing apparatus.

CLASS 10

Surgical, medical, dental and veterinary apparatus and instruments, artificial limbs, eyes and teeth; orthopedic articles; suture materials.

CLASS 11
Apparatus for lighting, heating, steam generating, cooking, refrigerating, drying, ventilating, water supply and sanitary purposes.

CLASS 12
Vehicles; apparatus for locomotion by land, air or water.

CLASS 13
Firearms; ammunition and projectiles; explosives; fireworks.

CLASS 14
Precious metals and their alloys and goods in precious metals or coated therewith, not included in other classes; jewellery, precious stones; horological and chronometric instruments.

CLASS 15
Musical instruments.

CLASS 16
Paper, cardboard and goods made from these materials, not included in other classes; printed matter; bookbinding material; photographs; stationery; adhesives for stationery or household purposes; artists' materials; paint brushes; typewriters and office requisites (except furniture); instructional and teaching material (except apparatus); plastic materials for packaging (not included in other classes); printers' type; printing blocks.

CLASS 17
Rubber, gutta-percha, gum, asbestos, mica and goods made from these materials and not included in other classes; plastics in extruded form for use in manufacture; packing, stopping and insulating materials; flexible pipes, not of metal.

CLASS 18
Leather and imitations of leather, and goods made of these materials and not included in other classes; animal skins, hides; trunks and travelling bags; umbrellas and parasols; walking sticks; whips, harness and saddlery.

CLASS 19
Building materials (non-metallic); non-metallic rigid pipes for building; asphalt, pitch and bitumen; non-metallic transportable buildings; monuments, not of metal.

CLASS 20
Furniture, mirrors, picture frames; goods (not included in other classes) of wood, cork, reed, cane, wicker, horn, bone, ivory, whalebone, shell, amber,

mother-of-pearl, meerschaum and substitutes for all these materials, or of plastics.

CLASS 21
Household or kitchen utensils and containers; combs and sponges; brushes (except paint brushes); brush-making materials; articles for cleaning purposes; steelwool; unworked or semi-worked glass (except glass used in building); glassware, porcelain and earthenware not included in other classes.

CLASS 22
Ropes, string, nets, tents, awnings, tarpaulins, sails, sacks and bags (not included in other classes); padding and stuffing materials (except of rubber or plastics); raw fibrous textile materials.

CLASS 23
Yarns and threads, for textile use.

CLASS 24
Textiles and textile goods, not included in other classes; bed covers; table covers.

CLASS 25
Clothing, footwear, headgear.

CLASS 26
Lace and embroidery, ribbons and braid; buttons, hooks and eyes, pins and needles; artificial flowers.

CLASS 27
Carpets, rugs, mats and matting, linoleum and other materials for covering existing floors; wall hangings (non-textile).

CLASS 28
Games and playthings; gymnastic and sporting articles not included in other classes; decorations for Christmas trees.

CLASS 29
Meat, fish, poultry and game; meat extracts; preserved, frozen, dried and cooked fruits and vegetables; jellies, jams, compotes; eggs; milk and milk products; edible oils and fats.

CLASS 30
Coffee, tea, cocoa and artificial coffee; rice; tapioca and sago; flour and preparations made from cereals; bread, pastry and confectionery; ices; sugar, honey, treacle; yeast, baking-powder; salt; mustard; vinegar, sauces (condiments); spices; ice.

CLASS 31
Grains and agricultural, horticultural and forestry products not included in other classes; live animals; fresh fruits and vegetables; seeds; natural plants and flowers; foodstuffs for animals; malt.

CLASS 32
Beers; mineral and aerated waters and other non-alcoholic beverages; fruit beverages and fruit juices; syrups and other preparations for making beverages.

CLASS 33
Alcoholic beverages (except beers).

CLASS 34
Tobacco; smokers' articles; matches.

CLASS 35
Advertising; business management; business administration; office functions.

CLASS 36
Insurance; financial affairs; monetary affairs; real estate affairs.

CLASS 37
Building construction; repair; installation services.

CLASS 38
Telecommunications.

CLASS 39
Transport; packaging and storage of goods; travel arrangement.

CLASS 40
Treatment of materials.

CLASS 41
Education; providing of training; entertainment; sporting and cultural activities.

CLASS 42
Scientific and technological services and research and design relating thereto; industrial analysis and research services; design and development of computer hardware and software.

CLASS 43
Services for providing food and drink; temporary accommodation.

CLASS 44
Medical services; veterinary services; hygienic and beauty care for human beings or animals; agriculture, horticulture and forestry services.

CLASS 45
Legal services; security services for the protection of property and individuals; personal and social services rendered by others to meet the needs of individuals.

A trademark may be used with goods or services in multiple categories, and a single application for registration may properly list a use classification for each different class of goods and services that applies. The General Remarks of the Nice Agreement offer the following advice on classifying uses with goods and services that do not appear to readily fit into a classification. This information is also helpful when searching for classes of goods or services that might create a likelihood of confusion between an existing trademark use and an applicant's trademark use, as an applicant may not initially consider searching within non-obvious or alternative classifications.

GOODS

If a product cannot be classified with the aid of the List of Classes, the Explanatory Notes and the Alphabetical List, the following remarks set forth the criteria to be applied:

(a) A finished product is in principle classified according to its function or purpose. If the function or purpose of a finished product is not mentioned in any class heading, the finished product is classified by analogy with other comparable finished products, indicated in the Alphabetical List. If none is found, other subsidiary criteria, such as that of the material of which the product is made or its mode of operation, are applied.

(b) A finished product which is a multipurpose composite object (e.g., clocks incorporating radios) may be classified in all classes that correspond to any of its functions or intended purposes. If those functions or purposes are not mentioned in any class heading, other criteria, indicated under (a), above, are to be applied.

(c) Raw materials, unworked or semi-worked, are in principle classified according to the material of which they consist.

(d) Goods intended to form part of another product are in principle classified in the same class as that product only in cases where the same type of goods cannot normally be used for another purpose. In all other cases, the criterion indicated under (a), above, applies.

(e) When a product, whether finished or not, is classified according to the material of which it is made, and it is made of different materials, the product is in principle classified according to the material which predominates.

(f) Cases adapted to the product they are intended to contain are in principle classified in the same class as the product.

SERVICES

If a service cannot be classified with the aid of the List of Classes, the Explanatory Notes and the Alphabetical List, the following remarks set forth the criteria to be applied:

(a) Services are in principle classified according to the branches of activities specified in the headings of the service classes and in their Explanatory Notes or, if not specified, by analogy with other comparable services indicated in the Alphabetical List.

(b) Rental services are in principle classified in the same classes as the services provided by means of the rented objects (e.g., Rental of telephones, covered by Class 38). Leasing services are analogous to rental services and therefore should be classified in the same way. However, hire- or lease-purchase financing is classified in Class 36 as a financial service.

(c) Services that provide advice, information or consultation are in principle classified in the same classes as the services that correspond to the subject matter of the advice, information or consultation, e.g., transportation consultancy (Cl. 39), business management consultancy (Cl. 35), financial consultancy (Cl. 36), beauty consultancy (Cl. 44). The rendering of the advice, information or consultancy by electronic means (e.g., telephone, computer) does not affect the classification of these services.

(d) Services rendered in the framework of franchising are in principle classified in the same class as the particular services provided by the franchisor (e.g., business advice relating to franchising (Class 35), financing services relating to franchising (Class 36), legal services relating to franchising (Class 45)).

Another problem with trademark searches is the difficulty inherent in searching for non-text trademark devices. Searching for simple text trademarks is straightforward, but searching for designs, scents, textures, and sounds is not so easy. The TESS system allows for design searches, but it is necessary to become familiar with the design codes TESS uses. The PTO publishes a design code guide to assist with this task, but non-text searching is still a common pitfall for do-it-yourself applicants. While a trademark with stylized wording should still have a plain text version of that wording in the searchable description of the mark, a mark that consists of a logo or non-text design is much harder to describe. While a musical sound trademark may contain a standard written musical representation that can be searched, a scent must be described without the benefit of a standard system of representation.

The PTO approved a scent trademark application for scented yarn in 1990 in the matter In re Clark. This fragrance was described in the application as a "high impact, fresh, floral fragrance reminiscent of Plumeria blossoms." Given the variation in the population of ability to perceive scents and ability to associate scents with other variable reference scents, such as Plumeria blossoms, it is easy to see how these types of trademarks can be extremely difficult to search. An applicant might think his scent smells like flowers, but he might not specifically describe it as a Plumeria scent. It is also difficult to determine exactly what might constitute a scent that is confusingly similar to a registered scent. Is a "high-impact, fresh, floral fragrance reminiscent of rose blossoms"

Figure 13.1.

confusingly similar? What about Gardenia blossoms? What if it is low-impact and weaker than a fresh scent?

13.4. The Examination Procedure

The Trademark Manual of Examining Procedure is the PTO's guidebook for trademark examining attorneys. It contains detailed information on relevant laws, government regulations, and the trademark application and examination procedures. The manual is comprehensive, and it can be referenced by following the link at the end of this section. The examination process is designed to ensure that trademark registration and protection is only granted where the mark in question meets all of the requirements to be a trademark and where there are no conflicts with pre-existing marks. As the goal of avoiding conflicts is usually the goal of applicants as well, the examination process largely mirrors that of the typical applicant's pre-application trademark search process, with the addition of publication to welcome objections from interested parties.

When an application is first received, the PTO reviews it to determine if it meets the minimum requirements for receiving a filing date. To receive a filing date, the application must contain the date of the first use of the mark in commerce, the goods or services with which the mark is used, a drawing or detailed description of the mark, and a specimen of the mark. If the mark is a descriptive mark, then evidence of distinctiveness acquired through secondary meaning must also be submitted. Applications for collective marks or certification marks must submit sufficient information for the PTO to verify that the marks are eligible for those types of registration. The applicant must also submit the appropriate fee, as published by the PTO. If these minimum requirements are not met, the entire submission, including the filing fee, is returned to the applicant. If the application does meet the minimum requirements, the PTO assigns it a serial number and sends the applicant a receipt.

Once the PTO assigns a filing date, the application undergoes a complete review that includes a search for conflicting marks, and an examination of the written application, the drawing, and any specimens. If the examining attorney determines that the mark cannot be registered, she will send the applicant a letter, called an office action, listing any grounds for refusal and any corrections required in the application. The applicant must respond to any office actions within six months of the mailing date of the letter, or the application will be deemed abandoned either in whole or as to whatever specific goods or services were at issue in the office action. The examining attorney may also request additional information, affidavits, declarations, or specimens deemed necessary to complete the examination.

After the applicant responds to any requests by the examining attorney, or to any objections, the application will be reexamined. There may be additional rounds of office action letters to the applicant raising issues and timely responses by the applicant, until the application is either approved or a final refusal is issued. If the applicant cannot overcome all objections, the examining attorney will issue a final refusal. Common bars to registration that applicants may encounter are discussed below. An applicant may potentially overcome a final refusal by appealing to the Trademark Trial and Appeal Board, or by requesting that the examining attorney reconsider the final refusal prior to the appeal filing deadline, although requests for reconsideration do not toll the appeal deadline.

Once the examining attorney is satisfied that an application appears to be entitled to registration on the Principal Register, the applicant's mark will be published in the Official Gazette to allow the public a chance to object to the registration. Interested parties typically have thirty days from the date of publication to object to the registration. If no objections are made, or if all objections are resolved in the favor of the applicant, then the mark will be registered and the applicant will receive a certificate of registration, if the application was an actual use application, or a notice of allowance, if the application was an intent to use application.

13.5. Bars to Registration

The PTO may refuse to register a mark on numerous grounds, and these grounds are exhaustively detailed in the Trademark Manual of Examining Procedure. The most common grounds for refusal to register a mark that have not already been discussed in detail above follow.

Likelihood of Confusion with a Registered Trademark: When a trademark examining attorney conducts a trademark search as part of the examination of an application, conflicts may be found with preexisting marks or other marks pending registration. The examining attorney will compare any potentially confusing marks and judge their similarity and likelihood of causing consumer confusion. The more similar the marks at issue are, and the closer the goods and services that the marks are used with are, the greater the chance that the examining attorney will reject the application on the basis of likelihood of confusion.

While it is possible for identical marks to be registered for use with different goods or services, those goods and services would have to be sufficiently different to convince the examining attorney that confusion in the marketplace as to the origin of the goods and services is unlikely. Marks may be considered similar if they sound, appear, or even have meanings that are similar. If the marks are identical or similar, and they are used with related goods or services, there is likely to be confusion. When a trademark examining attorney determines that there is a likelihood of confusion with a registered trademark, the application for new registration will be denied.

Mark is Merely Descriptive: Trademarks may not be merely descriptive terms. As discussed above, descriptive terms that are not generic may eventually acquire a secondary meaning in the marketplace that will allow them to be considered legally distinctive. Descriptive terms that have not acquired sufficient secondary meaning may not be registered as trademarks. The PTO considers a mark descriptive if it immediately describes an ingredient, quality, characteristic, function, feature, purpose or use of the specified goods or services.

Mark is Deceptively Misdescriptive: Deceptive marks may not be registered, and misdescription is considered by the PTO to be a form of deception. Misdescription may apply to ingredients, qualities, characteristics, functions, features, purposes, or uses of the goods or services with which the mark is used. In order to be a grounds for rejection of an application, the deception conveyed by the mark must be plausible and must be a material factor in a consumer's purchase decision. An example of a deceptively misdescriptive mark might be "Stryngth Organics" used on packages of non-organic dietary supplements, or "Honeybee Natural Leatherworks" used on synthetic-leather goods. An example of a potentially misdescriptive mark that would likely not be considered plausible, and therefore would not be subject to rejection on this basis, might be "Bulletproof Cosmetics" as used with makeup products. The public is unlikely to believe that makeup would provide a bulletproof barrier, and the public is unlikely to consider the ability of makeup to resist bullets as a material factor when purchasing makeup products.

Mark is Primarily Geographically Descriptive: A mark will be rejected if it is primarily geographically descriptive, which the PTO defines as a mark with a primarily geographic significance, that purchasers would be likely to think is the origin of the goods the mark is used with, and that actually conveys the geographic origin of the goods. An example might be "Florida Oranges" used on packages of oranges grown in Florida. However, these types of geographically descriptive marks may be protectable as geographical indications, and they may be registered as trademarks if they acquire sufficient secondary meaning in the marketplace to link the mark primarily with a specific product instead of primarily with a specific location.

Mark is Primarily Geographically Deceptively Misdescriptive: A mark will be rejected if it is primarily geographically deceptively misdescriptive, which the PTO defines as a mark with a primarily geographic significance, that purchasers would be likely to think is the origin of the goods the mark is used with, and that does not actually convey the geographic origin of the goods. An example would be "Georgia Peaches" used on peaches grown in South America.

Mark is Primarily Merely a Surname: A mark will be rejected if its primary meaning to the public is a surname. There are many blatant examples of registered trademarks that are primarily surnames, and the PTO will allow the registration of surname marks that have acquired sufficient secondary meaning in the marketplace to primarily associated the mark with a product rather than a surname. The word Steinway may be primarily recognized as a surname, but, if it is primarily associated with a specific product in the minds of consumers shopping for a piano, it may properly be registered as a trademark for use with piano products.

Mark is Merely Ornamentation: Decorative markings or designs that serve to dress up packaging or present products in an attractive manner are typically not able to be registered. In order to overcome this bar, such markings must acquire sufficient secondary meaning to serve the trademark function of identifying and distinguishing goods and services from others. When trade dress is recognized by the purchasing public not merely as attractive or distinct, but as originating from a specific source, then that trade dress may be registered.

Immoral or Scandalous Matter: Immoral or scandalous matter may not be registered as a trademark. A mark that is capable of multiple meanings, any one of which is considered immoral or scandalous, will be rejected. This rejection will occur even if the intent of the applicant was not to convey any immoral or scandalous message or meaning. Courts and the PTO seem to use the words immoral and scandalous interchangeably, and define them somewhat vaguely. Scandalous may mean "shocking to the sense of propriety, offensive to the conscience or moral feelings or calling out for condemnation." In re McGinley, 660 F2d. at 481 (Fed. Cir. 1981). Scandalous has also been defined to include all matter that is "vulgar" or "lacking in taste, indelicate, morally crude." In re Runsdorf, 171 USPQ 443, 444 (TTAB 1971). Obviously, these definitions are problematic as there is significant subjective variation between individuals regarding what one may consider "indelicate," and people don't typically equate "indelicate" with "offensive to the conscience" and "calling out for condemnation."

The PTO will use what it believes the views of a substantial composite of the general public would be on the mark in question when assessing potentially scandalous marks. This is some portion of the population that is not necessarily a majority, but that is not clearly defined. There is also no requirement or practice to poll any portion of the population and the PTO does not do so, although an applicant could theoretically do so at his own expense to support his application. Despite the vague definitions, an examining attorney will reject a mark if a substantial portion of the general public would consider the mark to be scandalous in the context of contemporary attitudes and the relevant marketplace. The attorney may rely on dictionary definitions, newspaper articles, magazine articles, and earlier decisions, although earlier decisions alone are not sufficient evidence of scandalous matter as the attitudes of the public and the specific marketplace of the mark may be different in different cases.

13.6. Duration

Trademark rights under the common law may last indefinitely, without any formal filings or registration, as long as the mark is in continuous use and has not become generic or otherwise invalid. Federal trademark registrations issued prior to November 16, 1989 initially lasted twenty years from their date of issue, and those issued after November 16, 1989 initially last for ten years. However, under federal law, a registered trademark may last indefinitely, but the holder of the trademark must periodically file both an affidavit of use and a renewal application. The Lanham Act requires a trademark holder to file an affidavit of use between the fifth and sixth years after initial registration, and another affidavit of use in the year preceding every tenth year thereafter. This affidavit must state that the trademark is being used on or with the goods or services originally stated in the initial registration, or explain why the trademark is not being used on or with those goods or services and why the lack of use does not constitute abandonment of the mark. The renewal application is due every ten years after the initial registration of the trademark. Failure to file a renewal application will cause the registration to be cancelled.

Chapter Summary

The United States Patent and Trademark Office oversees the federal trademark application and registration process. Although this process may be complex, and the use of an experienced attorney may be advisable to ensure a proper application, the PTO provides a variety of resources to assist applicants who wish to file their own applications. A thorough trademark search will prevent problems with registration and a smoother examination process. Successful applications may either be based on actual use of a mark in commerce or on the intent to use a mark in commerce within a certain timeframe. Registration in the Principal Register provides a number of important benefits that are in addition to the common law rights a trademark holder may already have. Registration on the Supplemental Register does not provide these same benefits, but may be useful to allow domestic mark holders to register those marks as trademarks in other countries. Registration in the Supplemental Register may also be useful for holders of descriptive marks who wish to put other potential users of those marks on notice that the marks are already in use in commerce. To maintain a registration, the trademark holder must periodically file an affidavit of use and a renewal application.

Key Terms

United States Patent and Trademark Office (PTO)
Principal Register
Supplemental Register
Constructive Use
Constructive Notice
Incontestable Status
Actual Use
Intent to Use
Official Gazette of the PTO
Certificate of Registration
Notice of Allowance
Office Action
Final Refusal
Affidavit of Use
Renewal Application

Review Questions

1. What is the difference between the Principal Register and the Supplemental Register?
2. What is the difference between an application for registration based on actual use and an application based on intent to use?
3. What are constructive use and constructive notice, and why are they beneficial to a trademark holder?
4. Under what circumstances may a surname be registered as a trademark?
5. How long may a federal trademark registration last?

Web Links

1. http://www.uspto.gov/trademarks/basics/—The United States Patent and Trademark Office website gateway for basic trademark information, with links to a variety of resources on understanding trademarks and the registration process.
2. http://tess2.uspto.gov/bin/gate.exe?f=tess&state=4801:uvr1zl.1.1—The PTO's Trademark Electronic Search System, which allows the public to conduct online trademark searches.
3. http://www.uspto.gov/news/og/trademark_og/index.jsp—The Trademark Official Gazette is published each Tuesday, and contains bibliographic information and a representative drawing for each mark published, along with a list of cancelled and renewed registrations.
4. http://www.uspto.gov/trademarks/resources/TMEP_archives.jsp—The Trademark Manual of Examining Procedure is published to provide trademark examining attorneys in the PTO, trademark applicants, and attorneys and representatives for trademark applicants with a reference work on the practices and procedures relative to prosecution of applications to register marks in the PTO. The Manual contains guidelines for Examining Attorneys and materials in the nature of information and interpretation, and outlines the procedures which Examining Attorneys are required or authorized to follow in the examination of trademark applications.
5. http://web2.wipo.int/nicepub/edition-20130101/taxonomy—The World Intellectual Property Organization page for the classifications under the Nice Agreement Concerning the International Classification of Goods and Services for the Purposes of the Registration of Marks.

Discussion Exercise

1. If a purely functional element of a product is exclusively found in only that product, and not in the products of competitors, why can't that element be registered as a trademark? What problems would arise if functional elements were allowed to be registered as trademarks?

Chapter 14

Protecting and Losing Rights

"In the Band-Aid commercials, they had a jingle, 'I'm stuck on Band-Aids because Band-Aids are stuck on me.' They now say, 'I'm stuck on Band-Aid brand because Band-Aid's stuck on me.' It sounds lousy, but it does the trick to avoid what is sometimes called genericide."
—David Wotherspoon

Chapter Outline

Chapter Objectives

- Learn the requirements to maintain trademark rights over time.
- Understand how successful brands can lose trademark status by becoming generic.
- Learn the various ways how trademark rights may be infringed and how trademark holders may protect against infringement.
- Learn the commonly available defenses to claims of trademark infringement.

14.1. Continuous Use and Abandonment

Trademark protection is only available for marks that are in actual use. Unlike patents or trade secret protection, which provide rights that are not dependent on actual use, trademark rights must be exercised or they are lost. That exercise must be genuine use of the mark in commerce, and not merely a token use to avoid abandonment. If a trademark is considered to be abandoned, it loses protection from infringement under the common law and its registration may be cancelled under federal or state law. Abandonment may be actual or constructive. *Actual abandonment* occurs when the trademark owner stops using the mark with the intent not to use the mark again. The owner intends to abandon the mark, and the rights of ownership are therefore intentionally resigned. *Constructive abandonment* occurs when the trademark owner does something or fails to do something that causes the mark to lose its distinctiveness or forfeits its registration. This occurs regardless of the actual intent of the trademark owner.

Once a trademark has been abandoned, it may be used by another party and may be registered by that party as the new owner in the Principal Registry. This is the case even if a registered trademark had already become incontestable under federal law. The issue of abandonment may arise when a new user attempts to register the mark and the old user objects, or it may arise when the PTO or another party seeks to have a registration cancelled for non-use, or it may arise in court as a defense to a claim of infringement. Proving or disproving abandonment can be a difficult task, as it often involves subjective questions of intent.

To prove actual abandonment, the intent of the owner to abandon the mark must be demonstrated. The most obvious evidence of abandonment would seem to be non-use of the mark, but this is insufficient alone as there may be many reasons why a trademark owner has temporarily stopped using a mark. A trademark owner may temporarily stop using the mark for economic reasons and, as long as the intent to resume use remains and the non-use is reasonable under the circumstances, the trademark will not be at risk of cancellation for abandonment. The law presumes that a trademark that has not been used for three years or longer has been abandoned, but it is certainly possible for abandonment to occur sooner than this.

Once non-use is established, the trademark owner has the burden to show why the non-use is reasonable or excusable under the circumstances. Courts will assess the trademark owner's reasons for non-use by the standard of what a reasonable business person having intent to use the mark would do under the same circumstances. If, for example, a trademark owner's business was destroyed and the business was involved in lengthy insurance litigation to receive insurance benefits needed to rebuild and resume the business, a period of non-use longer than three years would likely be excusable as long as the trademark owner still intended to resume use of the mark when the business resumes.

Likewise, a downsizing of business that reduces the trademark owner's business territory does not constitute abandonment of the mark. However, under the common law, the mark may be considered abandoned in any geography that the owner totally withdraws from, as common law trademark protection is only provided in the limited geographic areas that the owner actually conducts business in. Under federal law, any amount of interstate use of the mark in commerce will prevent abandonment and allow protection nationwide. If the trademark owner withdraws to a purely intrastate market, the trademark is at risk of cancellation as federal registration is only available to marks used in interstate commerce or which have an effect on interstate commerce.

Constructive abandonment may occur when the trademark owner fails to properly protect its mark. If another party uses the mark, or a confusingly similar mark, in commerce in a competing manner, the trademark owner has a duty to protect that mark and prevent such use. A trademark owner may protect its mark by licensing the use of the mark, but the license must be drafted carefully and policed carefully in order to prevent any unauthorized use or dilution of the mark. If a license is granted that imposes no restrictions on use of the mark, this "*naked license*" may cause a cancellation of the mark for abandonment.

A mark may potentially be considered constructively abandoned if the trademark owner fails to properly maintain federal registration of the mark once it is registered. An affidavit or declaration of continued use or excusable non-use must be filed within the year before the end of every ten-year period after the date of registration, or within six months of that deadline if a late fee is paid. If the trademark fails to file the required affidavit or declaration, the trademark registration will be cancelled. The same is true if the trademark owner fails to file the required applications for renewal in a timely manner. While these cancellations result from operation of law, not a determination of abandonment of the mark and certainly not conclusive evidence of abandonment, these failures to protect the federal registration of the mark are evidence of abandonment that may be used to challenge any remaining common law rights to the mark once the federal registration is cancelled.

14.2. Generic Terms

Generic marks may never be registered as trademarks under federal law and are not eligible for trademark protection under the common law with regard to the goods or services for which they are generic. A trademark must be capable of distinguishing the goods or services of the trademark owner, and a generic term is not capable of this function. Generic terms are typically the unprotected common names of products or services that are open for use by anyone to refer to or describe a product or service. In addition to a bar on the registration of a generic trademark, it is also possible to lose trademark registration and protection by allowing a trademark to become a generic term. The process by which a trademark loses its distinctiveness and becomes generic is called "genericization." Examples of genericized trademarks include aspirin, cellophane, dry ice, escalator, heroin, kerosene, lanolin, laundromat, linoleum, thermos, touch-tone, videotape, yo-yo, and zipper.

Somewhat counterintuitively, trademarks often become generic as a result of heavy and successful efforts to advertise and promote the trademark as a brand of specific products or services. While a trademark may be applied to a large number of products or services, marks that become generic are typically strongly associated with one specific product or service, or a number of very closely related products or services. The trademark becomes so widely known and dominant in the market that consumers begin to associate the trademark with the product itself instead of with the producer of the product. A trademark may become generic in all markets or only in specific markets, industries, or population segments.

Examples of trademarks that are in danger of becoming generic in the United States include Astro Turf synthetic turf, Band-Aid bandages, Bobcat skid loaders, Bubble Wrap packing cushioning, Bubbler water fountains, ChapStick lip balm, Cigarette Boat speed boats, Coca-Cola, Crock-Pot slow cookers, Dumpster frontloading waste receptacles, Formica countertop material, Frisbee flying disks, Hula Hoop plastic toy hoops, Jacuzzi spa tubs, Jet Ski personal watercraft, Memory Stick flash memory storage devices, Photoshop photo manipulation software, Ping Pong table tennis, Plexiglass acrylic glass, Post-It sticky notes, Q-tip cotton swabs, Realtor real estate agents, Styrofoam extruded polystyrene foam, Super Glue adhesive, Vaseline petroleum jelly, Velcro hook-and-loop fasteners, White Out correction fluid, Xerox copiers, and Zamboni ice resurfacers. These trademarks are in various stages of progression toward genericization. Some of them will recover and avoid losing trademark rights, but it is hard to imagine others avoiding that fate. How many people typically call a Dumpster "a frontloading waste receptacle," call Styrofoam "extruded polystyrene foam," or call Velcro "hook-and-loop fasteners"? Efforts to encourage the use of these generic terms instead of genericizing the trademark names are unlikely to be effective.

To avoid losing trademark protection through genericization, trademark owners with very popular trademark names must actively protect their brands by both educating the public about proper use of the trademark and taking legal action against anyone engaged in infringement by using the trademark as a generic term. Education efforts are often coupled with the promotion of alternative language called a *"generic descriptor."* A generic descriptor is a generic word or phrase added to the trademark to prevent the generic use of the trademark, or to call attention to the trademark as a brand and not a generic term. Velcro does this by avoiding the cumbersome use of "hook-and-loop fasteners" in favor of using the phrase "Velcro brand fasteners" in its advertising and packaging.

14.3. Tests for Infringement

The owner of a federally or state registered trademark may institute an infringement action to prevent or enjoin any unauthorized use or imitation of the mark that is likely to confuse consumers about the origin of those goods or services. An unregistered trademark owner may institute a state or federal action for unfair competition, which is distinct but substantially similar in terms of the factors involved in proving the case. The key in either case is proving a likelihood of confusion, and courts will consider the following factors in determining whether there is such likelihood.

Similarity of the Marks

The closer two marks are in terms of design, style, sound, color, overall appearance and presentation, and meaning, the more likely it is that likelihood of confusion will be found. Each of these factors will be evaluated both individually and as a whole. Even where no one single factor is identical to a protected mark, the collective similarity may be sufficient to find a likelihood of confusion. Generally, the more arbitrary the trademark is, the more likely the court will view similarities with suspicion. If a trademark name is arbitrary or fanciful, it is naturally much less likely that an alleged infringer would happen to create a very similar mark in good faith.

Similarity of the Goods or Services

Even where the marks in question are extremely similar, there can be no infringement where the goods or services the marks are used with are entirely unrelated. If the goods or services are not entirely unrelated, the court will determine how similar they are by trying to view them through the eyes of a consumer. Goods may be considered similar if they serve the same purpose or have the same function, relate to the same activities, or satisfy the same needs. Examples of non-identical categories of goods that may be deemed similar enough to warrant a determination that likelihood of confusion exists include toothbrushes and toothpaste, hair brushes and makeup, pet food and pet vitamins, and motor oil and brake fluid.

Character of the Market

Confusion is more likely when the marks in question are used in markets where consumers are likely to make impulse buys, rather than cautious and careful purchases. The classic example of impulse buy items are relatively low-cost products for sale at or near the cash register in a supermarket or convenience store. These items are expected to be purchased on a whim, with little thought or attention invested in the purchase decision. Under these circumstances, the likelihood of confusion between similar marks is very high. On the opposite end of the spectrum are automobile purchases. When buying a new car, consumers are far more likely to shop around, research makes and models, ask questions, examine the vehicles for sale, and test drive cars before making a purchase decision. It is extremely unlikely that a consumer would be confused by similar marks under these circumstances.

Consumer Sophistication

There is far less risk of consumer confusion when the consumer is highly sophisticated. Consumers with a high level of education, experience, business acumen, relevant technical knowledge or skill, industry knowledge, or other forms of relevant sophistication are much more difficult to confuse than the typical consumer of every day products and services. The more sophisticated the consumer, the less concern the court will have over likelihood of confusion. The sale of technical surgical implements with similar-sounding marks might be very confusing to the average consumer, but would probably be far less confusing when the consumer is an experienced surgeon, the purchasing manager for a large hospital, or a biomechanical engineer in the medical device industry.

Channels of Trade

Two similar marks used in the sale of similar products in the open retail market would be very likely to cause consumer confusion, but if one of those marks was used to sell those products exclusively at retail and another was used exclusively at wholesale, there may not be any likelihood of confusion at all. Similar situations may arise in the context of design or décor showrooms open exclusively to industry professionals versus retail showrooms, and in the context of professional stock houses serving professional contractors exclusively versus home improvement or hardware stores serving the general public. When the target markets do not overlap, the risk of confusion is dramatically reduced.

Intent to Infringe

The intent of the defendant to infringe or not is legally irrelevant. The law does not require any intent to deceive, and the level of protection available to the trademark owner is not dependent on the intentions of an infringer. Courts will nevertheless attempt to discern the defendant's intent and will often make decisions in very close cases on the basis of intent. Courts may also decide whether or not to grant equitable remedies, or the extent or severity of those remedies, on the basis of the intent of the infringing party. The credibility of the defendant is often significantly impacted by the court's perception of the defendant's intent to infringe. Even if the issue should have no legal significance, a court is more likely to apply additional scrutiny to the claims of a defendant who has obviously intentionally infringed on a trademark in order to benefit from the goodwill associated with that mark.

Actual Confusion

Actual confusion is not required in order to prove a likelihood of confusion or trademark infringement. It is sufficient to prove that a similar mark is likely to confuse any significant number of persons, and those persons are not required to be consumers. However, evidence of actual consumer confusion in the marketplace is certainly strong and compelling evidence that such confusion is likely. If enough evidence of actual confusion is presented, it may well be conclusive on the issue.

14.4. Dilution

Generally speaking, two parties may lawfully use extremely similar trademarks, or even the exact same trademark, and register those marks in the Principal Register, if the two parties use that mark for distinctly different goods or services and there is no likelihood of confusion created by that simultaneous use. The Remington® trademark of the Remington Arms Company, LLC and the Remington® trademark of Spectrum Brands, Inc. are examples of this scenario. Remington Arms Company, LLC manufactures firearms and ammunition, as it has since 1816, making it the oldest continuously operating manufacturer in the United States. Spectrum Brands, Inc. sells trimmers and other hair care products under the Remington name. These two companies seemingly have very different products with no real association, other than the name. The history behind the two companies is a lot closer than their current product lines would suggest.

The Remington trademark in both cases comes from E. Remington and Sons, a maker of firearms and a skilled manufacturing concern that often worked with other parties to create new products. E. Remington and Sons made sewing machines, farm implements, and the first typewriter with the QWERTY keyboard layout. E. Remington and Sons sold its typewriter business, which became the Remington Typewriter Company in 1886. That company merged with Rand Kardex in 1927 to become Remington Rand, which manufactured adding machines, filing cabinets, punched card tabulating machines, and other office equipment. In 1937, Remington Rand began making electric shavers, and in 1950, Remington Rand bought the Eckert-Mauchly Computer Company. In 1955, Remington Rand merged with the Sperry Corporation, which made automatic pilot products and other devices, to form the Sperry Rand Corporation, which still made and sold shavers under the Remington trademark.

In 1979, Sperry Rand sold its electric shaver business to Victor Kiam, who started the Remington Products Company using the Remington trademark. This business sold shavers and began making other small personal care appliances as well, buying the Clairol® personal care appliance business in 1994. The Remington Products Company was sold to the battery company Rayovac in 2003, and Rayovac changed its name to Spectrum Brands and now sells batteries and battery products while selling shavers, clippers, trimmers, massagers, makeup mirrors, heated hair rollers, blow dryers, curling irons, and flat irons all under the Remington trademark.

The reason for sharing this history is simply to illustrate both how two independent businesses can share a trademark without consumer confusion, and also how important it can be to choose and protect a unique trademark because markets that were unexpected at the start of a business venture might become an important line of business. While the interesting story of the Remington trademarks shows us how multiple companies with many product lines can successfully coexist, the story also shows us why large businesses should be concerned about sharing their trademarks with seemingly non-competitive enterprises.

When a business becomes large enough to build brands, those brands use trademarks more as a mark of goodwill than as a source of origin indicator. The law of trademarks began as a way to protect indications of origin, but today consumers care less about product origin and more about product reputation. Trademarks are serving more and more to associate lines of products and brand quality, and less to identify any specific manufacturer. By way of example, a consumer might buy a Remington product because of the brand's history of manufacturing quality products, even if the consumer has no idea if the product originated with E. Remington and Sons, Remington Rand, Sperry Rand Corporation, the Remington Products Company, or Spectrum Brands. The consumer probably doesn't know, and probably doesn't care which company actually made the product. The consumer is relying on the quality reputation of the brand, as indicated by the trademark, and not on the reputation of the specific manufacturer or even the reputation of the specific product.

In 1961, the Lanham Act was amended to prohibit any use of a mark that is likely to cause confusion, not only confusion by consumers about the origin of a product. This change is consistent with the modern trend of legal expansion of trademark rights. A trademark owner may now take legal action to protect the goodwill associated with its trademarked brands, even when there is no real consumer confusion at all. The concept of another party damaging the trademark owner by using the same trademark on unrelated products is called *dilution*. The theory is that, if a trademark is famous and has substantial goodwill associated with it, then it would be improper to allow another party to market its own, unrelated products or services under the same trademark and thereby benefit from the trademark owner's investment in the goodwill of the mark while potentially jeopardizing that same goodwill with potentially inferior products over which the trademark owner has no control.

When deciding actions to prevent or enjoin alleged dilution, courts will typically examine the *likelihood of expansion* of the trademark owner's business into the line of products or services that a non-competing second user is in. If the court deems it likely that the trademark owner will expand into that line of products or services, the court is likely to prohibit the second user from using the trademark in that manner. The court will also consider the public's perception of that likelihood. Even if the trademark owner admits that it is not planning to expand into the second user's line of products or services, the public may reasonably assume that the trademark owner may have done so and confusion may still result.

By way of example, if a new business starts making car batteries and decides to adopt the Remington name for its products, one or all of the Remington companies would likely be able to sue to prevent such a use of the trademark. Even if no Remington company makes car batteries and none plans to do so, the court may determine that the public is likely to be confused anyway as it would be reasonable to assume that Remington, a company with a long history of widely ranging products and a connection to Rayovac, a battery company, might well manufacture car batteries. The same outcome would be likely if the new company tried to use the Remington name on an electric toothbrush, a toaster oven, or a hand-held power tool.

This likelihood of expansion doctrine greatly expands the scope of trademark protection for famous trademarks. The traditional limiting requirement of actual use of the trademark in commerce and with the goods or services for which the trademark owner seeks protection is fading away. In its place is a series of related restrictions on the doctrine of likelihood of expansion. The *consumer-expectation test* limits the doctrine to those areas of the market that consumers would reasonably expect the trademark owner to expand. The *market reality test* limits the doctrine to those areas of the market where the same company commonly sells certain products or services, even if they are not related in use. An example might be a chemical company that manufactures paint and industrial lubricants. Although the two products are not related in use, they may be related in terms of market reality, as chemical companies often manufacture these types of products.

Finally, the *similarity of consumers test* limits the doctrine to uses where the target consumers are the same, regardless of whether the products or services are related or commonly sold together. An example of this might be a company selling hair dye under the Remington name. Even though consumers may not expect a small appliance manufacturer to make a chemical hair dye, and even though appliance manufacturers may not commonly make chemical hair dye products, the target consumers for small grooming appliances and hair dye are very often the same people. The potential for confusion exists and no actual confusion is required, therefore a court would be likely to prevent such a use of the trademark.

The result of the likelihood of expansion doctrine benefits strong brands far more than smaller, weaker brands. Indeed, the federal law protecting trademarks from dilution, added to the Lanham Act in 1996 and amended by the Trademark Dilution Revision Act of 2006, applies only to famous marks. Famousness is measured and determined by its distinctiveness, use, advertising, sales volume and geography, federal registration status, and similar criteria. Basically, the more well known the trademark is, the greater the likelihood that a court will prevent non-competing businesses from using the mark. Many states have passed their own anti-dilution statutes that are not so limited, and they often protect the interest of any trademark holder in preventing unauthorized use of their mark in any industry, regardless of the owner's actual use in that industry or any likelihood of confusion of product origin.

14.5. Passing Off and Reverse Passing Off

Passing off and reverse passing off were discussed in detail in Chapter 9. While these common law tort claims are very old and have been supplemented significantly with modern statutory causes of action, they are still crucial tools used to protect trademarks and the goodwill associated with an established brand. When a court examines a trademark owner's history of trademark protection when deciding whether or not a trademark has been abandoned, for example, the initiation of actions for passing off or reverse passing off, where appropriate, can be strong evidence of investment in protection of the mark and continued intent to use it. The same is true for control of trademark dilution. If a strong and established brand permits unauthorized users to pass off inferior products under the trademark name, the trademark will be diluted. The more this occurs, the less likely a later action to prevent dilution will be successful.

14.6. Secondary Liability

Secondary liability is a type of indirect trademark infringement that occurs when a party materially contributes to, facilitates, induces, or is otherwise responsible for actions by another that directly infringe a trademark. Interestingly, while this type of indirect infringement in increasingly common in the digital age, the Lanham Act contains no provisions directly addressing or prohibiting secondary liability. The courts, when addressing claims of secondary liability, have had to rely on tradition tort concepts to create appropriate causes of action and remedies. This decision seems appropriate considering that most concepts codified in the Lanham Act already originate in the common law of trademark and unfair competition. Secondary liability therefore comes in two varieties, *contributory liability* and *vicarious liability*, both of which are taken directly from common law tort theory.

Contributory liability for trademark infringement is basically a concept that holds liable those who do not directly infringe but who support or contribute those who do infringe. This concept developed even before the Lanham Act was passed, and it continued to develop and has remained valid since. The Supreme Court established a two-prong test for contributory infringement that was held to be valid after the Lanham Act in *Inwood Labs., Inc. v. Ives Labs., Inc.*, 265 U.S. 526 (1982). Contributory liability may be found where a defendant either actively induces another to infringe, or where a defendant knew or had reason to know that another party was infringing and the defendant continued to support or supply the activities of the infringer. The defendant's contributions to the infringing activity must be material, and the defendant must know or have reason to know that infringement is occurring in order for liability to attach.

An example scenario might involve a flea market business being held liable under a contributory liability theory when one or more of the vendors it provides space, electricity, and signage to is actively engaged in trademark infringement by selling counterfeit goods. The flea market business derives a substantial benefit from the infringing activity, and the business either knew or should have known about open and obvious counterfeiting taking place on its premises. It is often difficult for trademark owners to bring suit against small, mobile infringers who might leave the state and move to another flea market elsewhere once litigation is commenced. The option to bring suit against the enabling flea market venue, which is less likely to disappear once litigation begins, is very attractive.

Vicarious liability for trademark infringement has evolved primarily from the common law of agency. Courts will generally determine whether there was either a *joint tortfeasor* scenario or a *respondeat superior* scenario when evaluating a claim of vicarious liability. In the joint tortfeasor scenario, a court will decide if the defendant and the direct infringer had an apparent or actual partnership, or whether they acted in concert to commit infringement, pursuant to a common purpose. In a respondeat superior scenario, employers may be held liable for the infringing acts of their employees, as is generally the case in the context of other torts and statutory wrongs committed by employees in the scope of their employment.

14.7. Defenses

A number of defenses are available to claims of trademark infringement, some of which acknowledge the validity of the trademark and attempt to justify the use in question while others attempt to attack the validity of the trademark in the first place. The use and success of these defenses is obviously dependent upon the specific circumstances of each case, but the most commonly raised defenses follow.

First Amendment Protection

Restrictions on the use of trademarks are often restrictions, to some extent, on freedom of speech. Courts have universally recognized this concern, but their responses to the issue vary significantly. Some courts have held that trademark law either does not apply or must be very narrowly construed when a trademark is used in the context of a work of literary or artistic expression. This is typically because the trademark is not used to indicate the origin of any goods or services. Naturally the outcome would be different if a literary work was itself sold under a trademark without authorization. Other courts have tried to strike a balance between the risk of consumer confusion and the right of free expression. When trademarks are used in parody in the context of commercial advertising or on merchandise, courts tend to ignore the free speech concerns and resolve the matter as a normal commercial infringement issue. However, particularly expressive items, such as posters and lettered t-shirts, may warrant additional consideration as vectors for protected speech. While there is very little settled and consistent law regarding the extent to which First Amendment rights trump trademark restrictions, free speech remains a viable option for defendants in infringement actions involving expressive uses of protected trademarks.

Abandonment

As discussed above, abandonment of a trademark is grounds for cancellation of that mark. If a trademark has been abandoned, it may be freely used by another party and there can be no infringement until and unless a party reestablishes trademark rights in the mark. A defendant must prove that the trademark owner has failed to use the trademark, and then the trademark owner may provide a reasonable excuse for that non-use. If the owner fails to justify the non-use, the mark may be considered abandoned. A trademark may either be expressly abandoned, when the owner intends to stop using the mark and intends not to resume use in the future, or may be abandoned by operation of law, as when the owner fails to timely submit affidavits of continued use, fails to timely submit renewal applications, or fails to properly license or protect its trademark.

Genericized Mark

If a trademark has become generic in the market, an infringement defendant may attack the registration or lawful trademark status of that mark. Generic terms may not be protected as trademarks, and there can be no infringement of generic terms which are by definition indistinct and available to all in the public domain.

First Sale Doctrine

The first sale doctrine allows a party who lawfully purchased trademark goods to display, offer, and sell those goods under their original trademark. This is the law both under the common law and under the Lanham Act. An infringement defendant may therefore justify his use of the trademark at issue if he has simply resold a genuine, unaltered good under the trademark of the producer because his use of the mark in that context will not deceive or confuse the public as to the nature, qualities or origin of the good. However, the defendant may not represent himself as an agent or franchisee of the trademark owner, may not resell goods that are modified to be materially different from those authorized for sale by the trademark owner, and may not repackage the goods without notifying consumers that the goods have been repackaged.

Gray Market Goods

Gray market goods are goods that have legitimate trademarks, but that are manufactured outside of the United States and are imported to compete with domestically manufactured or marketed goods with the same trademark. The terms "grey market" implies that the goods are not illegal like black market goods, but are not quite kosher. Trademark law fails to address this situation because the imported goods bear a legitimate trademark, and so there is no trademark infringement unless the imports differ from domestic products in a materially significant way and they lack sufficient labeling to put consumers on notice of the difference. International trade laws may control this situation, but a defendant would not be liable for trademark infringement for selling equal quality gray market goods in the United States.

Laches

Laches is an equitable doctrine that prevents the enforcement of any right after a significant period of unexcused failure to enforce that right. An infringement defendant may defend against a common law or federal claim by establishing that the plaintiff unreasonably delayed in filing suit and, as a result of the delay, the defendant suffered prejudice. Courts will typically evaluate the strength of the trademark at issue, the diligence of the owner of the mark in protecting the mark from infringement, the knowledge the plaintiff had or should have had of the defendant's infringement, the potential harm to the plaintiff if relief is not granted, and the potential harm to the defendant if relief is granted. The less a plaintiff knew about the defendant's infringement during the delay, despite reasonable efforts to police the mark, the more likely the court will grant relief. The greater the harm to the defendant as a result of the plaintiff's delay, the more likely the court is to deny relief. A defendant might be harmed by the plaintiff's delay, for example, by assuming the plaintiff had abandoned the mark and then building up a significant business around the trademark at considerable cost. In any case, laches will typically only operate to shield the defendant from a claim for damages. The court will still grant injunctive relief to the trademark owner as long as the mark has not been abandoned.

Acquiescence

Acquiescence is similar to laches, but only arises if the plaintiff gave the defendant an express or implied representation that the plaintiff would not enforce its trademark rights against the defendant, and the defendant relied on that representation to his detriment. This is different from laches because acquiescence requires active representation from the plaintiff, not merely silence or failure to act as in the case of laches. If the defendant successfully proves acquiescence by the plaintiff, it may be a bar to both damages and injunctive relief.

Unclean Hands

The equitable doctrine of unclean hands prevents a plaintiff from recovering damages from a defendant when the plaintiff has engaged in some sort of misdeed relating to the trademark at issue. This doctrine represents the courts' reluctance to aid parties who are themselves engaged in wrongful conduct. This wrongful conduct may be illegal conduct, but it does not have to be illegal. A plaintiff engaged in fraud, engaged in efforts to deceive consumers through the use of its mark, engaged in trademark infringement itself, or in violation of other laws may find the doctrine of unclean hands to be a bar to recovery.

Fair Use

Fair use is a concept that allows a party to incidentally comment on a trademark in good faith for a purpose other than the normal purpose of trademarks. A defendant relying on this defense must prove that he used the plaintiff's mark in a manner other than as a trademark, that the mark was used fairly and in good faith, and that the use of the mark was only to describe the defendant's goods or services. The idea behind fair use is that, if a trademark owner chooses to adopt and use a mark that consists in part of a descriptive term or phrase, it is to be expected that another party may, at some point, need to reference that descriptive term or phrase in order to describe its own products or services.

Another form of fair use, called nominative fair use, arises when a defendant uses the plaintiff's trademark to describe the plaintiff's goods or services in order to describe its own goods or services. This may occur when the only practical way to reference the plaintiff's trademarked goods is by using the trademark name, as no generic term may be available or convenient. It may be impossible or impracticable to discuss a particular product for purposes of comparison, criticism, or reference without using the trademark, and people should not need to risk an infringement lawsuit each time they converse about common topics that happen to involve trademarks. Nominative fair use requires a defendant to prove that the goods at issue are not readily identifiable without use of the plaintiff's trademark, that the defendant only used the mark as much as reasonably necessary to identify the plaintiff's goods or services, and that the defendant did not misrepresent or suggest any form of association, sponsorship, or endorsement by the trademark owner.

Collateral Use

Collateral use is a specific type of fair use that permits a defendant to use and describe goods that bear the plaintiff's trademark in the repair, construction, or manufacture of some new good. If a mechanic buys, repairs, and re-sells old cars, for example, he may resell the car with all of the trademark labels on all of the parts that he installed in the car and he may describe the work he performed on the car with specific reference to the trademark names of the parts used. Indeed, the car itself would bear a trademark name of the make and model of the car, and the mechanic has no duty to remove those names prior to selling the vehicle.

Comparative Advertising

Comparative advertising is another specific type of fair use that allows the defendant to use the plaintiff's trademark to compare or contrast the defendant's goods or services to those of the plaintiff. Products may be packaged with language such as "compare to Trademark," or "compare the active ingredient in Trademark." This use allows the manufacturer of a generic product to inform consumers of the similarity of their products and name brand products. Comparative advertising is permitted as long as it is done in a manner that minimizes the likelihood of confusion between products of the defendant and the plaintiff. Use of the trademark name is often made with plain text, instead of the stylized logo of the plaintiff's trademark, and is often printed in smaller lettering than the defendant's own logo. These steps, although not specifically required, are prudent ways to avoid likelihood of confusion.

Eleventh Amendment Protection

Despite Congress' efforts to make states accountable for trademark infringement, the Eleventh Amendment prevents the federal courts from having jurisdiction in such cases, unless Congress is enforcing the Fourteenth Amendment, which is generally not the case, or unless the states waive their sovereign immunity, which has not happened. Unless this changes, states may not be accountable in federal court for infringement. However, states may generally be sued in their own state courts, or potentially in the state courts of another state.

Chapter Summary

Trademark owners have a lot of responsibility. If they wish to keep their protected trademark status, they must continue to use their marks and properly and thoroughly police them. Trademarks may be lost if the mark is not used enough, and they may be lost if they are used too loosely, either through naked licensing or through genericization. Trademark infringers may try to pass off counterfeit goods, or they may try to snatch away key domain names, and trademark owners must diligently work to stop these actions. Long delays in taking protective action may prevent recourse or even result in the loss of the trademark. To aid trademark owners, the law provides many causes of action against infringers. However, the law also recognizes the reasonable needs of other parties to engage in free speech about trademarked products, and to fairly use trademarks for descriptive and comparative purposes.

Key Terms

Actual Abandonment
Constructive Abandonment
Naked License
Genericization
Generic Descriptor
Dilution
Likelihood of Expansion
Consumer Expectation Test
Market Reality Test
Similarity of Consumers Test
Secondary Liability
Contributory Liability
Vicarious Liability
Joint Tortfeasor
Respondeat Superior
First Sale Doctrine
Gray Market Goods
Laches
Acquiescence
Unclean Hands
Fair Use

Collateral Use
Comparative Advertising

Review Questions

1. Under what circumstances may a trademark owner who does not intend to abandon her trademark nonetheless be held to have legally abandoned her trademark?
2. What is a "naked license" and why is it a problem for trademark holders?
3. How may a trademark in danger of becoming generic be saved?
4. List one way in which a trademark may be diluted.
5. What is the purpose of secondary liability?
6. What is a gray market good?
7. Give three examples of fair use of a trademark.

Web Links

1. http://www.wipo.int/wipo_magazine/en/2009/06/article_0010.html—World Intellectual Property Organization article on Xerox and preventing trademark "genericide."

Discussion Exercise

1. Should the law prevent the use of terms that have become generic as trademarks if they were not generic when initially registered? If you were so successful in marketing your product that consumers used your brand name rather than the generic product description, wouldn't that be a good thing? What do you call a Band-Aid if not a Band-Aid? An "adhesive bandage strip"? If you cut your finger, you probably ask for a Band-Aid, not an adhesive bandage strip. So why should that cause the Band-Aid brand to lose protection? Why should competitors be rewarded for failing to establish a popular competing brand name? Shouldn't competitors be required to sell "adhesive bandage strips" while you enjoy the success of the Band-Aid name? Why or why not?

Chapter 15

Trademark Remedies

"Don't find fault, find a remedy."—Henry Ford

Chapter Outline

15.1. Non-Monetary Remedies
15.2. Monetary Remedies
15.3. Criminal Penalties

Chapter Objectives

- Learn the different types of remedies available to trademark owners under different circumstances.
- Learn how the government may impose criminal penalties in certain types of infringement cases.

Under the Lanham Act, a plaintiff may receive specified statutory remedies, including injunctive relief, an accounting for profits, actual damages, treble damages, attorney's fees, and costs. 15 U.S.C.A. §1117. Remedies under the common law are similar, though treble damages, attorney's fees, and costs are generally not available. Courts may employ additional statutory remedies or create new remedies using the flexibility of injunctions.

15.1. Non-Monetary Remedies

The most important and most flexible non-monetary remedy is *injunctive relief.* A court may grant an infringement plaintiff an injunction against the defendant, which is an order to the defendant to do or refrain from doing something. Courts may be extremely creative with injunction orders in order to reach an equitable solution to a problem at hand. Typically, injunctions will order the defendant to stop engaging in allegedly infringing activities on a temporary basis. Temporary injunctions are granted early in the case, before the merits of the case have been decided. Courts will balance the risk of harm to the trademark holder if the injunction is not granted with the risk of harm to the defendant if the injunction is granted, and will also consider the interest of the public in not being deceived by infringing activities. If the plaintiff is successful on the merits of the case, the temporary injunction may become a permanent injunction.

Courts will try to create injunctions that prevent infringement, but that do not grant excessive rights to the trademark holder. Courts must remember that, while infringement is unlawful, ordinary competition may not be enjoined. It is therefore critical that injunctions be crafted carefully to respect ordinary competition. For example, many plaintiffs in infringement cases seek injunctions that prevent the defendant from manufacturing or selling its competing goods when it is alleged that the defendant unlawfully labeled those goods with the plaintiff's trademark. A balanced injunction will prevent the defendant from using the plaintiff's mark, but should not completely stop the defendant's business. As long as the defendant takes reasonable steps to ensure that the plaintiff's mark is not used, and that potential customers are put on notice that the defendant's product is not the plaintiff's product, the defendant should be allowed to continue to compete in the market. Otherwise, the plaintiff is unfairly protected from ordinary competition.

A court may also order the seizure and destruction of counterfeit goods and their means of production. This remedy may be appropriate where a large scale counterfeiting operation is discovered, and the risk that the goods or the means for producing the goods will be lost if not quickly secured and destroyed. Courts may order this remedy in an ex parte proceeding under very specific circumstances indicating that involving the defendant in a hearing on the matter is likely to cause the counterfeit goods or equipment to disappear.

A court may also order the cancellation of a federally registered trademark under the same conditions that the PTO may cancel a mark. This may be appropriate where the mark has been proven to be abandoned or to have become generic.

Finally, an order for an accounting may issue. This order typically goes hand-in-hand with a later order for damages based on the accounting, but that is not always the case. The accounting order will require the defendant, typically at his own expense, to hire an approved accountant or forensic accountant to examine the defendant's books, registers, receipts, bank accounts, credit lines, equipment, wages, payroll, and other income, costs, and expenditures in order to create an objective assessment of the profit or loss created by the defendant during nay period of infringement. When not used for the calculation of damages, an accounting order may be used to assess the volume of infringing sales, the pre-existing volume of sales prior to infringement, the level of market penetration achieved by the defendant before infringement, or to assess or ascertain any other aspect of the defendant's sales, financial, or business history.

15.2. Monetary Remedies

A plaintiff in an infringement action may recover a variety of monetary damages to restore the plaintiff to the position he was in prior to the infringement. The most basic of these is actual damages. A plaintiff may prove an amount of money that he lost directly because of the actions of the infringing defendant. This amount may include damages for lost profits and harm to the goodwill of the trademark, as well as amounts determined by an accounting to be the profits earned by the defendant due to infringing activity. However, a plaintiff may not recover more than his actual damages. This means that a plaintiff may recover the profits earned by the defendant or the sales reasonably determined to have been lost by the plaintiff, but a plaintiff may not recover both lost profits and profits gained by the defendant taking those sales. Such a scenario would allow the plaintiff to "double dip" and receive a windfall that does not represent the actual damages he incurred.

The Lanham Act also provides for the recovery of treble damages, but courts have interpreted this remedy to be available only in cases where the plaintiff is unable to demonstrate all of his actual damages. The court may then award up to triple the amount of actual damages proven in order to compensate the plaintiff. Treble damages are not available as a punitive measure or to deter future infringement, even though this is an effective method employed in numerous other statutes to control violations. Congress expressly restricted the use of treble damages under the Lanham Act to ensure compensation for a plaintiff, but to prevent punitive damages.

A plaintiff may recover his reasonable attorney's fees in appropriate cases, typically those where the defendant expressed a willful or malicious intent to profit by the infringement of the plaintiff's trademark. Attorney's fees may also be awarded in cases of bad faith litigation. Both of these types of cases are rare, and neither party typically receives attorney's fees in trademark litigation.

Finally, a plaintiff may elect to receive statutory damages instead of actual damages when a counterfeit mark identical to the trademark owner's mark is used by the infringer, or when the infringer is a cybersquatter. In the case of counterfeiting, the court may award statutory damages of no less than $1,000.00 nor more than $200,000.00 per counterfeit mark. In cases of intentional counterfeiting, the court may increase that amount to $2,000,000.00 per counterfeit mark. In cybersquatting cases, the court may award no less than $1,000.00 and no more than $100,000.00 per domain name, as the court considers just. Obviously, statutory damages can be very desirable in cases where actual damages would be very small or very difficult to prove.

15.3. Criminal Penalties

The Trademark Counterfeiting Act, 18 U.S.C. § 2320, was passed by Congress in 1984 to impose criminal penalties on anyone who intentionally traffics or attempts to traffic in goods or services and knowingly uses a counterfeit mark on or in connection with such goods or services. Individual violators may face fines up to $2,000,000.00 and up to ten years in prison. Corporate violators may face fines up to $5,000,000.00. For additional violations, an individual may be fined up to $5,000,000.00 and may face up to twenty years in prison, and a corporation may be fined up to $15,000,000.00. The government may also obtain an order to confiscate and destroy all infringing articles and equipment used to manufacture them.

A criminal defendant in a prosecution under the Trademark Counterfeiting Act may rely on any of the defenses discussed above, or any other defense or exception available in civil cases under the Lanham Act or otherwise. If the defendant is able to successfully attack the trademark, then there can be no conviction for trademark infringement.

Chapter Summary

There are a variety of remedies available to trademark owners to address infringement. Civil remedies are designed to put the parties back to where they were before the infringement occurred, and in rare and extreme cases, very significant monetary damages may be awarded. Courts use the flexibility of injunctions to create unique remedies that are specifically tailored to the facts of each case. In addition, the government may prosecute a willful trademark infringer under a criminal statute that carries significant fines and prison time.

Key Terms

Injunctive Relief

Review Questions

1. What is an injunction?
2. How might a court use an injunction to balance the interests of the plaintiff and the defendant before a case is resolved on the merits?
3. Why are the damages and fines available so much higher in cases of intentional infringement? Does the intent of the infringing party cause any more or less harm to the plaintiff?

Web Links

1. http://www.gpo.gov/fdsys/pkg/USCODE-2011-title18/pdf/USCODE-2011-title18-partI-chap113-sec2320.pdf—Official text of the Trademark Counterfeiting Act of 1984.

Discussion Exercise

1. When a plaintiff in a trademark infringement case claims to have suffered harm to her goodwill, how are damages calculated to address that harm? How can the value of goodwill, or lost goodwill, be determined?

Chapter 16

Special Topics

"I am explicitly not opening the giant can of worms that is the on-going current discussion of patent, copyright, and trademark reform."
—James Fallows

Chapter Outline

Chapter Objectives

- Distinguish between applications of trademark, copyright, and patent law.
- Understand strategic reasons for choosing between overlapping types of IP protection.

There are occasions when the protection offered by trademark overlaps with the protection offered by copyright and patent. Generally speaking, this phenomenon makes little practical difference in the market, but there are some exceptions where a traditional subject for copyright or patent protection, with finite terms of protection, may be protected indefinitely as a trademark. The decision of what type of IP protection to pursue in some cases is therefore complicated by this potential.

16.1. Trademark vs. Copyright

The general notion, as detailed in previous chapters, is that copyright protection covers original creative works of expression in a fixed medium and trademark covers names, slogans, and other devices used to identify and distinguish the source of goods or services in the marketplace. These distinct areas of law seem to be well defined and the choice of which protection applies to a particular subject should be only a matter of following these definitions. However, many subjects seem to fit both molds. The most common example is the corporate logo, which has more and more frequently been the subject of both trademark and copyright protection.

Traditional practice and wisdom suggests that a logo should be protected as a trademark. Trademark can apply to words, short phrases, colors, and simple designs that do not qualify for copyright protection, and a trademark may enjoy unlimited duration of protection, as long as it continues to be used in commerce and otherwise meets the definition of a trademark. So why would anyone bother with copyright protection as well? The answer is the extent of protection available. With a trademark, protection really only prevents others from using the trademark without permission to identify competing or confusingly similar goods or services in the marketplace. If the trademark is used in a different way, in a different market, or with different products or services, there may be no risk of confusion and the trademark could be lawfully used. Copyright, on the other hand, is far more restrictive. If a logo is original and sophisticated enough to qualify for copyright protection, and most simple logos are not, then it can be shielded from almost all forms of unauthorized copying or use. This advantage is in addition to trademark protection, as the two may simultaneously apply.

A more controversial situation arises when a traditional subject for copyright protection becomes the subject of trademark protection. A well-known example is Mickey Mouse. The Walt Disney Company owns copyrights to all of its characters, but the duration of those copyrights, in many cases, is nearing expiration, even despite the Copyright Term Extension Act of 1998, which extended the life of many Disney copyrights and is sometimes referred to as the "Mickey Mouse Protection Act" because of the lobbying efforts of the Walt Disney Company to get the Act passed. Even when these copyrights finally do expire and the cartoons enter the public domain, the characters themselves will still be subject to trademark protection. As long as the Walt Disney Company continues to use the characters as trademarks in commerce, competitors cannot do so. Given how vast and diverse the marketing and merchandising of Mickey Mouse has become, from theme parks to clothing lines to software and beyond, it would be hard to imagine a profitable area where a competitor could use the character without infringing on the Disney trademarks.

Another interesting example of the overlap between trademark and copyright is the use of trademark images as graphic art on clothing. This frequently occurs when companies with very strong brand recognition and loyalty produce clothing lines featuring their logo as the primary design or artwork on the garment, rather than placing the logo on a tag or more traditional discrete location for branding purposes. Examples abound in the sporting goods and active wear clothing industry, where Nike, for example, has created innumerable variations of prominently featured artwork including or embellishing its trademark swoosh logo. The logo itself is too simple to be eligible for copyright protection on its own, but it is a carefully protected trademark. When the logo is modified and featured as graphic art on clothing, the artistic presentation of the logo is subject to copyright protection.

Finally, music is traditionally protected by copyright, not trademark. As we learned earlier in this unit, however, sounds may properly be the subject of trademark protection when they otherwise serve the function of a trademark, such as the NBC chimes. Music that has become specifically associated with a particular commercial user's brand has started to find additional protection from trademark law. Examples include the song "Sweet Georgia Brown," which is a registered trademark of the Harlem Globtrotters, and the Looney Tunes theme song, which is a registered trademark of Time Warner, Inc.

16.2. Trademark vs. Patent

Trademark and patent law have many similar overlapping applications. As described earlier, a functional element may not be the subject of trademark protection. This is the case specifically to avoid circumventing the limited duration of patent monopolies by registering key functional elements of inventions as trademarks and thereby obtaining indefinite monopoly protection. However, a design patent and trademark protection may be obtained to cover the same non-functional element of an invention or design. This combination of protection allows businesses to obtain the much greater protection of a design patent for a relatively-short duration while establishing the design in commercial use. Once the design is established as a source-identifying element in commerce, it may be eligible for indefinite trademark protection. A good example of this combination protection is the classic Coke bottle, shown on the next page, which has been the subject of both design patent and trademark protection in the United States.

Figure 16.1

An example where trademark, copyright, and design patent all come into play in protecting the overall look and presentation of a product or service is the familiar homepage of Google. As shown below, the Google and Froogle logos are protected by trademark, the layout and specific content of the page is protected by copyright, and the overall design is subject to design patent protection.

Figure 16.2

©2004 Google

Chapter Summary

Trademark law is sometimes overlapping and compatible with copyright and patent law, and the combination of these forms of intellectual property protection can provide a broad spectrum of protection for the overall image, brand, and goodwill of businesses. Trademark protection may not be used to overtly circumvent the limited duration of patent or copyright protection, but some applications, such as the examples of Mickey Mouse and the classic Coke bottle, may provide a very broad level of protection well after the underlying patent or copyright expires.

Review Questions

1. How can trademark law be used to extend protection for the subject of a copyright?
2. How can trademark law be used to extend protection for the subject of a design patent?
3. How is the protection offered by trademark law different than that offered by a copyright?
4. How is the protection offered by trademark law different than that offered by a design patent?

Web Links

1. http://ipwatchdogs.com/patents/USD599372.pdf—The design patent for Google's homepage.

Discussion Exercises

1. What are some examples of products or services that would be permissible uses of the image of Mickey Mouse, without infringing on any Disney trademark?
2. If a new company began producing and marketing flower vases in the same shape as the classic Coke bottle, but without using the Coke or Coca-Cola names, would that use infringe on Coca-Cola's trademark?
3. Should trademark law be allowed to be used to extend protection to the subjects of copyright or design patent? The compromise system in each

case grants broad protection for a limited duration and then requires the subject to fall into the public domain. If trademark law prevents the bulk of practical public uses for these subjects, has trademark law circumvented the patent and copyright compromise?

Chapter 17

International Aspects of Trademark Law

"Insofar as international law is observed, it provides us with stability and order and with a means of predicting the behavior of those with whom we have reciprocal legal obligations." —J. William Fulbright

Chapter Outline

Chapter Objectives

- Learn about the many different international agreements governing trademarks.
- Understand the basic concepts of national treatment, non-self-executing force, and reservations.
- Learn the basic effect of the key provisions of the international agreements affecting trademark law in the United States.

17.1. National Treatment, Non-Self-Executing Force, and Reservations

There are certain big-picture considerations that apply when discussing international trademark law, just as they apply when discussing other aspects of international IP law. The most important issues, other than the specific treaties discussed below, include *national treatment, non-self-executing force,* and *reservations.* National treatment is the standard of protection granted by each country to the citizens and IP of other countries. Throughout the history of international IP protection treaty negotiation, there have been major disagreements about what may be protected and what the scope and duration of protection should be. These disagreements proved, largely, to be insurmountable and, as a result, the compromise position of national treatment was developed. The idea is simply that each country that is party to the treaty must give the citizens of other countries that are party to the treaty the same level of protection as they give to their own citizens. If the United States offers its citizens more protection than France, for example, offers to French citizens, then French citizens obtaining IP protection in the United States will enjoy that higher level of protection in the United States as well. All that is required is that everyone gets the same level of protection in a given country as citizens of that country get.

The concept of non-self-executing-force is simple enough. It just means that most treaties do not have the force of law on their own, and they are dependent on the enacting laws of each country to acquire the force of law. If the enacting legislation in a given country adopts the treaty's language exactly, then the law in that country is exactly the same as every other adopting country that uses the exact language of the treaty. The treaty itself has no actual force or effect. The problem arises when countries do not adopt the treaty language exactly, but instead opt out of certain provisions through the use of reservations. A reservation allows a country to decide not to adopt a particular provision of a treaty, as long as the omission of that provision doesn't defeat the essential purpose of the treaty. Unfortunately, the combination of variations in enacting legislation and reservations can prevent the desired uniformity of international law that the drafters of treaties typically hope to create.

17.2. Paris Convention for the Protection of Industrial Property

The Paris Convention for the Protection of Industrial Property was one of the first international intellectual property treaties, signed into effect in Paris in 1883. The Paris Convention offers protection for both patents and trademarks, and it is widely adopted. The two major provisions relating to trademarks are the requirement of national treatment for citizens of all member countries, and a six-month *priority advantage*. The priority advantage gives citizens of each member country who register a trademark in any member country six months to register that trademark in other member countries with the same effective date of registration as the initial registration.

17.3. Madrid Agreement Concerning the International Registration of Marks of 1891 and the Protocol Relating to the Madrid Agreement

The Madrid Agreement Concerning the International Registration of Marks of 1891 and the Protocol Relating to the Madrid Agreement, collectively referred to as the "Madrid System," provide a central system of international trademark registration. Rather than requiring individual registrations in each country, the Madrid System allows an application for registration in one member country to cause automatic registration in all member countries. The Madrid System used to allow a form of "central attack" on international registrations by cancelling them all if the original registration was cancelled. That is no longer the case, and each registration must be attacked individually if cancellation is desired by a party other than the registering party. The Madrid System now has approximately ninety members who have adopted the international trademark system, including most major international trading nations.

17.4. Trademark Law Treaty

The Trademark Law Treaty, administered by the World Intellectual Property Organization, is designed to simplify and homogenize a number of procedural aspects of international trademark registration by improving individual national trademark registration processes. The goal is to make trademark registration and maintenance in multiple countries less complicated and more efficient and predictable. The provisions of the treaty generally pertain to trademark applications, changes after registration, and renewal. There are a large number of procedural requirements under the treaty, but the major concerns follow.

Regarding application for registration, the treaty requires that member countries simplify the application process and encourages the use of the Nice Agreement Concerning the International Classification of Goods and Services for the Purposes of the Registration of Marks, while also limiting what information and support member countries may require in applications. Regarding changes after registration, the treaty allows trademark owners to record changes in ownership or changes of address for multiple trademark registrations with a single request for change, rather than one such request for each registration. Regarding renewals, the treaty standardizes the initial period of the registration and each subsequent renewal to a ten-year period.

17.5. Trade Related Aspects of Intellectual Property Rights (TRIPS)

The TRIPS Agreement is administered by the World Intellectual Property Organization and it provides certain minimum standards of protection for all of the types of IP discussed in this book. With regard to trademarks in particular, TRIPS is comprehensive. The World Intellectual Property Organization provides the following description of the provisions of TRIPS pertaining to trademarks and service marks:

> The basic rule contained in Article 15 is that any sign, or any combination of signs, capable of distinguishing the goods and services of one undertaking from those of other undertakings, must be eligible for registration as a trademark, provided that it is visually perceptible. Such signs, in particular words including personal names, letters, numerals, figurative elements and combinations of colours as well as any combination of such signs, must be eligible for registration as trademarks.
>
> Where signs are not inherently capable of distinguishing the relevant goods or services, Member countries are allowed to require, as an additional condition for eligibility for registration as a trademark, that distinctiveness has been acquired through use. Members are free to determine whether to allow the registration of signs that are not visually perceptible (e.g. sound or smell marks).

Members may make registrability depend on use. However, actual use of a trademark shall not be permitted as a condition for filing an application for registration, and at least three years must have passed after that filing date before failure to realize an intent to use is allowed as the ground for refusing the application (Article 14.3).

The Agreement requires service marks to be protected in the same way as marks distinguishing goods (see e.g. Articles 15.1, 16.2 and 62.3).

The owner of a registered trademark must be granted the exclusive right to prevent all third parties not having the owner's consent from using in the course of trade identical or similar signs for goods or services which are identical or similar to those in respect of which the trademark is registered where such use would result in a likelihood of confusion. In case of the use of an identical sign for identical goods or services, a likelihood of confusion must be presumed (Article 16.1).

The TRIPS Agreement contains certain provisions on well-known marks, which supplement the protection required by Article 6bis of the Paris Convention, as incorporated by reference into the TRIPS Agreement, which obliges Members to refuse or to cancel the registration, and to prohibit the use of a mark conflicting with a mark which is well known. First, the provisions of that Article must be applied also to services. Second, it is required that knowledge in the relevant sector of the public acquired not only as a result of the use of the mark but also by other means, including as a result of its promotion, be taken into account. Furthermore, the protection of registered well-known marks must extend to goods or services which are not similar to those in respect of which the trademark has been registered, provided that its use would indicate a connection between those goods or services and the owner of the registered trademark, and the interests of the owner are likely to be damaged by such use (Articles 16.2 and 3).

Members may provide limited exceptions to the rights conferred by a trademark, such as fair use of descriptive terms, provided that such exceptions take account of the legitimate interests of the owner of the trademark and of third parties (Article 17).

Initial registration, and each renewal of registration, of a trademark shall be for a term of no less than seven years. The registration of a trademark shall be renewable indefinitely (Article 18).

Cancellation of a mark on the grounds of non-use cannot take place before three years of uninterrupted non-use has elapsed unless valid reasons based on the existence of obstacles to such use are shown by the trademark owner. Circumstances arising independently of the will of the owner of the trademark, such as import restrictions or other government restrictions, shall be recognized as valid reasons of non-use. Use of a trademark by another person, when subject to the control of its owner, must be recognized as use of the trademark for the purpose of maintaining the registration (Article 19).

It is further required that use of the trademark in the course of trade shall not be unjustifiably encumbered by special requirements, such as use with another trademark, use in a special form, or use in a manner detrimental to its capability to distinguish the goods or services (Article 20).

Chapter Summary

There are a number of international treaties concerning trademark law to which the United States is a party. Each of these treaties is complex and contains a number of procedural requirements, minimum standards, and maximum requirements that member countries must respect. While the treaties themselves may be complex, their goal is to streamline and simplify international trademark application, registration, and maintenance. As more and more businesses conduct business on a global scale, the need for uniform trademark processes and consistent legal outcomes is more important than ever. These international agreements have been, and continue to be, effective tools in the effort to meet that need.

Key Terms

National Treatment
Non-Self-Executing Force
Reservations
Priority Advantage

Review Questions

1. What is national treatment?
2. How can a member country to a treaty omit a particular provision from its enactment of the treaty language?
3. What is the purpose of a priority advantage in international trademark registration?

Web Links

1. http://www.wipo.int/treaties/en/ip/paris/trtdocs_wo020.html—Paris Convention for the Protection of Industrial Property.
2. http://www.wipo.int/treaties/en/registration/madrid/—Madrid Agreement Concerning the International Registration of Marks.
3. http://www.wipo.int/treaties/en/ip/tlt/trtdocs_wo027.html—Trademark Law Treaty.
4. http://www.wto.org/english/tratop_e/trips_e/intel2_e.htm#trademark—Overview of the TRIPS Agreement from WIPO.

Discussion Exercises

1. Why would a country with a very high level of trademark protection for its citizens enter into an international agreement for national treatment with a country that provides significantly less protection in its country? Who benefits from such an agreement?
2. Does it make sense for countries with high requirements for trademark protection to agree to provide automatic registration upon application for registration in all other member countries? Could this kind of agreement put a domestic trademark applicant at a disadvantage?

Unit 3

Domain Name Basics

Chapter 18

Domain Names

"Domain names and websites are Internet real estate."
—Marc Ostrofsky

Chapter Outline

Chapter Objectives

- Learn the basic history and function of domain names.
- Understand the practice of cybersquatting.
- Learn the major law prohibiting cybersquatting and the options a victim of cybersquatting has to stop or prevent it.
- Learn about other restrictions on deceptive use of domain names, including those restrictions intended to protect minors from pornography online.

18.1. Introduction to Domain Names

A domain name is an alphanumeric representation of a numerical internet protocol address, or IP address. Websites on the Internet are each hosted on computers called servers, and each server is located on the Internet at a particular IP address. IP addresses are very difficult for humans to remember, as they are 32-bit binary numbers. When these numbers must be written out for some purpose, people generally write them in an easier notation format, such as 198.51.100.0. While this format is easier to read and use than a 32-bit binary expression, it is still far from memorable for most people. To make IP addresses easier to remember, computer scientists have used the same approach used in smart phones to store telephone numbers. Most people enter a telephone number into their phone and assign it to a new contact, with the name of the person the number belongs to. When they want to call a contact, they just need to recall the name of the contact they want to call, rather than the telephone number. Domain names serve this same function for IP addresses. Rather than trying to remember the numerical IP address for Google, an Internet user can simply use the domain name "google.com" to get there.

The Internet Corporation for Assigned Names and Numbers ("ICANN") is in charge of overseeing and accrediting domain name registrars, which "sell" domain names to the public. In reality, domain name registrars charge a fee to provide a registrant with an exclusive right to use a particular domain name. The registrant doesn't actually own the domain name, and it may be assigned to a new registrant if the original registrant fails to pay and re-register the domain name periodically. There are a limited number of domain names available for registration, and there is an ever-increasing number of registered websites. The inevitable shortage of domain names has been addressed to some extent by the creation of multiple top level domains. These include the familiar .com, as well as .net, .org, .gov, and .edu. Each country also has its own specific domain, such as .us for the United States or .ca for Canada. Despite the addition of these domains and others such as .tv, .biz, .info, .mobi, and others, there is still a limited quantity of top level domains available.

Naturally, individuals and businesses prefer to register domain names that make sense, either generally or with respect to their business or name. An insurance business called ABC Insurance, Inc. might wish to register the domain name ABC.com, or ABCInsurance.com, or even Insurance.com. These names are easy for customers to remember, and they make sense with respect to the business. The problem is that, as more and more people and businesses create webpages and register domain names, there are fewer and fewer top-level domain names available that make sense. This is compounded by the fact that people in the United States have come to expect a major commercial website to have a .com domain, which makes .com domain names a premium commodity. This combination of limited quantity and business necessity has led to the development of a very lucrative domain name speculation and resale business, which has resulted in individual domain name sales, in some cases, for millions of dollars each.

There are few restrictions on domain name speculation and resale in the United States with regard to generic domain names, and some of the most expensive domain names on the market have been generics, such as Insure.com, Fund.com, Sex.com, Porn.com, Poker.com, etc. While a successful business and brand may develop around a generic domain name, the generic terms comprising the domain name are usually incapable of constituting a trademark. Obviously, there are some exceptions to this rule, such as Apple.com, for companies with arbitrary names that have acquired secondary meaning and become trademarks.

More problems arise when domain name speculators begin systematically purchasing domain names that either are, or contain, the trademarks of other parties. As the popularity of the Internet and its potential for use in commerce grew, many established companies registered multiple domain names to create a web presence and to prevent others from using domain names containing their trademarks. Not all companies were so quick to realize the importance of domain names, and domain name speculators registered the obvious domain names containing their trademarks. This practice of buying up domain names with the specific intent of later selling them to corresponding trademark holders for a profit is called *cybersquatting*, and the domain speculators who engage in it are called cybersquatters.

18.2. Cybersquatting

Specifically, cybersquatting is any form of registering, buying, selling, or using a domain name with the bad faith intent to profit from the goodwill of a trademark of another. The classic example of cybersquatting occurs when an established business or organization fails to register the top-level domain name of its own trademark name or brand. If Example, Inc. sells widgets under the trademark name "Example," a cybersquatter might register www.example.com with the hope of later selling the domain name to Example, Inc. for a high price. Cybersquatters generally have no legitimate interest in the domain names they register.

Some cybersquatters simply register domain names without actually hosting websites on those domains, while others choose to upload content. In some cases, that content may be at least superficially relevant to the domain name. If a cybersquatter somehow managed to register the domain www.adobe.com, belonging to the Adobe Systems Incorporated software company, he might choose to upload information and pictures relating to the building material of the same name. While the cybersquatter's intent is to compel Adobe Systems Incorporated to buy the domain name at a high price, the content relating to the adobe building material gives the domain a superficial appearance of legitimacy.

Other cybersquatters use less savory techniques. Instead of uploading relevant generic content, a cybersquatter might choose to upload derogatory or malicious remarks about the target company's products or business practices until the company agrees to purchase the domain name. Cybersquatters may also engage in *typosquatting*, which is the practice of purchasing misspellings of popular domain names with the intent to commercialize the expected stream of unlucky visitors who expected to be directed to the legitimate domain. Another technique is to wait until popular domain names have expired, assuming the legitimate owner fails to renew their domain name registration, and then register those domain names in order to commercialize the residual traffic flow and to hopefully sell the domain name back to the original owner once they realize their mistake in allowing the original registration to lapse.

18.3. Anticybersquatting Consumer Protection Act

In response to business concerns about these practices, Congress passed the *Anticybersquatting Consumer Protection Act* ("ACPA") in 1999. The ACPA permits a cause of action against a domain name registrant who has a bad faith intent to profit from a mark and registers, traffics in, or uses a domain name that is identical or confusingly similar to a distinctive mark, identical or confusingly similar to or dilutive of a famous mark, or is a trademark protected by 18 U.S.C. § 706 (marks involving the Red Cross) or 36 U.S.C. § 220506 (marks relating to the "Olympics"). While the ACPA was designed to address the real and growing problem of cybersquatting, some critics have expressed concern that its provisions may be overly broad and that freedom of speech may be restricted by its application if websites that are legitimately used by consumers to complain about companies or their products are shut down. However, case law applying the ACPA has been reasonably respectful of such websites, much to the chagrin of the disparaged trademark owners.

When a court determines whether or not a registrant had a bad faith intent to profit under the statute, it may consider the following factors:

1. the registrant's trademark or other intellectual property rights in the domain name;
2. whether the domain name contains the registrant's legal or common name;
3. the registrant's prior use of the domain name in connection with the bona fide offering of goods or services;
4. the registrant's bona fide noncommercial or fair use of the mark in a site accessible by the domain name;
5. the registrant's intent to divert customers from the mark owner's online location that could harm the goodwill represented by the mark, for commercial gain or with the intent to tarnish or disparage the mark;
6. the registrant's offer to transfer, sell, or otherwise assign the domain name to the mark owner or a third party for financial gain, without having used the mark in a legitimate site;
7. the registrant's providing misleading false contact information when applying for registration of the domain name;
8. the registrant's registration or acquisition of multiple domain names that are identical or confusingly similar to marks of others; and
9. the extent to which the mark in the domain is distinctive or famous.

18.4. Uniform Domain Name Dispute Resolution Policy

Instead of filing a lawsuit under the ACPA, a trademark owner aggrieved by a cybersquatter has the option of using the *Uniform Domain Name Dispute Resolution Policy* ("UDRP") administered by the Internet Corporation for Assigned Names and Numbers. The UDRP provides a cheap and efficient administrative proceeding to resolve domain name disputes that is typically more cost effective than litigation. The remedies available in a ACPA lawsuit may be more attractive than the simple remedies of cancellation or transfer of the domain available in a UDRP proceeding, but the desirability of investing the time and money into a ACPA lawsuit probably depends on the collectability of any judgment against the alleged cybersquatter. The ACPA allows damages of between $1,000.00 and $100,000.00 per domain name involved in some cases. In most cases, however, the UDRP is a more desirable solution for dealing with small time cybersquatters.

ICANN commissioned the United Nations World Intellectual Property Organisation ("WIPO") to create a report on the conflict between trademarks and domain names, which was published in 1999. WIPO recommended a mandatory, arbitration-like administrative procedure to resolve allegations of abusive domain name registrations. In addition to being cheap and efficient, these proceedings would provide a reasonably neutral venue to resolve disputes that were often international in nature. Each domain name application for registration would require the registrant to consent to the UDRP procedure in the event that another party filed a complaint against the registrant. If the registrant does not consent, he may not register a domain name.

A complainant in a UDRP proceeding must prove three elements to succeed. First, she must show that the domain name in question is identical or confusingly similar to a trademark or service mark in which the complainant has rights. Second, the complainant must show that the registrant does not have any rights or legitimate interests in the domain name. Third, the complainant must show that the registrant registered the domain name and is using it in bad faith. Bad faith is determined by considering the following factors:

- Whether the registrant registered the domain name primarily for the purpose of selling, renting, or otherwise transferring the domain name registration to the complainant who is the owner of the trademark or service mark;
- Whether the registrant registered the domain name to prevent the owner of the trademark or service mark from reflecting the mark in a corresponding domain name, if the domain name owner has engaged in a pattern of such conduct; and
- Whether the registrant registered the domain name primarily for the purpose of disrupting the business of a competitor; or
- Whether by using the domain name, the registrant has intentionally attempted to attract, for commercial gain, internet users to the registrant's website, by creating a likelihood of confusion with the complainant's mark.

A UDRP complaint proceeding may cost as little as a few thousand dollars, compared to tens of thousands of dollars or more for major trademark litigation, and a successful complainant may quickly have the registration of the domain name at issue cancelled or transferred to the trademark owner.

18.5. Truth in Domain Names Act

The *Truth in Domain Names Act of 2003*, 18 U.S.C. §2252(B)(b), generally prohibits the use of false or misleading domain names to attract Internet users to pornographic websites and has specific provisions for the protection of minors. The Act specifically provides the following:

(a) Whoever knowingly uses a misleading domain name with the intent to deceive a person into viewing obscenity on the Internet shall be fined under this title or imprisoned not more than 2 years, or both.

(b) Whoever knowingly uses a misleading domain name with the intent to deceive a minor into viewing material that is harmful to minors on the Internet shall be fined under this title or imprisoned not more than 4 years, or both.

(c) For the purposes of this section, a domain name that includes a word or words to indicate the sexual content of the site, such as "sex" or "porn," is not misleading.

(d) For the purposes of this section, the term "material that is harmful to minors" means any communication that—

(1) taken as a whole and with respect to minors, appeals to a prurient interest in nudity, sex, or excretion;

(2) depicts, describes, or represents, in a patently offensive way with respect to what is suitable for minors, an actual or simulated sexual act or sexual contact, actual or simulated normal or perverted sexual acts, or a lewd exhibition of the genitals; and

(3) taken as a whole, lacks serious literary, artistic, political, or scientific value as to minors.

Chapter Summary

Domain names are an essential part of modern business, both for purposes of online commerce and for general advertising and brand promotion. The limited number of domain names available, especially at the desirable top-level .com domain, turns these domain names into valuable commodities. The activities of cybersquatters have created a surge in trademark protection litigation, primarily through the Anticybersquatting Consumer Protection Act. As an efficient alternative to litigation, WIPO and ICANN have created an administrative procedure for the resolution of domain name disputes that is fast and cheap, although its remedies are limited. As the deceptive use of domain names continues to create problems for Internet users, particularly with regard to sensitive populations such as minors, new laws will continue to impose restrictions on the way domain names may be used. The Truth in Domain Names Act is one such example.

Key Terms

Cybersquatting
Typosquatting
Anticybersquatting Consumer Protection Act
Uniform Domain Name Dispute Resolution Policy
Truth in Domain Names Act of 2003

Review Questions

1. What is cybersquatting?
2. What is typosquatting?
3. How might an alleged cybersquatter defend against a cybersquatting claim?
4. What are the advantages of resolving a domain name dispute though litigation under the ACPA instead of through an administrative proceeding under the UDRP?
5. What are the advantages of resolving a domain name dispute through an administrative proceeding under the UDRP instead of through litigation under the ACPA?
6. How can a sexually explicit website avoid liability under the Truth in Domain Names Act?

Web Links

1. http://www.wipo.int/amc/en/center/faq/domains.html—The WIPO page on the Uniform Domain Name Dispute Resolution Policy process with links and frequently asked questions.

Discussion Exercise

1. Should an accused cybersquatter who is using a domain name for a legit-
    imate, non-trademark-infringing purpose be required to give up his do-
    main name to the owner of an established trademark? What if someone
    registered the domain name www.panavision.com, even though the name
    Panavision is a registered trademark of a company running a theatrical
    motion picture and television camera and photographic equipment busi-
    ness, and uploaded a website featuring aerial views of Pana, Illinois? That
    would be a form of Pana-vision, wouldn't it? What if the name Panavi-
    sion wasn't used in association with any commercial goods and so wasn't
    used as an infringing trademark? Could the owner of the Panavision trade-
    mark take away the domain name? See *Panavision v. Toeppen*, available at
    http://cyber.law.harvard.edu/property/domain/panavision.html.

Unit 4

Geographical Indication Basics

Chapter 19

Geographical Indication

"A good reputation is more valuable than money." — Publilius Syrus

Chapter Outline

Chapter Objectives

- Learn the history and origin of geographical indication.
- Understand the modern role of geographical indication law in practice.
- Distinguish between geographical indication and trademark law.

19.1. Introduction to Geographical Indication

Geographical indication, like trademark, is a legal tool used to protect the reputation and integrity of products from a particular source. While trademark identifies a particular brand and protects the reputation of an individual trademark holder, geographical indication identifies the specific geographical origin of a product and protects the reputation of all producers of that product in that location. In a sense, geographical indication is a type of community trademark, arising from the reputation, history and culture of a particular product in a particular place. Any producer of that product may use the geographical indication, as long as they produce the product in that particular location, in accordance with any requirements established by historical production practice or law. These additional requirements of production, if any, beyond location, are typically designed to ensure the integrity and consistency of products bearing a particular geographical indication.

Geographical Indication, or "GI," describes an intellectual property concept that is more than a mere statement of product origin, such as "Made in China." GI is associated with various established protective terms, including *"Protected Designation of Origin," "Protected Geographical Indication," "Appellation d'Origine Controlée,"* and others. There are subtle differences among these terms, which are found in various national and international laws, but, for the broad purposes of this text, these distinctions are unimportant. Each of these terms is consistent with the World Trade Organization's *Agreement on Trade Related Aspects of Intellectual Property Rights* ("TRIPS") Article 22 definition of GI as any language, symbol, or mark that provides "indications which identify a good as originating in the territory of a Member, or a region or locality in that territory, where a given quality, reputation or other characteristic of the good is essentially attributable to its geographical origin." We will follow the generally accepted convention of describing this concept in its entirety as GI.

19.2. A Short History of Geographical Indication

The idea of protecting the reputation of products produced in specific locations from imitators and competitors is hardly new. Efforts have been made throughout the history of trade to clearly distinguish the origins of exclusive or specialized products, in order to promote those products in the market and command a higher price. Regions of ancient Greece were known for making excellent wines, and Thasian wine in particular remained highly popular and expensive into Roman times. A stone inscription from Thasos attests to the efforts made by that island state to protect its wine trade: there was legislation against speculating in wine "futures" and importing non-Thasian wine to part of the mainland coast of Thrace that Thasos ruled. These restrictions were intended to ensure that wine sold as "Thasian" really was produced locally, either on the island itself or on the mainland slopes, and that it was not blended with cheap imported wines.

Wine is the classic example of a product protected by GI, and so it is not surprising that the first well-organized legal efforts to protect products through forms of GI occurred in France with the *Paris Covention for the Protection of Intellectual Property* in 1883. This convention began with a union of eleven

European countries banding together to primarily protect their respective patents and trademarks, but the language of the convention provided protection specifically for GI: "The protection of industrial property has as its object patents, utility models, industrial designs, trademarks, service marks, trade names, *indications of source or appellations of origin,* and the repression of unfair competition."

The Paris Covention was also innovative in providing, specifically in its Article 10, protection against marks that falsely claimed a specific geographical origin. In such cases, the convention provided broad enforcement rights to any "producer, manufacturer, or merchant, whether a natural person or a legal entity, engaged in the production or manufacture of or trade in such goods and established either in the locality falsely indicated as the source, or in the region where such locality is situated, or in the country falsely indicated, or in the country where the false indication of source is used." Providing the right to bring enforcement actions to such a broad pool of potentially interested parties ensured that violations would be quickly and uniformly addressed. Remedies for such violations include a prohibition on importation of falsely marked products into member countries, or the seizure of such products already in member countries.

Europe has continued to develop a complex collection of national and international laws providing various levels of protection for GI, most notably with the *Madrid Agreement for the Repression of False or Deceptive Indications of Source on Goods* in 1891, which expanded protection against misleading GI labels, and the *Lisbon Agreement for the Protection of Appellations of Origin and their International Registration* in 1958. Both of these agreements significantly expanded the international recognition and protection of GI. However, the most significant modern source of international law governing GI is the TRIPS Agreement, which provides broad general GI protection and an international registry for geographical indications. TRIPS sets minimum starnards of protection for member countries to establish through their own national laws, though each country is free to enact stricter protections if they wish to do so.

TRIPS also provides a higher level of protection specifically for wines and spirits. Under Articles 22 and 23 of TRIPS, member countries must provide legal means to prevent the use of a GI identifying wines and spirits not originating in the place indicated by the GI, even where the true origin of the goods is indicated and, therefore, arguably not misleading the public. Protection must also be provided against cases where a protected GI is circumvented by its use in translation, or by its use accompanied by expressions such as "kind," "type," "style," "imitation" or similar statements. Further, the registration of any trademark which contains or consists of a GI identifying wines or spirits, must be refused or invalidated in the case of wines or spirits not having the origin associated with the GI.

While GI has become useful in protecting a broad range of both culinary and non-culinary products, as discussed later in the chapter, it continues to be most popular and effective in protecting the same alcohol products that motivated its spread and evolution in the first place.

19.3. The Policy Goals of Geographical Indication

The policy goals of GI are essentially the same as the policy goals of trademark, but applied in a community sense to all legitimate participants in the creation and maintenance of local product reputation. The protection of that reputation, the deterrence of misrepresentation and imitation products, the enhancement of consumer awareness, the continuation of successful traditions and market culture, and the reward of original or distinctive producers are all the aims of comprehensive GI legislation.

As GI has matured, developing nations have begun to recognize the value of GI in the protection of "traditional knowledge," which may include agricultural techniques, traditional or herbal medicines, and protection from "biopiracy." While many practical and financial barriers remain that prevent interested parties in developing nations from fully accessing the potential protections and financial benefits of GI, international development of GI protection systems and policy has shifted in favor of promoting these "traditional knowledge" interests, even where they may conflict with more established intellectual property systems, such as patent rights in the global pharmaceutical market.

"Traditional Knowledge" Example*

Figure 19.1

Turmeric *(Curcuma longa)* is a plant of the ginger family yielding saffron-colored rhizomes that is commonly used as a spice for flavoring in Indian cooking. It also has properties that make it an effective ingredient in medicines, cosmetics and as a color dye. As a medicine, it is traditionally used to heal wounds and rashes.

• In 1995, two Indian nationals at the University of Mississippi Medical Centre were granted US patent no. 5,401,504 on "use of turmeric in wound healing."

• The Indian Council of Scientific and Industrial Research (CSIR) requested the US Patent and Trademark Office (USPTO) to re-examine the patent.

• CSIR argued that turmeric has been used for thousands of years for healing wounds and rashes and therefore its medicinal use was not novel.

• Their claim was supported by documentary evidence of traditional knowledge, including an ancient Sanskrit text and a paper published in 1953 in the Journal of the Indian Medical Association.

• Despite arguments by the patentees, the USPTO upheld the CSIR objections and revoked the patent.

The turmeric case was a landmark case as it was the first time that a patent based on the traditional knowledge of a developing country had been successfully challenged. The legal costs incurred by India in this case have been calculated by the Indian Government to be about at US $10,000.

*Commission on Intellectual Property Rights, "Integrating Intellectual Property Rights and Development Policy—Report of the Commission on Intellectual Property Rights", London 2002. Picture at left by J.M. Garg, Wikimedia Commons. Picture at right by Sanjay Acharya, Wikimedia Commons.

19.4. Sources of Geographical Indication Law

Geographical indications are protected in accordance with international treaties and national laws under a wide range of concepts, including special laws specifically for the protection of geographical indications or appellations of origin, trademark laws in the form of collective marks or certification marks, laws against unfair competition, and consumer protection laws prohibiting unfair or deceptive acts and practices. In essence, these laws ensure that unauthorized parties may not use a geographical indication with respect to products that do not originate in the place designated by that indication. Applicable sanctions range from court injunctions preventing the unauthorized use to the payment of damages and fines or, in serious cases, imprisonment.

A number of treaties administered by the World Intellectual Property Association provide for the protection of geographical indications, most notably the Paris Convention for the Protection of Industrial Property of 1883, and the Lisbon Agreement for the Protection of Appellations of Origin and Their International Registration. In addition, Articles 22 to 24 of TRIPS deal with the international protection of geographical indications within the framework of the World Trade Organization. While TRIPS sets minimum standards that must be included in GI regulation, member countries are free to modify the model legislation to achieve the minimum standards as they see fit and to offer protections that exceed what TRIPS requires. The result is a very different set of laws applying to GI in each member country and, although each set of laws contains the same minimal protections, there is a wide variation in the specific levels of protection available to specific products. In all cases, the protections available for GI in other countries only apply if the GI is protected in its country of origin.

In the United States, which is part of the TRIPS agreement, the minimum standards required by TRIPS are met through the use of the existing body of trademark or certification mark law. Individuals, organizations or associations, or businesses may all register GIs to protect their own products or the products of a particular type from a particular area. The process for obtaining GI registration is the same as that described previously for trademarks or certification marks. However, the requirements of TRIPS still apply. The GI must still consist of indications which identify a good as originating in the United States, or a region or locality in the territory of the United States, where a given quality, reputation or other characteristic of the good is essentially attributable to its geographical origin. The GI must not be false or deceptive, and the GI cannot be a generic term in the United States.

If someone registers the name of a place as a trademark, certification or collective mark for a particular product, that registration does not necessarily prevent anyone else from using the term on unrelated goods provided that the public is not likely to be confused as to the source of the goods. A trademark, certification mark, or collective mark is not a monopoly right. The property right exists for these marks only in relation to a specific set of goods. The right extends to similar, related, or even unrelated goods depending on the specific factors of each case. A very well-known mark will have a wider scope of protection against infringing uses than a mark that is not known very well. Ultimately, the test is whether the average consumer would likely be confused as to the source of the goods between the two uses of the mark.

A trademark, certification mark, or collective mark registration does not necessarily prevent anyone from using the GI term to fairly describe where their products originate when their products are the same as those identified in the registration. Such use may be considered a fair use of descriptive terms. Fair use is a defense to a claim of trademark infringement. This concept developed very early on in U.S. jurisprudence as courts recognized that trademark law should not be able to take words entirely out of the public domain. In order to qualify for the fair use defense, use of a term must be purely descriptive and to determine if the use is purely descriptive, there must be an evaluation of how the term is used in the marketplace. If the term is used in a way that can be confusing to the public as to the source of the products, then the use is not really "fair" and the mark owner could bring a trademark infringement action against the use.

When a certification mark is registered, and someone else's goods meet the standards for certification, those goods may be labeled with the certification mark subject to the certification by the owner of the mark. Without that certification, the mark cannot be used. The owner must be able to control the use of the term on goods and, if the owner cannot do that or does not do that, the mark is subject to cancellation. If the owner discriminates against a producer who actually meets the standards, the mark is also subject to cancellation. With certification marks, the ability of the certification mark owner to "exercise legitimate control" over the use of the term by others is a critical issue. Often, a government or municipality is in the best position to control the use of a term by a group of producers. But a private association or agricultural collective is also in a good position to control the use of the term by producers. Either entity, a government or a private association, is acting as a private rightholder as the owner of the GI, which is a private right. In that way, the United States GI regime is consistent with TRIPS, which says that intellectual property rights are "private rights."

19.5. Geographical Indication in Practice

A GI can be a geographic place name, such as "Napa Valley," but it may also be a symbol, such as a picture of the Eiffel Tower, the Statue of Liberty, an orange tree, or the outline of a geographic area, such as the outline of the state of Florida, or a color, or anything else capable of specifically identifying the source of a good or service. GIs are usually names of places, but that is not always the case, and non-geographical names can be protected if they are linked to a particular place. The best example of this type of GI is Feta cheese, which is not named after anyplace in Greece, but which is identified as an inherently Greek product. Feta, however, may be considered a generic term in some countries and therefore not entitled to GI protection in those countries.

Common examples of GI include sparkling wine from the Champagne region of France, Indian basmati rice, Roquefort cheese from France, Gorgonzola cheese from Italy, lamb from New Zealand, and Kobe beef from Japan. Examples in the United States include Vidalia onions from Georgia, Idaho potatoes, Tennessee whiskey, Florida oranges, and Washington State apples. However, while GI is most frequently used to protect food and alcohol products, it is not limited to these applications. Examples of non-culinary uses of GI include Swiss watches, Czech crystal, Indian rugs, French *Poterie de Vallauris* pottery and *Toile de Chalet* cloth, Peruvian Chulucanas ceramic, and Russian Gorodets painting and Rostov enamel.

Non-Culinary GI Example*

Figure 19.2

Produced in the United Kingdom, Shetland wool has been used to make garments dating back to at least the 6th century BC. The wool for the Islands' knitting tradition is provided by the Shetland sheep, a hardy breed that produces a hard-wearing fleece. As early as the 18th century, travelers to Shetland noted the colorfully patterned knitwear. These multi-colored patterns called Fair Isle became popular and spread to the other islands of Shetland. Until fifty years ago the wool was spun by hand, but today most of the wool is spun by machine.

The Shetland Knitwear Trades Association (SKTA) was formed in 1982 to represent the knitwear producers of Shetland. Its primary aims are to protect and promote Shetland Knitwear and to provide a contact point for those wishing to make direct contact with Shetland based knitwear producers. "Shetland woolen outerwear" is protected in the United Kingdom in particular by a certification mark. The trademark system was chosen to protect the product because it is the only system available in the UK for the protection of geographical indications for handicrafts. A certification mark was chosen over an individual trademark because it is available for all producers to use.

*Directorate General for Trade of the European Commission, "Study on the protection of geographical indications for products other than wines, spirits, agricultural products or foodstuffs." 2009. Picture on left by Andrew, Wikimedia Commons. Picture on right by Dave Wheeler, Wikimedia Commons.

Producers in locations designated by a specific GI mark, producing in accordance with applicable production requirements, may label their products with these geographical indications just as they include their own trademarks in their labeling. Similar products produced elsewhere, or not produced in accordance with applicable production requirements, may not be labeled with these geographical indications. Through this labeling, consumers are able to ensure that they are purchasing products that are authentic, that originate from reputable locations, and that are made in the traditional manner. As a result, products carrying GI labeling are often able to command greater market recognition and a premium price.

If a geographical term is used as the common name for a kind of product, rather than an indication of the place of origin of that product, then the term no longer functions as a geographical indication. Such a generic term is not protected under the requirements of TRIPS, and so few countries offer them any protection. Examples of these types of terms that are at least arguably generic are cologne, Dijon mustard, Feta cheese, and Basmati rice. Countries where these products are produced as generics often produce them in multiple locations, and the original geographical specificity of the product names has been lost.

GI Protection for Basmati Rice*

Figure 19.3

Basmati is a variety of rice from the Punjab provinces of India and Pakistan. The rice is a slender, aromatic long grain variety that originated in this region and is a major export crop for both countries. Annual basmati exports are worth about $300,000,000 and represent the livelihood of thousands of farmers.

The "Battle for Basmati" started in 1997 when U.S. rice breeding firm RiceTec, Inc. was awarded a patent (US5663484) relating to plants and seeds, seeking a monopoly over various rice lines including some having characteristics similar to Basmati. Concerned about the potential effect on exports, India requested a re-examination of this patent in 2000. In response, RiceTec, Inc. withdrew a number of claims including those covering Basmati type lines. Further claims were also withdrawn following concerns raised by the USPTO. The dispute then moved from the patent to the use of the name "Basmati."

In some countries the term "Basmati" can be applied only to the long grain aromatic rice grown in India and Pakistan. RiceTec, Inc. also applied for registration of the trademark "Texmati" in the UK claiming that "Basmati" was a generic term. It was successfully opposed, and the UK has established a code of practice for marketing rice. Saudi Arabia (the world's largest importer of Basmati rice) has similar regulations on the labeling of Basmati rice. The code states that "the belief in consumer, trade and scientific circles [is] that the distinctiveness of authentic Basmati rice can only be obtained from the northern regions of India and Pakistan due to the unique and complex combination of environment, soil, climate, agricultural practices and the genetics of the Basmati varieties."

In 1998 the U.S. Rice Federation submitted that the term "Basmati" is generic and refers to a type of aromatic rice. In response, a collective of U.S. and Indian civil society organizations filed a petition seeking to prevent U.S.-grown rice from being advertised with the word "Basmati," The U.S. Department of Agriculture and the U.S. Federal Trade Commission rejected it in May 2001. Neither considered the labeling of rice as "American-grown Basmati" misleading, and deemed "Basmati" a generic term. The name "Basmati" (and the Indian and Pakistani export markets) can be protected by registering the name as a GI, but India and Pakistan will have to explain why they did not take action against the gradual adoption of generic status of Basmati over the last twenty years.

*Commission on Intellectual Property Rights, "Integrating Intellectual Property Rights and Development Policy—Report of the Commission on Intellectual Property Rights", London 2002. Picture from Wikimedia Commons.

19.6. Geographical Indication vs. Trademark

The distinction between GI and trademark is not always clear. This is particularly true in jurisdictions that protect GI through the use of trademarks and certification marks. Generally, a trademark is a sign used by an enterprise to distinguish its goods and services from those of other enterprises. A trademark gives its owner the right to exclude others from using the trademark, and trademarks may be arbitrary, so long as they are not deceptive. GI, on the other hand, provides specific information about a product and where that product is produced. GI may be used by any number of producers, so long as they all adhere to the location and required means of production necessary to meet the specification of the particular GI. A GI is usually not arbitrary, as it will typically include the name or symbol of a specific place.

A GI may be registered as a trademark, as often happens in jurisdictions that rely on trademark law to protect GI, as long as the GI component of the trademark is not misleading or registered in bad faith. A misleading GI trademark is one that is likely to mislead the public as to the true place of origin of the product in question.

Food for Thought: A Deceptive GI Trademark?*

Figure 19.4

The first American cream cheese was produced in New York by dairyman William Lawrence in 1872.

Despite having no connection to Philadelphia, the name Philadelphia® was chosen for the brand in 1880 in order to associate the cream cheese with the reputation for high-quality foods produced in that city at the time.

A trademark containing a misleading geographical indication must be refused or invalidated pursuant to TRIPS. So, how is the Philadelphia® brand permitted to exist as a registered trademark in the United States despite not originating or necessarily being produced in Philadelphia? Does it matter that the name was chosen specifically to associate the product with the reputation for quality foods in Philadelphia?

*Kraft Foods United Kingdom, "Philadelphia Brand History" available via <http://www.philadelphia.co.uk/philadelphia3/page?siteid=philadelphia3-prd&locale=uken1&PagecRef=584>.

Chapter Summary

Geographical indications play an important role in identifying and distinguishing a diverse range of products originating in specific locations and embodying specific production standards. While administratively very similar to trademark in the United States, where GI protection comes largely from trademark law, GI is a distinct form of intellectual property that has ancient origins and many unique modern applications. While GI has historically been underdeveloped in the United States, where its protections may have been perceived to be unfairly beneficial to European interests, that has changed dramatically in recent years. The United States boasts a wide variety of mature GI "brands" that are gaining recognition worldwide. In order to protect those brands at home and abroad, the United States must enhance its GI recognition and enforcement programs, which it has successfully done in accordance with the TRIPS Agreement. As more local and regional products in the United States gain distinction, GI law will continue to gain attention and enhanced protection.

Key Terms

Geographical Indication
Protected Designation of Origin
Protected Geographical Indication
Appellation d'Origine Controlée
Agreement on Trade Related Aspects of Intellectual Property Rights
Paris Covention for the Protection of Intellectual Property
Madrid Agreement for the Repression of False or Deceptive Indications of Source on Goods
Agreement for the Protection of Appellations of Origin and Their International Registration

Review Questions

1. Give two examples of GI from the United States and two examples of GI from abroad.
2. Can different countries have different levels of GI protection and still be incompliance with TRIPS?
3. How is GI protected in the United States?
4. How can GI be used to defeat a patent?

Web Links

1. http://www.wipo.int/geo_indications/en/about.html—World Intellectual Property Organization page on general geographical indication information.

Discussion Exercises

1. If a protected GI from country A has reached generic status in country B, but not in country C, should that GI still be protected in country C? If so, will producers in country B have an unfair competitive advantage over producers in Country C due to their ability to use the generic GI that is still protected in country C?

2. Is it reasonable to prevent producers who are not eligible to use a particular GI from using descriptive language containing that GI on their labels? For example, is it reasonable to prevent sparkling wines grown in California from using terms such as "Champagne-style" wine? Would this practice be likely to mislead the public as to the true origin of the products? What if the California origin is clearly printed on the label, such as "Champagne-style Sparkling Wine from California"?

Unit 5

Patent Basics

Chapter 20

Introduction to Patent Law

" ... the patent system added the fuel of interest to the fire of genius."
—Abraham Lincoln

Chapter Outline

Chapter Objectives

- Understand the rights granted to inventors under patent law.
- Explain the policy goals behind incentivizing inventors.
- Become familiar with the benefits to the public from patents.
- Grasp the balance struck between incentivizing inventors and benefitting the public.
- Understand how patents can address humanitarian needs.
- Identify common ways in which patents can be used in the corporate world.

Abraham Lincoln is the only United States President to hold a patent. His invention was a "Device for Buoying Vessels Over Shoals" and, although the device was never a commercial success, he was nonetheless a strong supporter of the patent system. Indeed, the United States has a long history of encouraging innovation through the use of patents. In the next several chapters, we will examine the patent system from its origins to the present day.

A *patent* embodies an exclusive grant of intellectual property rights from the United States government to an inventor. The PTO website carries the following definition of a patent:

> A patent is an intellectual property right granted by the Government of the United States of America to an inventor "to exclude others from making, using, offering for sale, or selling the invention throughout the United States or importing the invention into the United States" for a limited time in exchange for public disclosure of the invention when the patent is granted.

The scope of patent protection is very different from the scope of protection found in the other areas of intellectual property law presented so far. In many ways, the rights afforded an inventor under patent law are more robust. In fact, patent law, grants what many refer to as a *legal monopoly*. It is for this reason that the duration of patent protection is relatively shorter than the duration of protection found in other areas of intellectual property, such as trademarks, and copyrights. That is a balance that is struck—stronger protection for a shorter duration of time. It is this trade off that makes patent protection unique.

The first thing to note is that the grant of rights comes from the United States government. Unlike copyright law, trademark law and the law of trade secrets, patent protection comes *only* from the U.S. government. In order to acquire patent protection, an inventor must submit an application for the claimed invention to the PTO. As we will discuss in greater detail in Chapter 23, the application and review process involved in acquiring patent protection is rigorous and lengthy. The PTO examines applications for compliance with both procedural requirements and substantive requirements. Contrast this process to the relative ease of acquiring copyright protection, a trademark at common law, or as we will see in Unit 6, trade secret protection.

Notice that the rights granted under patent law do not include the right to *practice* an invention, but rather the *right to exclude* others from practicing an invention. For many patented inventions, there are requirements beyond gaining a patent that an inventor must meet in order to practice an invention. For example, pharmaceutical companies frequently protect new drug formulations using patents. The grant of a patent does not, however, give a pharmaceutical company the right to practice an invention. First, the Food and Drug Administration (the "FDA") must determine whether the new drug meets its safety requirements before it will give a green light for the sale of the new drug. Similarly, a newly patented consumer device must meet certain safety regulations before it can be sold to consumers and used in homes.

Another important feature of patent law is that the right to exclude others is so comprehensive that it includes a patentee's right to prevent another from practicing the invention *even* when a second inventor has reached the same invention by independent creation or reverse engineering. Compare this result with copyright law or, as we will see, trade secret law, where independent creation is a complete defense for infringement.

Perhaps the most distinctive characteristic of patent law is the bargained for exchange—the *quid pro quo*—between the government and the inventor. In this regard, the grant of an exclusive monopoly to an inventor is made in exchange for the inventor's promise to fully disclose and teach the public the invention. Let's explore this important concept in greater detail in the following section.

20.1. Origins of Patent Law and Policy Goals

As we explore the philosophical justification behind patent law, keep in mind two fundamental questions: From where do patent rights originate? And why should the law grant inventors the right to exclude others, essentially keeping technology out of public reach?

Congress' power to promulgate patent law comes from Article 1, §8, clause 8 of the Constitution which grants Congress the power to enact laws that "promote the progress of science and useful arts by securing for limited times to authors and inventors the exclusive rights to their respective writings and discoveries." As you may recall, this is the same Constitutional clause that grants Congress the right to enact copyright laws. These two areas of the law are cut from the same cloth—so to speak—but as we will see, are distinct in many ways.

The Constitution's grant of power to Congress also acts as a limit to that power. Congress has the authority to create laws that reward inventors, but may only grant patents for inventions that are *progressive* and *useful.* Hence, an invention must be *novel* and have *utility* before it will receive patent protection. We will discuss each of these requirements in greater detail in Chapter 22. Similarly, the Constitutional grant limits the duration of protection afforded to inventors to a *limited time.* Thus, the term of patent protection is relatively short—only 20 years from the effective filing date. Because the statute grants power and puts limits on that power, Congress must strike a balance between protecting intellectual property rights that incentivize inventors while limiting that which remains in the public domain.

At the heart of patent law, is the utilitarian concept that incentivizing innovation benefits the public. The patent system encourages inventors to innovate and disclose their knowledge by granting inventors the exclusive right to practice their invention for a period of time in exchange for the full disclosure of the invention. Thus, inventors must disclose the details of any invention in a patent application before patent protection will be granted. The public benefits from the disclosure of patented inventions in two ways. Initially, the public benefits from the fruits of the invention. Indeed, from disease curing pharmaceuticals, Wi-Fi networking, the telephone, and many versions of the light bulb, patented inventions bring beneficial advances to the public. Beyond this and perhaps more importantly, is the significant benefit that results after the term of patent protection. What happens to a patented invention after the expiration of the 20-year patent term? The invention falls into the public domain and the technology becomes free for anyone to practice. It is this disclosure of technology that adds to the building blocks of innovation and truly benefits the public.

Let's look at an example: pharmaceutical formulations are frequently protected by patents. A pharmaceutical company spends enormous resources in the research, development, testing, and approval of new drug formulas. Once the development phase has been completed, a pharmaceutical company may apply for a patent. If the patent issues, the pharmaceutical company will be allowed to exclusively practice the invention for the duration of the patent. (Keep in mind, the patent only confers the right to exclude others—not the right to market and sell the invention. The FDA must still give its approval for the new drug.)

The benefit to the pharmaceutical company is that during the duration of patent protection, it has a monopoly over the drug formula. Simple economic principles dictate that without any competition, a pharmaceutical company can set almost any price for its patented drugs. It is during this time that a pharmaceutical company can recoup the tremendous expense involved with drug development and build its brand as the exclusive source of the patented drugs. This represents the incentive to the patentee.

For the duration of patent protection, the public reaps the benefits of having access to life saving medications and beneficial vaccines. This is the initial benefit to the public. After the duration of the patent term, the drug or vaccine formula will fall into the public domain and competing pharmaceutical companies can freely practice the invention, making and selling the previously patented drugs. Because competing drug companies did not bear the initial expense of research and development, they can offer the drugs at a significantly lower cost. Hence, the public benefits from having access to generic drugs offered at sharply reduced prices. What is more, future technology will build upon the innovation that is embodied in the original patented drug formula and disclosed through the patent process.

Of course, there are critics of the patent system. Some say that granting a monopoly over an invention allows an inventor to exploit the patent, sometimes over charging for products that are important to people. The pharmaceutical industry is often a target of this critique. A pharmaceutical company can, and often does, charge very high prices for life-savings drugs, making many in need unable to attain the medical treatment they need. On the other side of this argument is the significant overall benefit that the public gains in having new drugs and the need to incentivize the pharmaceutical industry due to the high costs of development, approval, and liability associated with the drug development.

20.2. A Short History of United States Patent Law

The concept of incentivizing innovation has a long history. Two of the earliest known systems of patent law take us back to the *Venetian Statute of 1474* and the *Statute of Monopolies* enacted in England in 1624. Many of the fundamental concepts in our current system of patent laws resemble the concepts found in these early statutes. The drafters of the United States Constitution recognized the benefit of a system that rewards innovators and accordingly included Art. 1, §8, clause 8 of the Constitution granting Congress the power to enact laws that "promote the progress of science and useful arts …." It is from this power granted to Congress that our current system of patent laws has emerged and evolved. From the first patent laws enacted in 1790 until the most recent changes signed into law in 2011 as part of the *Leahy-Smith America Invents Act* ("AIA"), Congress has, from time to time, updated and added to our system of patent law.

Prior to the enactment of the first federal patent statute, a number of individual states had established patent laws. The Act of 1790 unified patent rights under one federal scheme providing a stronger level of certainty and predictability of patent rights among the states. Among other requirements, this first statute required that an invention was *new* and *useful*. As we will see throughout the next several sections, these concepts have endured and continue to be a central requirement of patentability. On July 31, 1790, only a few months after the enactment of the first federal patent statute, the first U.S. patent was granted to Samuel Hopkins for a process of making potash. At that time, the patent process was much different than it is now. A patent could be granted by approval of the Secretary of State, the Attorney General, or the Secretary of the Department of War. After only three years, Thomas Jefferson, the then Secretary of State, revised the patent statute emphasizing the need to limit monopolies granting them only when it benefits the public. This philosophy has also endured and is reflected in our current system of patent laws.

Amendments made to the patent statute since Jefferson's 1793 draft to reflect changes in technology and the culture of the nation. In 1952, Congress fully revised and established the basis for today's patent laws by passing the Patent Act of 1952. In many ways, the 1952 Act codified much of the judicial precedent that had emerged since the prior patent act. For example, as we will see in Chapter 22, a claimed invention must be nonobvious before it will be patented. This standard of patentability emerged as judicial precedent and was codified in the 1952 Act in § 103. On September 16, 2011, Congress passed the AIA bringing major legislative reform to the patent statute in an attempt to address many issues found in the patent system. Specifically, parts of the new legislation were designed to simplify sections of the patent code that have historically given rise to a tremendous amount of litigation and to bring the United States' system of patent law more in line with the patent laws found in other parts of the world. We will discuss many of the important changes under the AIA throughout the upcoming chapters.

20.3. Patents in Practice

An important balance must be struck between protecting the interests of inventors and acting in the best interests of the public. The public benefits when patent law promotes progress. It is also equally important that patent rights are robust so that inventors are rewarded for their efforts. Let's look at the real-world impact patents can have.

20.4. Building a Modern World and Addressing Humanitarian Needs

Patented technologies have had a great impact on history and, in many cases, have shaped the course of history. Indeed, incentivizing innovation is rooted in the goal of bringing beneficial advances to the public. Nevertheless, critics of the patent system point to the fact that a patent keeps innovation in the hands of the patentee for a period of time and out of reach of the public, making it possible for a patent owner to exploit a granted monopoly charging inflated prices during the patent period. Many see this as a fault of the patent system.

Still, many technological advances that add to our quality of life and address humanitarian crisis' come from patented technologies. In February, 2012 the PTO announced its *Patents for Humanity* program. This initiative encourages inventors to develop advances that address humanitarian challenges around the world, specifically in the areas of medical technology, food and nutrition, clean technology, and information technology. The goal is to create lasting solutions for some of the most dire needs in under-served regions of the world. To incentivize inventors, the PTO has established a fast-track for patent prosecution. From this program, technologies that have emerged include a water purification system that removes impurities from water, including 99.9% of bacteria, viruses and other pollutants; genetically improved crops that provide more protein and higher nutrition yields of specific vitamins; and an information device that promotes literacy. Other inventions addressed critical problems like malaria and HIV.

Similarly, a cooperative of corporate leaders have formed an initiative called *Eco-Patent Commons* which encourages patentees to pledge their innovations, creating a collection of patents that aim to protect the environment. Examples of such innovations are those that address an environmental issue, such as a manufacturing or industrial process that reduces the impact on the environment or demonstrates improved energy efficiency. Under this program, patents are pledged by corporations and inventions are easily shared with other corporations, thus promoting the protection of the global environment. Programs like this facilitate advances that can help protect our environment on a global level.

20.5. Corporate Patent Strategies

In addition to providing benefits to the public, patents give inventors market power. The right to exclude others comes with its own bundle of rights. A patentee can license patented technology to many licensees generating an income stream during the patent term. On the other hand, a patentee can grant an exclusive license to one licensee in exchange for a higher royalty rate. A patentee can assign a patented invention in exchange for a lump sum and retire to a tropical island. Still other patentees may practice the invention exclusively, ultimately leveraging their monopoly into an established position in the market. Patents provide protection to inventors in the marketplace. For instance, for a sole proprietor that has only an innovative idea, taking an idea to the marketplace, unprotected by a patent can be a tricky business. However, protecting the idea by reducing it to practice and obtaining a patent can provide a sole proprietor the ability to exploit the invention without fearing that the idea will be stolen by a larger company that has an established customer base and a ready manufacturing facility. In short, patent protection gives a patentee options in the marketplace.

Let's look at an example. Entrepreneur Sara Blakely designed and patented a line of shape wear when she was unhappy with the options available. When she obtained a patent for her innovative undergarments, she went to famous department stores and clothing manufacturers to sell her idea. Having a patent allowed her to freely share the technology with established manufacturers without fearing that the idea would be copied. The patent provided a platform to start a company on a small level that has now grown into Spanx®, a multi-million-dollar company with numerous product lines.

In business, patents can be used in many ways—sometimes as a shield and sometimes as a sword. Indeed, there are corporations that employ defensive patenting strategies while others employ offensive patenting strategies. Some acquire a portfolio of patents in an effort to protect a company's interests or to use as a tool to force negotiation or settlement with a competitor. Other corporations acquire what is known as a *patent thicket,* a collection of patents that cover the same or very similar subject matter. This is done in an effort to keep competitors from *designing around* valuable inventions. We will discuss designing around in more detail in later chapters. Still other companies, known as *patent assertion entities* ("P.A.E.") or sometime referred to as *patent trolls,* acquire patents for the sole purpose of enforcing the patent rights without any interest in practicing the invention. We will discuss P.A.E.s in greater detail in Chapter 27.

Chapter Summary

Patent law grants rights that allow inventors to exclude others from practicing an invention for a period of 20 years from the effective filing date. These rights come only from the U.S. government. There are no patent rights under common law. Accordingly, inventors must go through a lengthy application process that examines the substantive and procedural requirements. Because the rights granted to a patentee are so comprehensive, these rights are sometimes referred to as a *legal monopoly.*

Our patent laws and copyright laws originate from the same Constitutional grant of power. Patent law *incentivizes* inventors to innovate and share their knowledge with the public. The public benefit is twofold: the inventor discloses the knowledge behind the innovation while the public enjoys the benefit of technological advances. This quid-pro-quo between the inventor and the public is at the heart of patent law. For this reason, an inventor's disclosure of knowledge is critical to fulfilling the philosophical justification behind patent law.

There is a strong history of incentivizing inventors to benefit the public. Some of the oldest statutory schemes that protected inventors date back to 1474. Based on the United States Constitutional grant of power to enact patent laws, Congress promulgated the first set of U.S. patent laws in 1790 and has continued to improve upon the laws. Recently, Congress passed the America Invents Act which provided revisions to many areas of patent law. The new law aims to simplify the patent regulations and reduce some of the litigation originating from patent disputes.

In addition to the many inventions that have built our modern world and brought many of the conveniences that we enjoy today, patented inventions have an impact on our quality of life. Many life-saving technologies and innovations that protect our environment are patented inventions. Recently, the PTO introduced an initiative to incentivize inventors to address some of the world's most critical humanitarian crises. Technologies addressing the need for water purification and life saving medications have all come from this program.

Patent protection provides a means for market power and gives corporations the options of leveraging their patent protection in the market. Some corporations use patents in a defensive manner while others use patents in an offensive way, seeking to merely enforce rights without practicing the invention embodied.

Key Terms

Patent
Right to Exclude
Legal Monopoly
Quid pro quo
Incentivize
Venetian Statute of 1474
Statute of Monopolies
Leahy-Smith America Invents Act
Patents for Humanity
Eco-Patent Commons

Review Questions

1. In what ways does patent law differ from copyright law and trademark law?
2. What is the bargained for exchange between inventors and the government?
3. How does the public benefit from a patented invention?
4. What are some of the criticisms of the patent system?
5. What is the America Invents Act?
6. What is the benefit to patentees under the *Patents for Humanity Program*?
7. How can a sole proprietor benefit from patenting an invention?
8. Give an example of defensive patenting? Offensive patenting?

Web Links

1. Google has a patent searching site. See: http://www.google.com/?tbm=pts. Using the name of a product, a company or an inventor, search for some familiar patented inventions.
2. Spanx® inventor and entrepreneur tells the story of how an idea and a patent became a corporate success. See: http://www.spanx.com/corp/index. jsp?page=sarasStory&clickId=sarasstory_aboutsara_text.

Discussion Exercise

1. Pharmaceuticals provide a good example of how the public can benefit from patented inventions both during the patent period and when the patent falls into the public domain. Can you think of another example? What is the benefit to the public during the patent term? How does the public benefit when the patent term has ended?

Chapter 21

Patentability

" ... anything under the sun that is made by man."—Diamond v. Chakrabarty, 447 U.S. 303 (1980)

Chapter Outline

Chapter Objectives

- Know the three types of patents granted by the PTO.
- Become familiar with the four categories of patentable subject matter.
- Understand business method patents and the challenges in balancing issues of patentability.
- Grasp the concept of blocking patents.
- Identify the three judicially carved out areas of excluded subject matter.
- Recognize that laws of nature, natural phenomena and abstract ideas are not patentable but can be incorporated into patentable subject matter.

The quote above, in which Chief Justice Burger famously quoted the legislative history on patentable subject matter, seems to imply that patentable subject matter is limitless. However, this quote is often taken out of context and misconstrued. As we will see in the next several sections, there are limits to what is patentable.

In the last chapter, we saw that patent protection is a unique form of intellectual property, granted only through application to the PTO. Unlike the process for gaining copyright protection in a new novel or trademark protection for corporate branding, the grant of a patent involves a substantive examination of the underlying subject matter of an invention. Indeed, before a patent will be granted, an invention must be evaluated for several criteria including, whether the invention functions as it should, whether it is obvious, and whether it is new compared to that which is in the public domain. In the next few chapters we will discuss these standards of patentability in detail. The first level of evaluation involves a determination of whether the innovation falls within the scope of patentable subject matter. Indeed, not all innovation can be patented. Even when an invention meets the standards of patentability, it must fall into the scope of patentable subject matter. Let's look at the statutory guidelines and judicial precedent that shape the issue of patentable subject matter.

21.1. Types of Patents

There are three types of patents granted by the PTO, *utility patents*, *design patents* and *plant patents*. Utility patents are by far the most common and although the scope of this book will focus mainly on the law governing utility patents, let's take a moment to discuss design and plant patents.

A design patent can be granted for the *new*, *original* and *ornamental* characteristics of a product. Patent protection for designs extends *only* to the configuration or shape of a product, not to the utilitarian or functional features of that product. Design patents are frequently used for industrial designs such as cars and even the shape of a smart phone. The image on the next page shows the design patent for an iPhone®. Only the overall appearance of the iPhone® is protected by the design patent, not the functional elements, such as the "bounce-back effect" or "tap to zoom" technology."

Car designs are often protected by a design patent. The Volkswagen Beetle shown on the next page is protected by a design patent. Because design patents protect only the ornamental features of the car, if the car's design performs a function, such as adding stability at high speeds, the car's functional features would *not* fall under the protection of a design patent.

Figure 21.1

U.S. Patent   May 26, 2009   Sheet 1 of 12   US D593,087 S

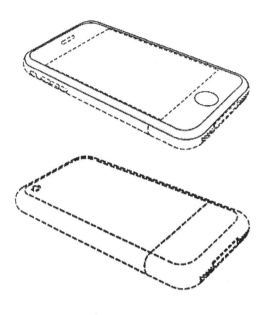

Figure 21.2

U.S. Patent   Jun. 26, 2001   Sheet 3 of 3   US D444,102 S

Functional features can only be covered under a utility patent. It is, however, possible for a product to be patented under a utility patent to protect the functional features *and* a design patent to protect the ornamental designs of a product. Consider the Dyson® vacuum cleaner in the image below. The vacuum's unique appearance is protected by a design patent while the functional features of the vacuum are protected by a utility patent. Using this strategy, an inventor can protect both utilitarian features of a product in addition to the design features. Design patent protection lasts only 14 years from the date of grant while the duration of a utility patent is 20 years from the effective filing date.

Figure 21.3

U.S. Patent   Jan. 22, 2013   Sheet 1 of 7   US D674,977 S

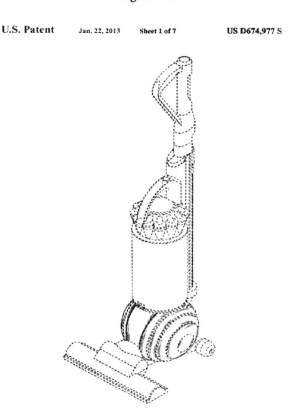

Let's turn to plant patents. A plant patent can be granted for asexually reproduced plant varieties. Asexual reproduction means that a plant is reproduced without the use of genetic seeds. Reproduction is instead accomplished by methods including rooting the cuttings from a plant, grafting, layering or, budding. Asexually reproduced plants can also be protected by utility patents and indeed, in many cases are. For instance, Monsanto®, a multinational corporation that produces, among other things, genetically modified seeds regularly protects its genetically modified plants using utility patents. We will discuss the Monsanto soybean seeds in much more detail in Chapter 25 in the section on *exhaustion*.

Although the standards for obtaining a plant patent are similar to the standards for obtaining a utility patent, these standards are more easily met for plant patents. An important difference between plant patents and utility patents is that a utility patent is not limited to plants that are asexually reproduced, and can be a basis of protection for plants that are reproduced using seeds. Accordingly, utility patents are widely used in protecting genetically modified plants.

21.2. Patentable Subject Matter

The first hurdle an inventor must overcome is the determination of whether the subject matter of the claimed invention falls under the rubric of patentable subject matter. Patent protection is granted only to an invention that falls into one of the four eligible categories of invention found in § 101 the patent statute.

> "Whoever invents or discovers any new and useful process, machine, manufacture, or composition of matter, or a new and useful improvement thereof, may obtain a patent therefor, subject to the conditions and requirements of this title." 35 USC § 101.

The four categories enumerated by Congress are intentionally broad and modified by the term, "any." Accordingly, courts have interpreted the question of patentable subject matter to be broad and limited only by carved out limitations which we will discuss below. As a result, whether a claimed invention falls into the scope of machine, manufacture, process or composition of matter should be read liberally to be inclusive.

Let's discuss each of these categories individually. A *machine* has been defined as a "mechanical device or combination of devices that perform some function or produce a certain effect or result." Machines include items that you are likely familiar with such as a coffee maker, video game system, baseball pitching machine, factory machine, and components of a smart phone. Even tweezers or a safety pin would fall under this category.

An *article of manufacture* has been defined as an article "produced from raw or prepared materials by giving the materials new forms qualities, properties or combinations, whether produced by hand or machine." Thus, anything that is manufactured or produced in this way can be an article of manufacture. A few examples are a tennis racket, golf ball or guitar.

A *composition of matter* has been defined by the Supreme Court as "the composition of two or more substances ... whether they be the result of chemical union, mechanical mixture, or whether they be gases, fluids, powders or solid." Pharmaceuticals are typically patented as compositions of matter, as are formulations for low-VOC paint. Consider a patented paint formula owned by Valspar Paint® that claims a unique formula containing a lower percentage of volatile organic content, making the paint less toxic and more environmentally friendly. This patent can be found on the PTO website, www.uspto.gov, or on Google Scholar; search for U.S. Pat. No. 6,762,230.

The last enumerated category of patentable subject matter is a *process*. A process, or method as it sometimes referred to, has been defined as "an act or a series of acts or steps performed upon the subject matter to be transformed and reduced to a different state or thing." A process patent can embody a method for making something or achieving a certain result. The Amazon.com "one-click" method of purchasing goods on an internet site is an example of a patented process. This process for purchasing goods on the internet allows customers to bypass the need for entering credit card and address information in connection with their purchases. The patented process speeds up customer transactions and has given Amazon a competitive edge in the internet retailing business. This patent can be found on the PTO website, www.uspto.gov or on Google Scholar; search for U.S. Pat. No. 5,960,411.

The category into which a claimed invention falls is inconsequential with regard to the duration of patent protection and a patentee's right to enforce the patent. In fact, it is common for an invention to fall into more than one category. For example, a safety pin may fall into the category of a machine *and* an article of manufacture. After all, it can be used to *perform the function* of fastening two pieces of fabric to one another and is produced or manufactured, making it both a machine *and* an article of manufacture. Similarly, a formulation of low-VOC paint that is produced using a unique method can be patented as a composition of matter or as a process.

21.3. Business Method Patents and Software Patents

Before we move on to the substantive requirements of patentability, let's take a moment to discuss business method patents and software patents. A business method patent claims a new way of doing business and falls under the rubric of process or method patents. For years, it was widely believed that business methods were not patentable. In fact, at one time, the *Manual for Patent Examination Procedures* ("MPEP"), a guide for PTO examiners, specifically identified methods of doing business as an example of subject matter that was *not* patentable. Accordingly, for many years the PTO routinely denied patent protection to applications for business methods. This section of the MPEP has been replaced with language that no longer prohibits business methods from patent protection.

In *State Street Bank and Trust Company v. Signature Financial Group, Inc.*, 149 F.3d 1368 (Fed. Cir. 1998), the United States Court of Appeals for the Federal Circuit ("CAFC") put an end to the longstanding practice of denying patent protection to all business methods. In *State Street Bank*, the claimed invention at issue was a method of mutual fund accounting that uses a *hub and spoke* as a means for accounting funds as they are channeled in and out of mutual funds. Assets are pooled in an investment portfolio, known as the *hub* and then directed among several mutual funds, known as the *spokes*. This method allows funds to flow between several mutual funds in the same family, providing certain tax benefits.

The court held that the hub and spoke accounting method was a patent-eligible business method, reversing the long standing proposition that business methods were not patentable. The immediate result was a flood of patent applications for business methods, and a dramatic increase in the number of these patents that were issued. In fact the pendulum seemed to swing in the opposite direction—some argue, too far—granting business method patents liberally. Since that time, many of these patents have been successfully challenged and found invalid.

Although courts have reviewed the question of patentability of business methods, there has yet to emerge a definitive test for the patentability for business methods. For some time, courts relied on what is known as the *machine or transformation test* which requires that an invention be tied to a particular machine or apparatus, such as a computer, or that it transforms a particular article into a different state before a business method patent can be granted. However, in the recent case *Bilski v. Kappos*, 561 U.S.__ (2010), the Supreme Court held that although the *machine or transformation* test can be useful in determining patentability, it is not the only test in the determination.

Under the AIA, post-grant scrutiny of business method patents will be allowed in certain circumstances. The Transitional Program for Covered Business Method Patents ("TPCBMP"), discussed in greater detail in Chapter 23, allows a person charged with infringing a business method patent to challenge the validity of the patent before the Patent Trials and Appeal Board ("PTAB"). This provision will provide a less expensive alternative to much of the litigation that resulted from the period of liberally granting business method patents following the *State Street Bank* case.

Despite some relative confusion surrounding business methods, it is now clear that business methods fall under the rubric of patentable subject matter. There are many examples of business method patents that have changed traditional business practices in areas such as e-commerce and electronic marketing. For example, *Priceline.com* holds a patent that employs a reverse auction method where several sellers compete for a buyer's bid rather than a traditional auction in which several purchasers compete for a seller's product.

Software patents are also the focus of much controversy. Indeed, there are many who believe software should not be patentable at all. Critics point to the fact that software patents are the focus of a large percentage of law suits, particularly suits initiated by Patent Assertion Entities.

Nevertheless, software is patentable subject matter. The PTO grants patents for software that satisfies the standards of patentability and courts have routinely upheld the patentability of software patents. A patent for software typically covers the methodology or function that the software is intended to serve — not the software code. Software code can be protected under copyright law. Accordingly, most software patents are process patents. Some examples of software patents that have been granted are software directed towards voice recognition, software directed towards automated language translation, and software directed towards associating online information with geographical areas. Software patents can cover a wide range of topics.

As with other areas of patentable subject matter, software patents that are drafted too broadly and do no more than recite an abstract idea directed towards the objective they attempt to solve, will be struck down or eventually invalidated. As we will discuss in the next few sections, abstract ideas cannot be patented. For this reason, software patents must be drafted narrowly focusing on specific methodologies and algorithms rather than merely claiming abstract ideas alone.

21.4. Improvements

A patent may also be awarded for an improvement or a new use of a patented or a non-patented item. An inventor who adds something new or incorporates new technology to prior innovation may receive a patent for the improvement. The key to patentability is that the improvement must provide something *novel*, or *new*. The reality is that most inventions are, at least in part, improvements over existing innovation. Even Thomas Edison, one of the most important U.S. inventors, patented improvements over already existing technologies, including the incandescent lamp.

An interesting situation can arise when a claimed invention is an improvement over patented subject matter. Remember, a patent does not give a patentee the right to practice an invention, just the right to exclude others from practicing the invention. For example, if a second inventor develops and patents an improvement over an existing patented product, the second inventor cannot practice the improvement patent unless the first inventor grants a license or gives permission to practice the original patented invention. Similarly, the inventor of the original invention cannot practice the patented improvement without the permission of the new inventor. This situation involves what are known as *blocking patents.* Let's look at a fictitious example.

Imagine that an inventor has developed and patented the first garden hose. It is made with a threaded fitting on one end designed to attach to an outdoor water spigot and a nozzle on the other end. (Assume for the purposes of this example that the standards of patentability have all been met.) Suppose a second inventor improves on the garden hose by inventing and patenting an oscillating sprinkler that attaches to the end of the patented garden hose. The inventor of the sprinkler has added a novel improvement to the patented hose. Yet, inventor number two, the inventor of the sprinkler, cannot practice his invention in connection with the patented garden hose without gaining permission or a license from the garden hose inventor. Similarly, the garden hose inventor cannot practice the invention of the sprinkler without gaining permission or a license from the inventor of the sprinkler.

Figure 21.4

UNITED STATES PATENT OFFICE.

THOMAS A. EDISON, OF MENLO PARK, NEW JERSEY

ELECTRIC LAMP.

SPECIFICATION forming part of Letters Patent No. 223,898, dated January 27, 1880.

Application filed November 4, 1879.

To all whom it may concern:

Be it known that I, THOMAS ALVA EDISON, of Menlo Park, in the State of New Jersey, United States of America, have invented an Improvement in Electric Lamps, and in the method of manufacturing the same, (Case No. 186,) of which the following is a specification.

The object of this invention is to produce electric lamps giving light by incandescence, which lamps shall have high resistance, so as to allow of the practical subdivision of the electric light.

The invention consists in a light-giving body of carbon wire or sheets coiled or arranged in such a manner as to offer great resistance to the passage of the electric current, and at the same time present but a slight surface from which radiation can take place.

The invention further consists in placing such burner of great resistance in a nearly-perfect vacuum, to prevent oxidation and injury to the conductor by the atmosphere. The current is conducted into the vacuum-bulb through platina wires sealed into the glass.

The invention further consists in the method of manufacturing carbon conductors of high resistance, so as to be suitable for giving light by incandescence, and in the manner of securing perfect contact between the metallic conductors or leading-wires and the carbon conductor.

Heretofore light by incandescence has been obtained from rods of carbon of one to four ohms resistance, placed in closed vessels, in which the atmospheric air has been replaced by gases that do not combine chemically with the carbon. The vessel holding the burner has been composed of glass cemented to a metallic base. The connection between the leading wires and the carbon has been obtained by clamping the carbon to the metal. These leading-wires have always been large, so that their resistance shall be many times less than the burner, and, in general, the attempts of previous persons have been to reduce the resistance of the carbon rod. The disadvantages of following this practice are, that a lamp having but one to four ohms resistance cannot be worked in great numbers in multiple arc without the employment of main conductors of enormous dimensions; that, owing to the low resistance of the lamp, the leading-wires must be of large

dimensions and good conductors, and a glass globe cannot be kept tight at the place where the wires pass in and are cemented; hence the carbon is consumed, because there must be almost a perfect vacuum to render the carbon stable, especially when such carbon is small in mass and high in electrical resistance.

The use of a gas in the receiver at the atmospheric pressure, although not attacking the carbon, serves to destroy it in time by "air-washing," or the attrition produced by the rapid passage of the air over the slightly-coherent highly-heated surface of the carbon. I have reversed this practice. I have discovered that even a cotton thread properly carbonized and placed in a sealed glass bulb exhausted to one-millionth of an atmosphere offers from one hundred to five hundred ohms resistance to the passage of the current, and that it is absolutely stable at very high temperatures; that if the thread be coiled as a spiral and carbonized, or if any fibrous vegetable substance which will leave a carbon residue after heating in a closed chamber be so coiled, as much as two thousand ohms resistance may be obtained without presenting a radiating-surface greater than three-sixteenths of an inch; that if such fibrous material be rubbed with a plastic composed of lamp-black and tar, its resistance may be made high or low, according to the amount of lamp-black placed upon it; that carbon filaments may be made by a combination of tar and lamp-black, the latter being previously ignited in a closed crucible for several hours and afterward moistened and kneaded until it assumes the consistency of thick putty. Small pieces of this material may be rolled out in the form of wire as small as seven one-thousandths of an inch in diameter and over a foot in length, and the same may be covered with a non-conducting non-carbonizing substance and wound on a bobbin, or as a spiral, and the tar carbonized in a closed chamber by subjecting it to high heat, the spiral after carbonization retaining its form.

All these forms are fragile and cannot be clamped to the leading wires with sufficient force to insure good contact and prevent heating. I have discovered that if platinum wires are used and the plastic lamp-black and tar material be molded around it in the act of carbonization there is an intimate union by com-

21.5. Excluded Subject Matter

Although § 101 defining patentable subject matter should be viewed expansively, there are certain limitations that have been judicially carved out. Specifically, there are three categories of subject matter that are outside the scope of patentability: 1) laws of nature, 2) abstract ideas, and 3) physical phenomena. Indeed, the Supreme Court in *Bilski v. Kappos* stated that these three classes of subject matter are "part of the storehouse of knowledge of all men ... free to all men and reserved exclusively to none."

Accordingly, these three categories, sometimes referred to collectively as *natural phenomena,* are viewed as the building blocks of technology and must be kept in the public domain for future inventors to build upon. Keep in mind, the policy goal of patent law as defined in the Constitution is to promote the progress of science and useful arts. Allowing patentees the right to exclude others from natural phenomena can impede progress rather than promote it. Although patent protection does not extend to natural phenomena alone, an invention can — and almost always does — incorporate some natural phenomena and can still be patent eligible. The invention must be considered as a whole.

Nevertheless, it can be difficult to identify the point at which an invention properly incorporates natural phenomena, keeping it in the realm of patent ability and situations in which a claimed invention does no more than claim an element of natural phenomena, making it ineligible for patent protection. This was the case in three very important Supreme Court cases: *Bilski, supra; Mayo Clinic v. Prometheus,* 566 U.S. ___ (2012); and *Association of Molecular Pathology v. Myriad Genetics, Inc.,* 569 U.S. ___ (2013). We'll discuss these cases in detail as we examine each category of natural phenomena in depth.

21.6. Laws of Nature

Laws of nature include things like gravity and Einstein's theory of relativity. Despite the tremendous effort and skill required in discovering such phenomena, even the first person to ascertain, understand or articulate the principles of the laws of nature cannot patent the subject matter. Remember, a patent allows an inventor the right to exclude others. Can you imagine if Einstein had been able to patent the theory of relativity or Sir Isaac Newton, the law of gravity? Dropping your pencil could be an infringement!

The initial discovery of the laws of nature almost always requires a high level of expertise and a tremendous amount of talent and effort. Nevertheless, laws of nature may never be patented. This was the situation in the recent case *Mayo Clinic v. Prometheus*. In a unanimous Supreme Court decision, it was held that a process for administering a certain drug was not patentable because it amounted to no more than the application of a law of nature. The patented process claims a method for administering medication to patients. Too much of the medication would be harmful while too little of the medication would be ineffective. Thus, the amount of medication administered needed to be tailored to each patient based on the patient's ability to metabolize the drugs.

The patented process instructed doctors to administer the medications, determine the level of metabolites that resulted in the patient's blood, then adjust the dosage of the medication based on the results. The Court held that the claimed invention was nothing more than the application of a law of nature specifically, the relationship between the patient's ability to metabolize the drug and the appropriate dosage of the drug. In other words, it was the manner in which a patient's blood reacted to the medication, nothing more. Despite the effort and expertise involved in identifying the proper dosage of medication based on each patient's rate of metabolizing the medication, the Court compared the claimed invention to Einstein's discovery of the theory of relativity and Newton's discovery of gravity, holding that it was outside the scope of patentable subject matter.

21.7. Abstract Ideas

Abstract ideas are similarly outside the scope of patentable subject matter. In *Bilski v. Kappos, supra*, the Supreme Court focused on this very topic. At issue was a claimed business method for a procedure that instructed buyers and sellers how to hedge against price fluctuations in various sectors of the economy. When the Court looked at the claimed invention, it held that the claim was nothing more than a method of hedging risk in the field of commodities trading—an abstract idea. Allowing petitioners to patent risk-hedging would preempt use of this approach in all fields and effectively grant a monopoly over an abstract idea. From a policy point of view, granting patent protection for the concept of hedging could have far-reaching implications. Because patent law allows a patentee to exclude others from practicing an invention, traders and brokers who have long practiced the procedure of hedging trades would be precluded from business as usual.

Likewise, in the1853 case *O'Reilly v. Morse*, 56 U.S. 62 (1853), the Court held that the patentee, Morse, had claimed no more than an abstract idea.

Morse claimed the use of "electromagnetism, *however developed*, for marking or printing intelligible characters, signs, letters at any distance...." Can you guess why this claim was held as an unpatentable abstract idea? The Court held that Morse hadn't stated a method for accomplishing the objective set out in the patent claim. Instead, the patent application merely claimed an abstract idea.

21.8. Physical Phenomena

Physical phenomena, sometimes referred to as products of nature, have also been identified as being outside the scope of patentable subject matter. A new mineral or new plant found in the wild is simply a product of nature, not patentable subject matter. Indeed, there is nothing inventive or new in identifying subject matter that exists in its natural state. Similarly, there are instances in which a process for extracting something found in nature is found to be inventive and accordingly, quite possibly patentable subject matter. For instance, natural gas is not patentable because it is a naturally occurring substance. However, a novel and nonobvious method of obtaining natural gas from the earth may be patentable. Similarly, carrot juice is not patentable, but a novel and nonobvious method of extracting a higher yield of juice per unit weight of carrots may be patentable. Natural phenomena itself is not patentable, but a claimed invention that incorporates natural phenomena may be patentable. In fact, many patented pharmaceuticals incorporate components that are naturally occurring substances and not patentable on their own.

In *Association for Molecular Pathology v. Myriad Genetics, Inc., supra,* the Supreme Court struck down a patent on isolated genetic material because the patent claimed nothing more than a product of nature. We will discuss this case in more detail in Chapter 27.

Chapter Summary

The Patent Office issues three types of patents: utility patents, design patents, and plant patents. Utility patents are the most common and will be our focus in the next several chapters. Design patents can be granted for new and ornamental designs while plant patents are awarded for plants that are asexually reproduced.

To obtain patent protection, a claimed invention must fall into one of the four categories of patentable subject matter: a *machine or device*, an *article of manufacture*, a *composition of matter*, or a *process or method*. These categories are broad and should be read to be inclusive. *Business method patents* are process patents and were, for a time, thought to be outside the scope of patentable subject matter. This practice was eventually changed in *State Street Bank and Trust Company v. Signature Financial Group, Inc.*, *supra*, resulting in the liberal granting of business method patents. Patents are also available for new uses or *improvements* over existing patented or non-patented items. An improvement must add something inventive in order to be patent eligible.

Despite the broad categories of patentable subject matter, patent protection does not extend to three judicially carved out areas of subject matter: laws of nature, abstract ideas and physical phenomena. These three categories of subject matter must remain in the public domain as they are the building blocks of all innovation. These three categories of subject matter are not patentable on their own but may be, and almost always are, incorporated into patentable technology.

Key Terms

Utility Patent
Design Patent
Plant Patent
Machine or Device
Article of Manufacture
Composition of Matter
Process or Method
Business Method Patent
Manual for Patent Examination Procedures
Improvements
Laws of Nature
Abstract Ideas
Physical Phenomena

Review Questions

1. List one example of each: a machine, an article of manufacture, a composition of matter, and a process.
2. Which elements can be protected under a design patent?

3. Can an invention fall into more than one category of patentable subject matter?
4. Explain the significance of the *State Street Bank* case?
5. What is the key for gaining an improvement patent?
6. Explain the concept of *blocking patents*.
7. List the three judicially carved out areas of subject matter known as natural phenomena.
8. Why is natural phenomena unpatentable?
9. Why was the claimed invention in the *Bilski* case held to be outside the scope of patentable subject matter?
10. Do you agree with the Court's ruling in *Mayo Clinic v. Prometheus*?

Web Links

1. Browse and search many familiar items that are protected by a design patent. See: http://search.designpatents.us/.
2. The PTO provides a guide to filing an application for a design patent. See: http://www.uspto.gov/web/offices/com/iip/pdf/brochure_05.pdf.

Discussion Exercise

1. A patented invention can fall into more than one category of patentable subject matter. Can you identify an item that might fall into more than one category? Such as a composition of matter and an article of manufacture? An article of manufacture and a machine or device? A composition of matter and a process?

Chapter 22

Standards for Obtaining a Patent

"The good patent gives the world something it did not truly have before, whereas the bad patent has the effect of trying to take away from the world something which it effectively already had."
—Giles Sutherland Rich, United States Court of Appeals for the Federal Circuit

Chapter Outline

Chapter Objectives

- Understand the procedure of patent prosecution.
- Recognize the requirements for patentability.
- Appreciate that novelty requires an invention to be new compared to the prior art.
- Identify the sources of prior art that can defeat patentability.
- Learn what makes prior art relevant to the question of novelty.
- Distinguish between the critical time at which prior art can defeat novelty under the 1952 Act and the AIA.

- Understand that inventors must file for protection in a timely manner.
- Distinguish between the concept of novelty and nonobviousness.
- Understand the four-part test for nonobviousness.
- Identify the secondary considerations courts consider in making a determination of obviousness.
- Understand that the utility standard requires that an invention is useful and that it must function in the manner intended.
- Appreciate that the utility requirement does not bar inventive products that apparently promote deception.
- Recognize that a patent application must be drafted with definiteness so that it enables a person having ordinary skill in the art to practice the invention.
- Know that an inventor must disclose the best mode for practicing an invention in a patent application.

Once it has been established that a claimed invention falls within the ambit of patentable subject matter, it must then be determined whether the substantive requirements of patentability have been met. When it is submitted to the PTO, a patent application will be evaluated with regard to each requirement. This process is called *patent prosecution*. Each element of patentability must be met in order for a patent to be granted. Failure to meet even one of the necessary standards of patentability will prevent a patent from issuing. Specifically, a claimed invention must be *novel, nonobvious,* and have *utility*. Once these standards have been met, an inventor must still meet the requirement of *adequate disclosure* and **enablement**. We will discuss each of these standards in detail.

Under the AIA, there have been many changes to some of the substantive requirements for patentability. It's important to have an understanding of both statutory schemes because patents granted before the implementation of the AIA will be subject to the former rules while patents granted after March 16, 2013 (the implementation of the first-to-file provision of the AIA) will be subject to the new rules. Consequently, the former rules will be relevant for a little less than 20 years from the implementation of the AIA.

22.1. Novelty

A central concept to patentability is *novelty*. An invention that is not novel or *new* compared to the *prior art* is not patentable. After all, the Constitutional language gives Congress the power to "promote the *progress* of science and useful arts." Section 102 of the patent statute which provides the basis for novelty has undergone several changes under the AIA. Despite these changes, the most fundamental concepts of novelty remain the same. Novelty is a critical point evaluated during prosecution and can also be raised as a basis for invalidity as a defense to an accusation of infringement. In other words, a defendant in a patent suit may challenge a patent's novelty alleging that the claimed invention was not novel at the time of prosecution and is accordingly invalid. We'll discuss this strategy in more detail in Chapter 25 on defenses.

As we will see, there is more than one layer to the novelty inquiry. As an initial matter, novelty asks whether a claimed invention is *new* compared to what already exists in the prior art. To answer this question, there are several inquires: What are the sources of prior art? What prior art is relevant? And prior to what point in time? Additionally, novelty requires that an inventor has submitted an application to the PTO in a timely fashion. In the following sections, we will examine these concepts and inquiries one-by-one.

22.2. Sources of Prior Art

Prior art can come in many forms: a previously patented invention, printed publications that teach the invention, public use of the invention, and many other activities taking place in the public domain. Keep in mind an important principle of patent law is that a balance must be struck between rewarding innovation through patent protection while keeping subject matter in the public domain free for all to practice.

Before we continue to discuss the various sources of prior art, there is an important change under the AIA regarding the geographical origin of prior art. The 1952 Patent Act made a distinction between prior art that originated from within the United States and that originating outside United States. Under the AIA, this distinction has been eliminated and prior art will be considered from anywhere in the world regardless of geography. Do you see why this an appropriate change? In 1952, when the last patent act was enacted, the world was a very different place. People did not have the same kind of access to activities taking place all over the globe that we have now and it made sense to make a distinction between activities that occurred inside and outside the U.S.

Let's look at the sources of prior art that will defeat novelty under the former rules and under the new rules. Under the 1952 Act, if a claimed invention was *known or used by others* in the United States or if it was *patented or published* by another person anywhere in the world before the date of invention, it would be deemed prior art and defeat novelty. This part of the statute focused on activities of third parties, not activities of the inventor. Under the AIA if the claimed invention was *patented, published, in public use, on sale or otherwise available* to the public by anyone before the **effective filing date**, this activity will be deemed prior art and will defeat novelty making the claimed invention unpatentable.

A key factor in determining whether prior art will defeat novelty is that it must be *publically available.* Certainly, written materials available through libraries or the patent office, as well as printed and electronic publications are regarded as publically available. But, what about more limited publications? In *Massachusetts Institute of Technology v. AB Fortia*, 774 F.2d 1104 (Fed. Cir. 1985), the question was whether an oral presentation made to an audience of less than 500 people was public for the purposes of novelty. Here, the meeting was open to anyone interested in the field and written copies of the presentation were made available to the audience without any restrictions on the use of the printed materials. Under these facts, the presentation and materials were deemed publicly available and accordingly, prior art.

On the other hand, when documents are distributed with the understanding that the contents will remain confidential, the material will not be considered publically available regardless of the number of copies distributed. In *Northern Telecom, Inc. v. Datapoint, Corp.*, 908 F.2d 931 (Fed. Cir. 1990), reports that were distributed to employees and retained in a restricted access corporate library were not deemed publically available for the purposes of a novelty inquiry. In this case, there was a corporate policy in place to keep documents of this type confidential. The court reasoned that although many employees had access to the documents, the public did not and accordingly, the documents were not deemed prior art.

22.3. Which Prior Art Is Relevant?

Often, the phrase *relevant prior art* is used in connection with the prosecution of a patent application. Not all prior art will be relevant to the question of novelty. In order to defeat patentability, prior art must include each and every *element* of a claimed invention. For the purposes of our discussion on novelty and prior art, it's important to understand that a patented invention is made up of *claims*. (In chapter 23 we will discuss the claims of an invention in greater depth.) Each claim is made up of *elements* or *limitations*. Think of elements and limitations as the details that make up a claim. In order for prior art to defeat the patentability of a claim, it must contain all of the elements, or details, in the claim. This is known as the *all elements* rule or the *mirror image rule.* Prior art that contains all the elements of a claimed invention will defeat novelty and render the claimed invention unpatentable. This is sometimes referred to as being *anticipated by the prior art.*

Moreover, for prior art to defeat novelty, it must be *enabling.* For example, when prior art is a published article that describes an invention, it must do so in a way that enables a *person who is skilled in the art* to actually practice the invention based on the writing. The prior art must clearly describe the innovation sufficiently enough to teach the invention or it may not defeat novelty.

Even a drawing of a claimed invention can be enabling and defeat novelty. Where all the features of the invention are included in a drawing in such a way that teaches the invention, the drawing may be regarded as prior art that defeats novelty. As Judge Learned Hand acknowledged in *Jockmus v. Leviton,* 28 F.2d 812 (2d Cir. 1928): "Words have their equivocations quite as much as figures; the question always must be what the art necessarily gathered from what appeared." In this case, because a figure of a type of candle socket found in a catalog clearly depicted the elements of the simple invention and was accompanied by a brief description of the invention, the figure was enabling and deemed prior art defeating novelty.

22.4. Prior to What?

At what point does prior art defeat novelty? Under the 1952 Act, the *critical date* for determining relevant prior art is date of *invention.* Thus, prior art in existence before the date of invention defeats novelty. This standard begs the question: what is the date of invention? The process of inventing can take many steps; from an inventor's conception of the initial idea to experimenting, building prototypes, and finally having the invention function as it should. Thus, determining the date of invention can be a complicated question.

The date upon which an idea was *reduced to practice* is said to be the date of invention. Reduction to practice is typically the date on which the invention worked for its particular purpose. Because the process of inventing is not something that always happens instantaneously, inventors must rely on documentation to prove the date on which an invention was reduced to practice. Inventors are encouraged to keep detailed notes on their progress and even date and witness their work. As you can imagine, the documentation of such a complex process can be an arduous task.

In contrast, under the AIA, prior art will be considered from the *effective filing date.* Any relevant prior art in existence before the filing date, or *critical date*, will defeat novelty. This is a significant change from the standard under the 1952 Act and creates a more objective standard by which to judge novelty

There is an important caveat to note. As stated previously, the issue of novelty comes up in two distinct situations: during patent prosecution and when patent invalidity based on a lack of novelty is raised as a defense to infringement. When it comes to filing patent applications, novelty will be judged under the standard found in the AIA and prior art will be looked at from the effective date of filing. On the other hand, when a defendant asserts a lack of novelty as a defense, the standard which governs whether prior art will defeat novelty depends on when the patent application was filed. Patents filed before March 16, 2013 will be judged using the standards found in the 1952 Act and prior art will be examined from the date of invention. After all, this is the standard that was used to determine patentability. For patents filed after the implementation of the AIA, novelty will be judged using the standard found in the AIA and prior art will be examined from the effective filing date.

22.5. A Timely Application

Another important component of novelty requires that inventors file a patent application with the PTO in a timely manner from the point at which the invention is made known to the public. The main issue here is that patent law favors the disclosure of innovation and technology. Indeed, disclosure is a fundamental driving principle behind patent law. Inventors are encouraged to disclose the innovation behind their inventions by applying for patent protection as soon as possible once the invention has been reduced to practice. Timely disclosure is important for yet another reason. An inventor who exploits an invention for several years before applying for a patent and then finally applies for patent protection can ultimately enjoy a monopoly lasting longer than the 20 year duration of patent protection, thus expanding the duration of patent protection. Let's take a look at the specific rules in this area.

The 1952 Act included a complicated system of *statutory bars* that focused on activities taking place within one year before the *date of application*. The AIA has eliminated the statutory bars and instead provides a one year grace period before the effective filing date allowing for certain activities. Although the language of the statutory bars in the 1952 Act and the one year grace period of the AIA are worded differently, the objective is still the same. The law allows inventors one year to engage in some public activities before their activity will defeat novelty. This layer of novelty tries to strike a balance by allowing inventors to start marketing their inventions or engaging in a preliminary negotiation, but also encourages timely application. The law recognizes that these activities may be a necessary part of determining a potential market for the invention and can be part of a business decision on whether to move forward with the expensive process of filing for a patent. If, however, these activities extend for a period exceeding a year before the date of application, the activity will defeat novelty and a patent will not be granted.

22.6. Nonobviousness

Another substantive requirement of patentability is that a claimed invention must be *nonobvious*. The inquiry of whether a claimed invention is nonobvious is a different inquiry than the inquiry focusing on novelty. Even if a claimed invention satisfies the question of novelty, it may still be unpatentable if the invention is deemed obvious under the standards set forth in § 103 of the statute. As you recall, the question of novelty asks whether the invention is *new* compared to the existing prior art. Compare this to the question of obviousness which asks whether the elements, as they were put together in the claimed invention, would have been *obvious* in light of the existing prior art to a *person having ordinary skill in the art*—sometimes referred to as *PHOSITA*. In other words: Would PHOSITA have combined the elements of the invention in the same manner given the prior art? There are several elements to this question that we will examine in detail.

To paraphrase the statutory standard found in § 103 under the AIA: Even assuming that the claimed invention is novel, a patent may not be obtained if the differences between the claimed invention and the prior art are such that the claimed invention would have been obvious to a person having ordinary skill in the relevant prior art as it existed *at the time of filing*. Notice that the statute as it reads under the AIA measures obviousness from the *effective date of filing* while the standard under the 1952 Act measures obviousness from the time of *invention*. Accordingly, new patent applications will be judged on the issue of nonobviousness under the standards found in the AIA while claims of invalidity based on nonobviousness will be judged using the relevant statute according to whether the patent was filed before or after the implementation of the AIA. Like the issue of novelty, the question of obviousness arises first at the time of application and can subsequently be raised by a defendant as a basis for patent invalidity. Because anything that would have precluded a patent from issuing can invalidate a patent, defendants often raise invalidity based on obviousness. In either situation, the substantive analysis of whether an invention was obvious is the same. Keep this in mind as we go through the analysis below.

The framework for determining obviousness is detailed in a Supreme Court case called *Graham v. John Deere Co.*, 383 U.S. 1 (1966). The inquiry involves a four part analysis that looks at: (1) the relevant prior art, (2) the differences between the claimed invention and the prior art, (3) the level of skill of a *person having ordinary skill in the prior art* or PHOSITA, and, (4) whether the claimed invention, as a whole, would have been obvious to a PHOSITA. Let's look at each of the elements of the analysis in detail.

The first part of the inquiry requires an analysis of the relevant prior art. Here, as with the inquiry of novelty, the prior art can include previously patented work, printed publications and other public references. The second part of the obviousness inquiry requires an examination of the differences between the prior art and the claimed invention. Here, the claimed invention must be looked at as a whole as compared to the prior art. In this regard, when a claimed invention combines several already existing elements, although each reference of prior art will be viewed separately, each must be compared to the claimed invention as a whole. Next, the analysis requires a determination of the level of skill of a PHOSITA. A PHOSITA is a fictitious person who has the knowledge and skill level of the ordinary person who is skilled in the relevant art at the time of the invention. For example, if the claimed invention involves pharmaceuticals, a PHOSITA might be an ordinarily skilled biochemist. A PHOSITA is also assumed to have knowledge of *all* the prior art and be a person of ordinary creativity. The last question is whether the claimed invention would have been obvious to a PHOSITA in light of the prior art.

Let's consider the facts in the *Graham v. John Deere* case. The claimed invention was a device designed to absorb the shock from a plow shank as it is plowed through rocky terrain. Typically, a plow would be damaged or break when it hit an obstacle such as a large rock. The patented device combined several already existing mechanical elements including a spring clamp that allowed the plow shank to be pushed upward when the plow hit a large obstacle. The spring clamp then allowed the shank to fall back into normal position once the rock was passed over. The controversy in the case focused essentially on the hinge, spring and shank combination and whether the combination of these elements was an obvious extension of the prior art.

Using the four part test as detailed above the Court analyzed whether the claimed device was obvious. Looking at the first part of the inquiry, the Court found that the prior art did not disclose the same arrangement of elements as the claimed invention. The differences between the prior art and the claimed invention was in the placement of the hinge relative to the plow shank making the shank *free-flexing*. This difference, the Court reasoned, would have been an obvious extension over the prior art because any other placement of the spring would have been ineffective. The Court concluded that a person having ordinary skill in the art would have immediately seen that the solution would be to combine the elements in the same way the claimed invention combined the elements making the claimed invention obvious and as follows, invalid.

The final question of an obviousness analysis requires a legal conclusion of whether, given the analysis of the first three parts of the inquiry, the claimed invention would have been obvious. While the first three inquiries of the analysis are objective, the last inquiry is a question of law and not always an easy one to answer. To make this final determination of whether the claimed invention is obvious, the PTO and courts can look to several *secondary considerations* that may tend to show that an invention was obvious or that it was nonobvious. Here, evidence of *commercial success* is a factor that may tend to prove that the invention was nonobvious. Similarly, *a long felt need in the industry* that is addressed and solved by the claimed invention can tend to show that the invention is nonobvious. Evidence of *previous failures* to address the relevant need in the industry also tend to show that invention is nonobvious. The *commercial acquiescence* of competitors, such as requests to license the technology, can also tend to show that a claimed invention is nonobvious. Do you see why these secondary considerations tend to make a claimed invention more or less likely to be obvious? If the claimed invention had been obvious, it is likely that those in the industry would have conceived of the invention prior to the claimed invention.

Similarly, when an invention produces an *unexpected result*, it is more likely that it is nonobvious. Let's look at an example.

Figure 22.1

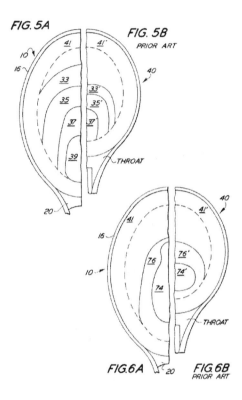

U.S. Patent   Dec. 28, 1976   Sheet 2 of 4   3,999,756

Shown above is the patent for a tennis racket that was designed to be larger than conventional tennis rackets at the time. Generally, the larger version of a patented item is an unpatentable modification. However, in this case, the oversized racket exhibited an unexpected result. The center of percussion, or the "sweet spot" as it more commonly known, in this larger racket is disproportionately larger than the increase in the size of the racket. This unexpected result confirmed that the larger racket was not just an obvious improvement over a conventional racket, but an inventive improvement over a conventional racket.

The factors set forth in the *Graham* case have long provided a guideline for the obviousness inquiry and were recently revisited by the Supreme Court in *KSR International, Co. v. Teleflex, Inc.*, 550 U.S 398 (2007). Since *KSR v. Teleflex*, the Graham factors continue to control the test for obviousness, but a few more guidelines have been articulated. The issue in *KSR v. Teleflex* was whether a claimed invention that combines several already existing elements resulted in something obvious. As you recall, a claimed invention must be viewed as a whole when compared to the prior art. In this regard, the *KSR* Court affirmed the proposition that when a new invention "simply arranges old elements with each performing the same function it had been known to perform and yields no more than one would expect from such an arrangement, the combination is obvious."

Moreover, for some time, courts had been relying on what is known as the *teaching, suggestion, motivation* test to answer the final part of the inquiry of whether a claimed invention was obvious. This test prescribed that when the prior art taught, suggested or motivated a person who was skilled in the relevant art to combine the elements found in the prior art, the resulting invention was likely obvious. In *KSR v. Teleflex*, the Court held that the teaching, suggestion, motivation test taken alone, reflected a narrow conception of obviousness, but could still provide helpful insight into the question of obviousness and should not function as the only test available.

In the case of *Crocs, Inc. v. U.S. International Trade Commission*, 598 F.3d 1294 (Fed. Cir. 2010), at issue was a footwear assembly in which a molded foam base forms the top of the shoe and includes a strap also made of foam that is attached to the foam base so that the strap supports the wearer's Achilles. The question in this case was whether the prior art had combined the elements in a similar way, making the Crocs assembly obvious. Although the prior art had combined a strap and base, the prior art actually taught against using foam for the strap. Indeed, the prior art taught that the foam strap would stretch and deform, likely sliding down the wearer's Achilles. In the Crocs, however, the combined elements did not yield predictable results. Because both the base of the shoe *and* the strap are constructed of foam there is friction between the two pieces that allows the strap to stay in place rather than constantly sliding down the wearer's Achilles, making the resulting combination nonobvious and patentable.

Figure 22.2

U.S. Patent   Feb. 7, 2006   Sheet 1 of 12   US 6,993,858 B2

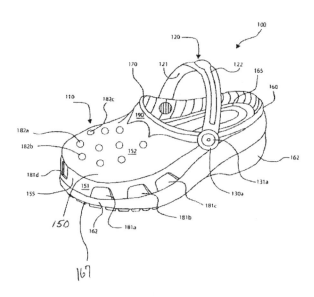

As you may imagine, *hindsight bias* can be a pitfall in determining whether an invention is obvious. After-the-fact, many new inventions can seem obvious. As we will discuss shortly, a patent application must be drafted with *definiteness* and be *enabling*— it must be drafted to teach the invention. This contributes to hindsight bias. Yet, as previously discussed, obviousness must be measured as of the critical point designated in the patent statute: at the time of invention for patents granted under the 1952 Act and at the effective date of filing for all patents after the implementation of the AIA.

22.7. Utility

In addition to being novel and nonobvious, a claimed invention must have *utility*. Section 101 of the statute defining patentable subject matter limits patentability for "new and *useful*" inventions. By virtue of the motivation of most inventors, the utility standard is typically an easy goal to meet. As the old adage goes: "Necessity is the mother of invention." Accordingly, most inventions result from some kind of need and therefore, necessarily meet the utility requirement.

If, however, the claimed invention does not have a stated use, the application may be denied based on a lack of utility. This was the case in *Brenner v. Manson*, 383 U.S. 519 (1966). Manson, chemist, discovered a process to produce a steroid that was similar to another steroid which had been proven to have tumor-inhibiting properties. The steroid produced by Manson's process had not yet been proven to have the same tumor-inhibiting effects. It was merely Manson's presumption that the claimed compound may prove to have the same properties as the adjacent steroid. The Court denied the patent stating that the utility requirement had not been met.

This case illustrates an important point. Because it is possible that Manson's produced steroid may have, under some circumstances, had tumor inhibiting qualities, it could prove to be a useful component in the research of tumor inhibition. Allowing Manson to hold a patent and essentially, a monopoly on the claimed compound, would have allowed him to exclude others from practicing the invention thus, keeping other scientists from using a potentially beneficial steroid. Such an outcome could impede progress by keeping the process for producing the steroid out of the hands of other scientists.

In addition to being *useful* in the sense of having a purpose, utility requires that an invention is useful in the sense that it functions as it should or accomplishes its stated goal. If a claimed invention is found to be inoperative or incapable of achieving the result claimed by the applicant, it will be rejected based on a lack of utility. The PTO Manual of Patent Examining Procedures ("MPEP") provides some colorful examples of inventions that lacked utility in this sense: an invention that allegedly changed the taste of food by using a magnetic field; a perpetual motion machine; a flying machine utilizing a "flapping or flutter function"; and a method for controlling the aging process were all deemed to lack utility based on the fact that the claimed invention was inoperative and therefore lacking utility.

Nevertheless, the utility standard will not act as a bar for inventions that are seen as deceptive. In *Juicy Whip, Inc. v. Orange Bang, Inc.*, 185 F.3d 1364 (Fed. Cir. 1999), the CAFC found that although a patented invention essentially aimed to deceive customers purchasing fountain beverages, the invention did not lack utility. The patent claimed a drink fountain machine that appeared as if the tank was full and circulating juice. At the time the juice was dispensed, however, the beverage was immediately mixed rather than dispensing the same liquid that appeared to be circulating in the tank. The patentee, Juicy Whip, brought an infringement action against Orange Bang. In its defense, Orange Bang argued that the tanks lacked utility because the purpose of the patented invention was to deceive consumers. The Court cited several examples of patented products that deceive customers including, laminated floors intended to simulate wood and a method for producing imitation grill marks on food without using heat holding that the utility standard does not require the PTO to evaluate whether a patent promotes deceptive trade practices.

22.8. Definiteness, Enablement and Best Mode

In addition to the substantive requirements of novelty, utility and nonobviousness, a patent application must meet the statutory requirement that it describe the invention using " ... full, clear, concise, and exact terms as to enable any person skilled in the art ... to make and use the same, and shall set forth the *best mode* contemplated by the inventor...." Remember, a key element of patent law is that when the duration of patent protection concludes, the invention will fall into the public domain and become free for anyone to practice. The patent application becomes the written record of the invention and accordingly, it's important that the document is drafted so that the public can learn from the patent itself. The quid pro quo between the government and the inventor is that the inventor promises to disclose the technology behind the invention in exchange for a limited monopoly in the patented subject matter. When a patent is described with *definiteness*, it can teach the invention to the public and thus satisfy the policy goals of patent law. Moreover, the description of the invention must be sufficient to the point that it *enables* a person skilled in the relevant art to practice the invention. A patent is said to be enabling when a person who is skilled in the relevant art can practice the invention without *undue experimentation* just by reading the patent. This means that an electrical engineer should be able to practice an invention directed to a unique system of electrical circuitry just by reading the patent. The statute further requires that an inventor disclose the best mode, or best way, of practicing the invention. We will discuss each of these standards in greater detail as they relate to the application for a patent in Chapter 23.

During the examination process, if claims are found to be indefinite, too vague or fail to enable, an examiner will reject the claims. Similarly, a defendant accused of infringement may assert that the patent lacks definiteness as part of a defense, claiming invalidity. The policy here is that an indefinite claim does not provide adequate notice of the boundaries of the claims and, by implication, what activity remains in the public domain. This is critical information for future inventors and encourages innovation.

The inquiry of definiteness is fact specific. Different areas of technology necessitate the use of varying levels of precision in the language of a claim. Claim language will be regarded as definite when "those skilled in the art" can understand what is claimed simply by reading the claims together with the written description of the invention. The MPEP outlines several guidelines for determining when language will be deemed indefinite. For instance, the use of subjective terms to describe the features of a claimed invention may be held indefinite. Consider the use of the phrase *aesthetically pleasing look and feel*. In *Datamize, LLC v. Plumtree Software, Inc.*, 417 F.3d 1342 (2005), this phrase as used to describe a claimed computer screen was found indefinite where the written description provided no guidance regarding the parameters of what would render the appearance *aesthetically pleasing*. The court found the phrase to be subjective. After all, what is aesthetically pleasing to one person may not be pleasing to another making the phrase lack the necessary level of definiteness. Similarly, when patent language referenced the phrase "similar apparatus" in describing a type of nozzle, the claims were held to be indefinite because it was not clear what was referenced by the term "similar."

Chapter Summary

There are several substantive requirements for patentability that must be met before a patent will be issued. A patent application is submitted to the PTO for prosecution in order to determine whether the substantive requirements have been met.

The first substantive requirement that must be met is novelty. A claimed invention must be new compared to what is in the public domain. In order to evaluate whether a claimed invention is new there are several inquiries: What are the sources of prior art? At what point in time will prior art have an effect on novelty? Has the inventor filed a patent application within one year of certain public activities?

The sources of prior art can include previously patented inventions, printed publications, and public uses of the invention. Prior to the passage of the AIA, there was a distinction between prior art that originated in the U.S. and prior art that originated outside the U.S. This distinction has been eliminated under the AIA and prior art can be considered regardless of its geographic origin. In order for prior art to be relevant and defeat novelty, it must contain all the elements of a claim and must be enabling. Prior art is enabling when it teaches the claimed invention. Prior is measured from the time of invention for all patent applications filed under the 1952 Act. Under the AIA prior art is measured from the time the effective date of filing.

In addition to being novel a claimed invention must be nonobvious. The test for nonobviousness asks whether the invention is an obvious extension of what exists in the prior art. Here, the test requires an evaluation of the prior art, the differences between the prior art and the claimed invention and whether, given the prior art, a person having ordinary sill in the art would have found the invention obvious. The ultimate question of obviousness is a subjective one and often difficult to answer. Courts look to secondary factors to determine whether the invention was, in fact, obvious.

A claimed invention must also have utility, meaning that it must be useful. To satisfy the question of utility, a claimed invention must have a stated use and must be capable of accomplishing what it sets out to do. Utility does not require the PTO to evaluate the deceptive nature of an invention.

Finally, a claimed invention must be described with definiteness and must enable a person having ordinary skill in the art to practice the invention. An inventor must also disclose the best mode known for practicing the invention.

Key Terms

Novelty
Prior Art
Relevant Prior Art
Anticipated
Reduced to Practice
Effective Filing Date
Critical Date
Nonobvious
PHOSITA
Hindsight Bias
Utility
Definiteness
Enablement
Best Mode

Review Questions

1. Why are the rules found in the 1952 Patent Act still relevant?
2. Explain the concept of novelty.
3. List three sources of prior art.
4. Why is the geographical origin of prior art no longer a relevant distinction?
5. What does it mean for prior art to be enabling?
6. What makes prior art relevant?
7. Explain the difference between the critical date for determining when prior art can defeat novelty under the AIA and under the Patent Act of 1952.
8. Why are inventors given a one-year grace period during which to file for a patent?
9. How does the question of nonobviousness differ from the question of novelty?
10. What are the secondary considerations used in an obviousness analysis?
11. Explain the concept of utility.

Web Links

1. The PTO's website includes an electronic version of the Manual of Patent Examination Procedure. See: http://www.uspto.gov/web/offices/pac/mpep/mpep-2100.html to explore Chapter 2100 on patentability. This chapter details the standards for patentability used by PTO examiners. Click on the links to learn more about patentable subject matter, prior art, obviousness and much more.

Discussion Exercise

1. There are several substantive requirements that must be satisfied before a patent will be issued: novelty, utility, nonobviousness, definiteness, enablement and best mode. Explain how each of these standards fulfills the objectives of patent law.

Chapter 23

Obtaining a Patent

"Our patent system is the envy of the world." —David Kappos, Former Director of the USPTO

Chapter Outline

Chapter Objectives

- Become familiar with the process for patent prosecution before the PTO.
- Appreciate that the patent application becomes the document that teaches the world the technology behind the invention.
- Understand that changes in the patent statute award inventors priority based on the first inventor to file instead of the first to invent.

- Become familiar with the appeals process for patent prosecution.
- Understand the function of a provisional patent application.
- Identify the purpose of the abstract section of the patent application.
- Explain the interaction between the written description of the patent application and the claims of a patent.
- Learn about the lexicographers rule and its purpose.
- Appreciate that the claims are the heart of the invention and are the basis for defining the inventor's rights.
- Recognize the objectives for the various post-grant proceedings found under the AIA and the impact of reducing litigation.

Unlike the other areas of intellectual property we have studied so far, patent rights are only granted by application to the PTO—the same government agency that grants registrations of trademarks. And while rights for trademarks and copyrights may be protected under common law or through federal registration, patent rights are only awarded through a rigorous application process. There are no common law patent rights. The procedure for obtaining a patent is governed by the patent statute as it has been interpreted by the courts. It's a complex system that requires knowledge of the patent system in addition to knowledge of the subject matter sought to be patented. In the next several sections, we will examine the process for obtaining a patent.

23.1. The Prosecution Process—
Filing Before the PTO

The procedure for preparing and submitting a patent application is a lengthy and complex process referred to as *patent prosecution*. Only the inventor or a patent agent or patent attorney acting on behalf of the inventor may submit an application to the PTO and engage in the negotiations regarding the application.

The patent application becomes the written record of the invention once the patent is issued. As previously discussed, the bargained for exchange between the inventor and the government requires that the inventor *teach the invention to the public*. Hence, teaching the world an invention, hinges on the patent application's effectiveness to convey the elements of the invention. From a reading of the issued patent, a person skilled in the relevant art should understand the fundamentals of the claimed invention and practice the invention based on the written record found in the application. It is for this reason that the patent application and the prosecution process are such a vital part of patent practice.

23.2. The Examination Process by the USPTO

Generally, the date on which an application for a patent is received by the PTO will become the *effective filing date* and will establish priority under the new first inventor to file system. The application will then be assigned to an *examiner* in one of the many PTO examiner *art groups*. Each group specializes in a specific practice area. For example, a patent application filed by a pharmaceutical company for a new drug will be assigned to an examiner in the art unit specializing in biotechnology. Similarly, an application filed for medical equipment will be assigned to an examiner that has specialized knowledge in the area of mechanical engineering.

The examiner will review the application for the substantive requirements of patentability and for the procedural requirements of filing. It is rare that an application will result in an issued patent after the first review by an examiner. In fact, very few applications are approved without some negotiation between the inventor and the examiner. Thus, most applications are rejected after the examiner's first review. An application can be rejected entirely, based on all of the claims or in part, based on only certain claims. The examiner will explain the reason or reasons for the rejection in an *Office action*. The burden of proof is on the examiner to prove that the claimed invention does not qualify for patent protection; accordingly, the basis for each objection must be clearly stated, identifying the relevant rule of law.

In response to an Office action, an applicant may submit a response contesting the basis for the examiner's rejection or amending the claims of the application in order to comply with the examiner's objections. An applicant can also abandon the application completely, deciding not to pursue patent protection at all. If the applicant chooses to respond to the Office action, the examiner will review the applicant's response and the amended application along with the arguments set forth by the applicant. At this point, the examiner can again either reject some or all of the claims, usually in the form of a final rejection—which may not be truly final, we'll talk about that in a minute—or grant the patent. This negotiation between the examiner and the applicant is known as the *prosecution process*.

If the patent is granted, the applicant must pay an issue fee and the patent will be published in the Official Gazette for Patents. Once issued, a patent has the presumption of validity. This means that an opposing party has the burden of proof in alleging that the patent is invalid. After all, the prosecution process is so extensive that the law gives weight to the examination procedure and puts the burden of proof on the challenger.

Let's go back to the *final rejection* for a moment. *Final* is a bit of a misnomer, an applicant still has a few more bites at the apple. In fact, even after a final rejection, an applicant can request an interview with the examiner. This is a chance for the applicant to speak directly to the examiner, either by phone or in person. An applicant can also appeal a rejection to the *Patent Trial and Appeal Board* ("PTAB"). (Prior to the passage of the AIA, an appeal would be made to the Board of Appeals and Patent Interferences.) From here, an applicant may still appeal a rejection to the C.A.F.C. and eventually, may file an appeal to the Supreme Court, although it is rare that such appeal will be heard. Nevertheless, the few cases that have been litigated before the Supreme Court have helped to shape the scope of patentable subject matter.

Take for instance, the previously discussed case, *Bilski v. Kappos*. Upon application to the PTO, the patent examiner rejected Bilski's claimed invention on the basis that it was an unpatentable abstract idea. Bilski appealed the decision to the Board of Patent Appeals and Interferences where the examiner's rejection was affirmed. When Bilski appealed the Board's decision to the C.A.F.C., the claimed invention was again held unpatentable. Bilski then appealed the C.A.F.C. decision to the Supreme Court where, once again and finally, Bilski's claimed invention was deemed an unpatentable abstract idea.

The prosecution process can take anywhere from one to three years, and sometimes even longer. Patent prosecution is a complex and costly procedure. The chart on the next page, taken from the PTO website, diagrams the process.

23.3. Conducting a Patent Search — Should You Even Apply for a Patent?

An important step in the patenting process is the *patent search*. An inventor, or the inventor's patent attorney or patent agent, must perform a search of the records of currently patented inventions and expired patents to determine whether the claimed invention is novel compared to already patented inventions.

Patent attorneys and patent agents specialize in conducting thorough patent searches to determine whether there is prior art that may defeat novelty and preclude an invention from being patented. The PTO's website includes several search functions that allow inventors to conduct a patent search using a variety of parameters including, searching by key words that describe an invention and searching by the name of an inventor or the owner of a patent. In addition to researching patentability, those wishing to keep pace with technological advances and research and development in a particular field can mon-

Figure 23.1

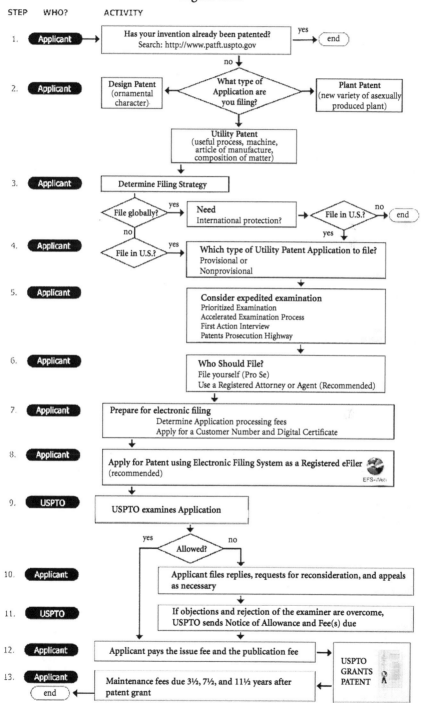

itor newly patented inventions. Similarly, inventors and corporations can keep track of a competitors' newly patented technology by searching for patents issued to a particular individual or corporation.

Patent searches can also be conducted using a system established by the PTO consisting of a set of numbered classifications and sub classes for different categories of inventions known as the *Patent Classification system.* This system is designed for use by PTO examiners, but is widely used by patent attorneys and agents in conducting patent searches, as well. The system is made up of a number of *classes* that are broken down into many *subclasses.* Let's look at an example. Nike®, Inc. owns patent 8,272,971 titled Golf Ball with Reduced Flight Path Length. See the image below. The patent is listed as being in U.S. Class 473/281 and also 473/165. Class 473 covers *Games Using Tangible Projectiles.* Within this class are numerous subclasses including, subclass 165 which covers *Particular Projectiles, (e.g., reduced flight path balls)* and subclass 281 which covers *Practice Projectiles having Air Resistance.* Nike's patented golf ball claims various elements that induce drag and minimize the ball's flight path and is accordingly listed in subclasses 281 and 165. By virtue of the number of classes and subclasses and the fact that many inventions can be included in more than one subclass, a search using the patent classification system can be confusing and requires a great attention to detail.

Figure 23.2

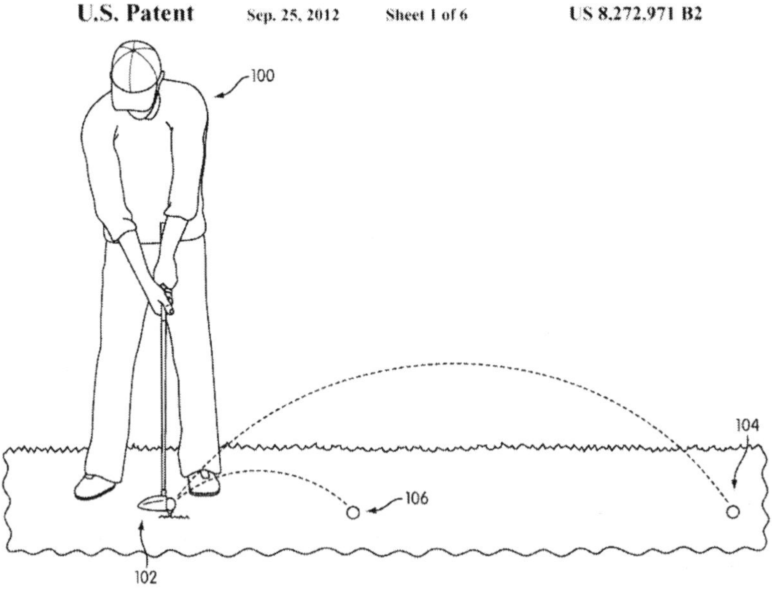

The PTO has also set up a system of *Patent and Trademark Depository Libraries* all over the country that are open to the public. These designated libraries receive and house copies of US patent and trademark materials making them available to the public.

23.4. Provisional Applications

In certain instances, an applicant may wish to file what is known as a *provisional patent application.* The requirements for a provisional application are significantly less burdensome than the requirements for filing a full patent application. Filing a provisional application can act as a placeholder allowing an inventor to establish an effective filing date even before the entire application is prepared. Typically, a provisional application is not examined to determine whether the invention meets the substantive standards of patentability and instead is simply recorded to hold the filling date until a full patent application has been submitted. This practice is likely to become even more widely used since the AIA has changed the US patent system to *first inventor-to-file* rather than *first-to-invent.* Accordingly, it is an inventor's race to file that may make provisional applications an important part of patent practice.

Once a provisional application is filed, an applicant has 12 months to file a full patent application in order to benefit from the earlier filing date of the provisional application. If the applicant fails to file the non-provisional application before the expiration of the 12 months, the application will become abandoned.

23.5. The Patent Application

Once an invention has been reduced to practice, the parameters of the invention must be set forth in clear and concise terms and submitted to the PTO for the prosecution process. The patent statute provides specific guidelines regarding the various sections required in an application.

A patent application has two functions. Its primary function is to convince the PTO examiner of the patentability of the invention. The second function is to serve as the documentation that will teach the world the invention. Remember, the policy goal of patent law is to encourage innovation to benefit the public. This benefit is realized when the invention falls into the public domain after the term of patent protection, becoming free for all to practice. The written application plays a critical part in teaching the invention and fulfilling the policy goal of patent law. In the following sections, we will examine many of the important sections found in a patent application. As we go through the sections, keep in mind the functions of the application and how each section plays an important role.

23.6. Abstract

The *abstract* is similar to an executive summary of the invention. It's typically one paragraph long and should be preferably no longer than 150 words. It provides a very basic summary of the invention appearing on the first page of an issued patent.

The abstract can be very useful during a patent search. Because patent applications are lengthy and complex, the abstract allows patent examiners or the public to quickly read the brief description of an invention to determine the nature of the invention and whether it is relevant. The abstract gives notice of prior art to a future inventor or to a PTO examiner during a search for relevant prior art. For this reason, the wording of the abstract should be brief and concise so that a quick reading will reflect the nature of the invention and whether the patent may be prior art. Many practitioners choose to draft the abstract after drafting the *specification* and the claims, using the finished claims as a guideline for what to include in the abstract paragraph. We will discuss the claims in greater depth a later section.

Let's look at an abstract on the next page for a very popular patented invention. Do you recognize what it is? It's the abstract from the Twitter® patent.

23.7. Specification

The specification is the written body of the patent application. It is made up of several parts including, a written description, drawings (when necessary) and the claims. Let's look at each section in detail.

23.8. Written Description, Enablement and Best Mode

The *written description* is the main body of the invention. It should describe the invention, give the background of the invention and explain the uses of the invention. As previously discussed in Chapter 22, the written descrip-

Figure 23.3

(12) **United States Patent**
Dorsey et al.

(10) Patent No.: **US 8,401,009 B1**
(45) Date of Patent: **Mar. 19, 2013**

(54) **DEVICE INDEPENDENT MESSAGE DISTRIBUTION PLATFORM**

(75) Inventors: Jack Dorsey, San Francisco, CA (US); Christopher Isaac Stone, Berkeley, CA (US)

(73) Assignee: Twitter, Inc., San Francisco, CA (US)

(*) Notice: Subject to any disclaimer, the term of this patent is extended or adjusted under 35 U.S.C. 154(b) by 346 days.

(21) Appl. No.: 12/177,589

(22) Filed: Jul. 22, 2008

Related U.S. Application Data

(60) Provisional application No. 60/951,415, filed on Jul. 23, 2007.

(51) Int. Cl.
H04L 12/28 (2006.01)

(52) U.S. Cl. 370/389; 370/390; 709/206; 709/244

(58) Field of Classification Search 370/389, 370/352, 713/153, 188; 709/206, 220, 223; 707/10
See application file for complete search history.

(56) **References Cited**

U.S. PATENT DOCUMENTS

5,706,211	A	1 1998	Beletic et al
5,745,692	A	4 1998	Lohmann II et al.
6,226,668	B1	5 2001	Silverman
6,275,570	B1	8 2001	Homan et al.
6,301,245	B1	10 2001	Luzeska et al.
6,301,609	B1	10 2001	Aravamudan et al.
6,405,035	B1	6 2002	Singh
6,408,309	B1 *	6 2002	Agarwal 707/999.104
6,463,462	B1	10 2002	Smith et al.
6,594,345	B1	7 2003	Vinson
6,633,630	B1 *	10 2003	Owens et al. 379/93.24
6,661,340	B1	12 2003	Saylor et al.
6,665,722	B1	12 2003	Elliott
6,683,194	B2	1 2004	Chang et al

6,694,362	B1	2 2004	Secor et al.
6,708,217	B1	3 2004	Colson et al.
6,745,021	B1	6 2004	Stevens
6,813,634	B1	11 2004	Ahmed
6,816,878	B1	11 2004	Zimmers et al.
6,832,341	B1	12 2004	Vijayan
6,839,562	B2 *	1 2005	Smith et al. 455/466
6,891,811	B1	5 2005	Smith et al.
6,965,777	B1	11 2005	Cast et al
7,116,994	B2	10 2006	Hatch

(Continued)

FOREIGN PATENT DOCUMENTS

WO   WO 01 80534 A1   10 2001

OTHER PUBLICATIONS

"Transit Cooperative Research Program, TCRP Report 92, Strategies for Improved Traveler Information," Transportation Research Board of the National Academies, Multisystems, Inc., 2003, 122 pages, Cambridge, MA.

Primary Examiner — Dang Ton
Assistant Examiner — Brian O'Connor

(57) **ABSTRACT**

A system (and method) for device-independent point to multipoint communication is disclosed. The system is configured to receive a message addressed to one or more destination users, the message type being, for example, Short Message Service (SMS), Instant Messaging (IM), web form input, or Application Program Interface (API) function call. The system also is configured to determine information about the destination users, the information comprising preferred devices and interfaces for receiving messages, the information further comprising message receiving preferences. The system applies rules to the message based on destination user information to determine the message endpoints, the message endpoints being, for example, Short Message Service (SMS), Instant Messaging (IM), E-mail, web page output, or Application Program Interface (API) function call. The system translates the message based on the destination user information and message endpoints and transmits the message to each endpoint of the message.

22 Claims, 3 Drawing Sheets

tion must be drafted to describe "the manner and process of making and using" the invention in "full, clear, concise and exact terms as to enable any person skilled in the art" to practice the invention. When the written description is drafted to meet this standard it is said to be *enabling*. This is the crux of the bargained for exchange between the public and the inventor. The inventor must "teach" the world the invention and in return, the inventor enjoys a period of time during which to exclude the public from practicing the invention.

In addition to being adequately described and enabling, the written description must provide the *best mode*, or the best way, for practicing the invention that is known to the inventor at the time the application was filed. The best mode requirement ensures that the public gains the benefit of the inventor's knowledge and is a key part of the bargained for exchange between the inventor and the government. Before the passage of the AIA, failure to disclose the best mode could provide a basis to invalidate a patent. Under the AIA, although the inventor is still required to disclose the best mode of practicing the invention, failure to disclose the best mode is no longer a basis for patent invalidity. We'll discuss this in greater detail in Chapter 25 when we examine patent invalidity as a defense to infringement.

An important tool available for an applicant is the *lexicographer rule*. In the written description, an applicant may assign specific definitions to certain words or phrases in the patent. The terms as defined in the written description will be read to reflect the inventor's intended meaning throughout the application. Similarly, if claim interpretation becomes necessary, the definition given by the applicant will govern the interpretation of the word.

Importantly, the written description must be drafted to *support the claims*. This means that the written description must describe all the elements and limitations of the claims. We will see in the next section that the claims are the boundaries of the invention. Elements and limitations of the claims set out the specific parameters of the claims. In this regard, the written description section must completely describe each limitation of the claims. If the written description fails to support any element of a claim, that element and perhaps the entire claim could be rendered invalid.

23.9. Drawings and the Written Description of the Drawings

Although it is not a requirement that every patent application include drawings, drawings must be included when necessary to adequately describe the invention. Remember, the primary purpose of the application is first to convince the examiner of the claimed invention's patentability, but equally important is that the application must provide enough instruction so that it teaches the invention to the public. Accordingly, if drawings facilitate the understanding of an invention, they must be included in the application.

Notice that the following drawing includes numbers identifying various components of the invention. These identifying numbers can be referenced throughout the written description and in the claims in order to facilitate an accurate understanding of the patent.

Figure 23.4

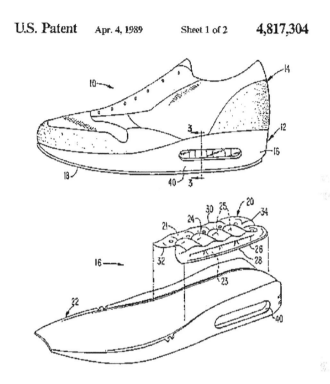

23.10. Claims

The *claims* of a patent are often referred to as the "heart of the invention." They define the boundaries of the invention and provide the source of a patentee's legal rights in the invention. For this reason, the claims must be written using technical language and a great attention to detail. Because the claims provide the invention's parameters, an accusation of infringement will hinge on the interpretation of the claims. Only activity that falls within the parameters of the claims will result in a finding of infringement. It's important to understand the relationship between the claims and the written description. As previously discussed, the written description must *support* the claims. This means that the written description must explain all the elements and limitations of the claims. An important caveat in this regard, is that the written description is not binding, only the claims are binding. Instead, as we will see when we discuss claim interpretation, the claims are given the broadest interpretation in light of the written description and must be consistent with what is disclosed in the written description. In Chapter 24, we will talk about claims in more detail as we discuss an important part of an infringement analysis, claim interpretation.

23.11. Inventor's Oath

Each individual who is an inventor or joint inventor must submit an *inventor's oath or declaration* before a patent will be issued. In the oath an inventor must state that he or she is the original inventor of the claimed invention. The oath is made using the form on the next page.

23.12. Post-Grant Proceedings and Challenges

There are several proceedings that can take place with the PTO after a patent has been granted. This is an area in which there have been many changes under the AIA—certain procedures have been eliminated while others have been added. Because one of the objectives behind the AIA was to reduce litigation costs, allowing certain challenges to take place before the PTAB, rather than in courtroom will alleviate a certain amount of litigation in the courts. Let's look at a few post-grant proceedings now.

23.13. Reissue

Reissue is a procedure that allows a patentee to correct a mistake found in an issued patent. If, for example, a patentee discovers that the patent has been issued with a defective specification or drawing that could render the patent inoperative or invalid, the patentee may correct the language of a claim or correct a drawing in order to accurately reflect the invention. This proceeding is only available when the error is the result of an innocent mistake and not based

Figure 23.5

PTO/SB/01A (09-12)
Approved for use through 01/31/2014. OMB 0651-0032
U.S. Patent and Trademark Office; U.S. DEPARTMENT OF COMMERCE
Under the Paperwork Reduction Act of 1995, no persons are required to respond to a collection of information unless it displays a valid OMB control number.

DECLARATION (37 CFR 1.63) FOR UTILITY OR DESIGN APPLICATION USING AN APPLICATION DATA SHEET (37 CFR 1.76)

Title of Invention	

As the below named inventor(s), I/we declare that:

This declaration is directed to:

☐ The attached application, or

☐ United States application or PCT international application number _____

filed on _____

☐ As amended on _____ (if applicable);

I/we believe that I/we am/are the original and first inventor(s) of the subject matter which is claimed and for which a patent is sought;

I/we have reviewed and understand the contents of the above-identified application, including the claims, as amended by any amendment specifically referred to above;

I/we acknowledge the duty to disclose to the United States Patent and Trademark Office all information known to me/us to be material to patentability as defined in 37 CFR 1.56, including for continuation-in-part applications, material information which became available between the filing date of the prior application and the national or PCT International filing date of the continuation-in-part application. The above-identified application was made or authorized to be made by me/us.

WARNING:

Petitioner/applicant is cautioned to avoid submitting personal information in documents filed in a patent application that may contribute to identity theft. Personal information such as social security numbers, bank account numbers, or credit card numbers (other than a check or credit card authorization form PTO-2038 submitted for payment purposes) is never required by the USPTO to support a petition or an application. If this type of personal information is included in documents submitted to the USPTO, petitioners/applicants should consider redacting such personal information from the documents before submitting them to the USPTO. Petitioner/applicant is advised that the record of a patent application is available to the public after publication of the application (unless a non-publication request in compliance with 37 CFR 1.213(a) is made in the application) or issuance of a patent. Furthermore, the record from an abandoned application may also be available to the public if the application is referenced in a published application or an issued patent (see 37 CFR 1.14). Checks and credit card authorization forms PTO-2038 submitted for payment purposes are not retained in the application file and therefore are not publicly available.

All statements made herein of my/our own knowledge are true, all statements made herein on information and belief are believed to be true, and further that these statements were made with the knowledge that willful false statements and the like are punishable by fine or imprisonment, or both, under 18 U.S.C. 1001, and may jeopardize the validity of the application or any patent issuing thereon. I hereby acknowledge that any willful false statement made in this declaration is punishable under 18 U.S.C. 1001 by fine or imprisonment of not more than five (5) or both.

FULL NAME OF INVENTOR(S)

Inventor one: _____ Date: _____

Signature: _____ Citizen of: _____

Inventor two: _____ Date: _____

Signature: _____ Citizen of: _____

☐ Additional inventors or a legal representative are being named on _____ additional form(s) attached hereto.

This collection of information is required by 35 U.S.C. 115 and 37 CFR 1.63. The information is required to obtain or retain a benefit by the public which is to file (and by the USPTO to process) an application. Confidentiality is governed by 35 U.S.C. 122 and 37 CFR 1.11 and 1.14. This collection is estimated to take 1 minute to complete, including gathering, preparing, and submitting the completed application form to the USPTO. Time will vary depending upon the individual case. Any comments on the amount of time you require to complete this form and/or suggestions for reducing this burden, should be sent to the Chief Information Officer, U.S. Patent and Trademark Office, U.S. Department of Commerce, P.O. Box 1450, Alexandria, VA 22313-1450. DO NOT SEND FEES OR COMPLETED FORMS TO THIS ADDRESS. **SEND TO: Commissioner for Patents, P.O. Box 1450, Alexandria, VA 22313-1450.**
If you need assistance in completing the form, call 1-800-PTO-9199 and select option 2.

on a deceptive intention to change the patent scope. Reissue is an important part of making patent law efficient. Because the issued patent will serve as the document that teaches the world the invention and give notice of the parameters of the invention, it is important that it accurately reflect the invention.

23.14. Post-Grant Review and Inter Partes Review

A *post-grant review* can be initiated only within the first nine months after a patent has issued. A third party challenger may initiate the proceeding based on a claim of patent invalidity. Here, invalidity can be based on any grounds including, a lack of novelty, obviousness, lack of enablement and a number of other challenges. Compare, the *inter partes review* which may be initiated on a much more limited range of challenges, but may be brought at any time nine months after a patent has issued. Here a challenge may be based on a more limited range of challenges: a lack of obviousness or lack of novelty stemming from the existence of certain categories of prior art.

Both a post-grant review and inter partes reexam will take place before a panel of three administrative judges with the PTAB. Under either proceeding, the parties have a right to participate in the process, including the patentee who has the right to respond to challenges of validity of the patent by amending the claims in the patent. However, an amendment may not expand the scope of patentable subject matter. Either the third-party challenger or the patentee can request an oral hearing, request discovery and take depositions. At the conclusion of the proceeding the three member panel will issue a certificate that invalidates the patent, reaffirms the patent or adds the modified claims to the patent. Either party can appeal the board's decision to the C.A.F.C.

In many ways, these two proceedings function in much the same way a litigation would. The parties are both given an opportunity to participate in the process and both maintain the right to appeal a decision. These post-grant challenges are likely to resolve many of the same issues that would be raised at trial, but in a more time and cost efficient manner.

23.15. Transitional Program for Covered Business Methods

The *Transitional Program for Covered Business Methods* ("TPCBM") is a new proceeding available under the AIA which allows a defendant charged with infringing a business method patent to challenge the validity of that patent. This post-grant proceeding was created in response to claims that many of the business method patents that were issued after the *State Street Bank Case, supra,* were not valid. Recall that for a time, it was thought that business methods were beyond the scope of patentability and applications during this time were consistently denied. After *State Street Bank*, the pendulum swung in the other direction, allowing business method patents to be issued more freely, in many cases where they should not have been.

23.16. Ex Parte Reexam

An *ex parte reexam* can be initiated by a patentee, a third-party or the director of the PTO when there is a substantial new question of patentability. However, unlike other post-grant proceedings, third parties do not have the ability to participate in the proceeding. Hence, it is more likely that a third-party would bring a challenge under a post-grant review or an inter partes review. At the conclusion of the ex parte reexam, the PTO will issue an office action similar to an office action issued in connection with the original exam and ultimately will issue a certificate that either affirms the validity of the claims, amends the claims or cancels the claims.

Chapter Summary

In order to gain patent protection, an inventor must submit an application to the PTO. The patent application will become the written record of the patent. In most cases, the date on which an application is filed will become the effective filing date and serve as the critical date to establish priority among inventors. The critical date will also be used to measure prior art for the purposes of establishing novelty and nonobviousness.

A PTO examiner will review a patent application for compliance with the substantive standards of patentability and reject a patent in part or in whole by issuing an Office action. Applicants can respond by amending the claims or abandoning the application. Appeals of an examiner's rejection can be made to the PTAB, then to the CAFC and ultimately to the Supreme Court.

Before filing a patent application, an inventor must conduct a patent search of the prior art. Applicants can submit a provisional patent application to serve as place holder establishing priority even before the full patent application has been prepared. Applicants have one year from filing the provisional application in order to file the full patent application or the provisional application will be abandoned.

A patent application has many required parts. The abstract acts as an executive summary and should describe the invention in less than 150 words. The written description portion of the application must be written to support the claims and must describe the invention with specificity in order to teach the invention and enable a person having ordinary skill in the art to practice the invention. The claims are the heart of patent and establish the boundaries of patent protection.

Once a patent has been issued there are several post-grant proceedings that can be initiated before the PTO. Reissue allows a patentee to correct mistakes found in a patent. Inter partes review and post-grant review provide the basis for challenging a patent's validity before the PTO. The Transitional Program for Covered Business Methods allows defendants accused of infringing a business method patent to challenge the validity of the patent before the PTO. An ex parte reexam allows for a reexamination of an issued patent.

Key Terms

Patent Prosecution
Examiner
Art Groups
Office Action
Patent Trial and Appeals Board
Court of Appeals for the Federal Circuit
Patent Search
Patent Classification System
Patent and Trademark Depository Library
Provisional Application
Abstract
Specification
Written Description
Claims
Reissue
Post-Grant Review
Inter Partes Review
Transitional Program for Covered Business Methods
Ex Parte Rexam

Review Questions

1. What is patent prosecution?
2. Explain the significance of the patent application.
3. Why is an issued patent given the presumption of validity?
4. Explain the appeals process for a rejected patent application.
5. What are the reasons to conduct a patent search?
6. Explain the reason that the practice of filing provisional patent applications may become more common.
7. Explain the function of the abstract portion of a patent application.
8. What is the lexicographers rule?
9. Explain the relationship between the written description and the claims of a patent.
10. When would a patentee initiate a reissue proceeding?
11. Explain the difference between an inter partes review and a post-grant review.
12. When would a party initiate a review using the transitional Program for Covered Business Methods?

Web Links

1. The PTO's website has useful information for all facets of patent practice. In the following link, is an outline for several patent searching strategies. See: http://www.uspto.gov/products/library/ptdl/services/step7.jsp. Try searching for some popular patented products.

Discussion Exercise

1. The abstract section of a patent application provides a concise summary of the invention in less than 150 words. Try your hand at drafting an abstract for one of the following: a hammer, a set of binoculars, a pencil, an energy drink consisting of several ingredients, a method for baking a chocolate chip cookie, or another example.

Chapter 24

Scope and Enforcement of Patent Rights

"The right of property is simply the right of dominion. It is the right, which one man has, as against all other men, to the exclusive control, dominion, use, and enjoyment of any particular thing."
—Lysander Spooner, *The Law of Intellectual Property*

Chapter Outline

Chapter Objectives

- Recognize that joint inventors enjoy an equal benefit of patent rights even when their contribution is not the same.
- Distinguish between employee and employer rights in inventions developed in the scope of employment.
- Explain the process for determining ownership among competing inventors.
- Appreciate the contractual nature of patent rights between the government and an inventor.
- Recognize the usefulness of the patent as a document.

- Grasp the concept of infringement and that all elements must be present to establish infringement.
- Distinguish between literal infringement and infringement under the doctrine of equivalents.
- Understand the concept of claim interpretation and that courts use intrinsic and extrinsic evidence in claim construction.
- Identify the ways a defendant can be liable for indirect infringement.

The right conferred by a patent is the right to exclude others. But, what does this really mean? What is the bundle of rights granted to the owner of a patent? We know that patents give patentees market power. From popular technologies like Twitter® and the iPhone®, patents can be the basis for establishing an entire corporation or even an empire. But it's important that patent rights are balanced against the public interest. The public interest is served when inventors create new and useful innovations. Yet, patent rights must be clearly defined. When patent rights are unambiguous and implemented under a uniform set of laws, future inventors are free to innovate without fear of litigation. Creating a system of rights that permits the emergence of future technologies is critical. As we examine the rights of patentees and the interest of the public, this is the balance that must be struck. Let's look at these issues in the next few sections.

24.1. Inventorship

The issue of inventorship may seem simple, but there are situations in which questions of inventorship can arise. As a general rule, the individual or individuals that *conceive* of the idea that ultimately results in a patent are credited as the inventors. In situations of *joint inventors* or employee-inventors, questions of inventorship and ownership can arise.

Without an agreement stating otherwise, joint inventors share an equal interest in the resulting patent. This means each inventor has the right to practice the invention and enforce the right to exclude others. A joint inventor even enjoys the right to license the patent without the permission of a joint inventor. Moreover, joint inventors do not owe an accounting to one another. The implication is that one inventor can license the invention and enjoy an income stream without sharing that income stream with a joint inventor. This arrangement can be modified by contract before the patent issues or the inventors can agree to each assign their rights to a common entity, thereby keeping the inventors' interest in the patent united.

Nevertheless, absent an agreement stating otherwise, each joint inventor has an equal right to exploit the patent. For this reason, among the members of a collaborative group, it is crucial to accurately determine inventorship. Typically, many parties contribute to the development of an invention but, not each contributor will be deemed a joint inventor. The general rule is that a joint inventor must contribute some *conception* or something *inventive* to the resulting invention to be a joint inventor. In most cases, it is typical that one inventor conceives of the original concept to which the other inventor adds inventive content. Importantly, it is not necessary that inventors contribute equally to the invention or that each inventor contribute to all the claims in the patent. In fact, even where an inventor contributes to only one claim, the inventor will have ownership in the entire patented invention. Joint inventors must apply for a patent jointly and each inventor must make the required oath we discussed in the last chapter. Failure to name a joint inventor can result in the invalidity of a patent.

Let's turn to the issue of employee-inventors. Most employers address the issue of patent ownership at the beginning of the employment relationship through a contract requiring all employees to assign any inventions conceived of by the employee in the scope of employment to the employer. The employee will still be credited as the inventor, but will assign all rights to the employer. Without such an arrangement, the employee may retain ownership in a resulting patent. However, when an employee has developed a patented invention using the employer's facility and tools, or has invented during working hours, the employer may retain what are known as *shop rights*. Shop rights include a limited right for an employer to practice an invention without permission from the inventor and without paying a licensing fee to the employee-inventor.

Issues of ownership can also arise when federally funded research results in a patented invention. Many universities and small businesses benefit from federal funds used to conduct research. In many instances, this research results in a patented invention and the question arises: who has ownership in a resulting patent? The *Bayh-Dole Act* enacted in 1980, sought to address patent policy in this area. Prior to the enactment of Bayh-Dole, inventors were obligated to assign any resulting patents to U.S. government. This deprived the true inventors from enjoying any resulting patent rights. It also put the ownership of the resulting patents in the hands of the U.S. Government rather than in the hands of innovators who may be in a better position to exploit a patented innovation. The Bayh-Dole legislation sought to address these issues by creating a system that benefits both inventors and the federal government. The provisions of the Bayh-Dole Act allow inventors the option of retaining title to patents that result from federally funded research. In return, the U.S. government retains rights to practice the invention anywhere in the world under a license provided by the inventor.

24.2. Priority

At times, more than one inventor has developed the same invention at the same point in time, making *priority* among competing inventors an issue. Under the 1952 Act, priority was awarded to the *first to invent*, even if the first inventor was not the first to file an application for a patent. However, as previously discussed, establishing the date of invention can be a complex inquiry as inventors often must produce documentary evidence to prove the date of invention. Under the 1952 Act, priority among inventors was established in an administrative hearing before the PTO in what was known as an *interference proceeding*. Each competing inventor would present evidence in an attempt to prove the date of invention, thus establishing priority among the competing inventors.

Under the AIA, a patent is granted to the first inventor *to file* a patent application with the PTO, making priority among inventors determined by the effective filing date—a more objective measure than establishing the date of invention. Nevertheless, under the AIA, it is still possible that priority issues among inventors will arise. In addition to the objective component of the effective filing date, priority is still established when the first *inventor* files. Accordingly, the AIA has instituted a *derivation proceeding* to resolve issues of priority. During a derivation proceeding, an inventor must prove that she conceived of the claimed invention rather than *deriving* the idea from the true inventor.

24.3. The Patent

Once a patent has issued for a claimed invention, the inventor enjoys the right to exclude others from the boundaries of the patented invention. This right is based on a contractual relationship between the inventor and the government: the inventor has agreed to disclose the knowledge behind the patented invention while the government provides the legal authority for the inventor to enforce the right to exclude others. In contractual terms, the inventor's *offer* is embodied in the patent application as it is filed and the government's *acceptance* is embodied in the issued patent. Because the relationship is contractual in nature, there is an inherent duty of good faith and fair dealing. Accordingly, an inventor has a *duty of candor* towards the PTO. If an inventor withholds material information or makes a material misrepresentation, the resulting patent can be found invalid. It is the inventor's duty of candor that makes the prosecution process efficient. We will discuss the duty of candor and inequitable conduct in more detail in Chapter 25.

The cover sheet of an issued patent contains many important and useful elements. Review the cover sheet below of a patent for a game playing system. The filing date of the application is always found on the cover sheet, giving

Figure 24.1

US 20130007892A1

(19) **United States**
(12) **Patent Application Publication** (10) Pub. No.: US 2013/0007892 A1
INOOKA (43) Pub. Date: **Jan. 3, 2013**

(54) ELECTRONIC CONTENT PROCESSING SYSTEM, ELECTRONIC CONTENT PROCESSING METHOD, PACKAGE OF ELECTRONIC CONTENT, AND USE PERMISSION APPARATUS

(75) Inventor: Hidehiro INOOKA, Tokyo (JP)

(73) Assignee: SONY COMPUTER ENTERTAINMENT INC., Tokyo (JP)

(21) Appl. No.: 13/611,243

(22) Filed: Sep. 12, 2012

Related U.S. Application Data

(63) Continuation of application No. PCT/JP2010/007066, filed on Dec. 3, 2010.

(30) Foreign Application Priority Data

Apr. 14, 2010 (JP) 2010-093513

Publication Classification

(51) Int. Cl.
G06F 21/24 (2006.01)
(52) U.S. Cl. 726/27

(57) ABSTRACT

A game playing system includes a use permission tag provided for use in a game disk for a user of a game, a disk drive, and a reproduction device for reproducing the game. The disk drive reads out a disk ID from the game disk. When the game is to be played, the reproduction device conveys the disk ID and a player ID to the use permission tag. The use permission tag stores the terms of use of the game and determines whether a combination of the disk ID and the player ID conveyed from the reproduction device fulfills the terms of use or not.

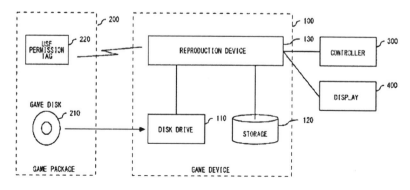

GAME PLAYING SYSTEM 1000

notice to the world as to the duration of patent protection. As you recall, a patent term is 20 years from the date of filing. Accordingly, a competitor wishing to start practicing a patented manufacturing process once the invention falls into the public domain will have notice of when patent protection will end. Similarly, a biomedical researcher wishing to conduct research using a patented protein or a method of isolating a gene sequence will benefit from knowing the duration of patent protection.

Even before patent protection has ended, there may be interest in licensing the patented technology. An inventor and any *assignees* are listed on the patent cover sheet for such practical purposes. An assignee becomes the owner of patent when an inventor transfers the entire bundle of rights to the assignee. In employment relationships, where an employee has agreed to assign any inventions to the employer, the employee-inventor will be credited as the inventor while the employer will be listed as the assignee.

Look carefully at Figure 24.1. It is a cover sheet for a patent application directed to Sony Playstation®. The numbers found to the left of each heading on the cover sheet are used consistently by international agreement. The cover sheet of a patent issued in Germany or Japan will list an inventor-applicant next to (75), an assignee next to (73), and the date on which the patent was filed next to (22). This system allows anyone, regardless of the language they speak, to determine the ownership and duration of a patent originating from anywhere in the world.

24.4. Infringement

A patentee's right to exclude others is a fundamental part of patent law. These rights are set forth in the Patent Act in 35 U.S.C. §154 and 35 U.S.C. §271. Section 271(a) provides that:

> " ... whoever without authority makes, uses, offers to sell, or sells any patented invention, within the United States, or imports into the United States any patented invention during the term of the patent therefor, infringes the patent."

Any of the enumerated activities found in the statute can constitute infringement. Notice that even *offering* to sell a patented article can constitute infringement. Even assuming an alleged infringer is unsuccessful in selling a patented item or fails to profit from the infringing activity, liability for infringement may be established based on the mere offer to sell.

The rights conferred upon a patentee are comprehensive and indeed, sometimes referred to as a legal monopoly. Thus, even when a second inventor develops the same invention through independent creation or reverse engineering, the second inventor will be precluded from practicing the invention. Contrast this with copyright law. An artist or author can be excused of copyright infringement by validly claiming independent creation. Similarly, as we will see, under trade secret law, the independent discovery of a patented process or reverse engineering a patented formula does not infringe a trade secret.

In this regard, a patentee's right to exclude others is more robust than the rights found in the other areas of intellectual property. The extent of this monopoly is, however, limited by the fact that the duration of patent protection lasts for a relatively short period of time, only 20 years from the effective date of filing. Moreover, it's important to note that the statute only covers infringing activity that takes place within the United States. The United States patent laws do not extend beyond the borders of the United States. To gain international patent rights, inventors must look to the laws of the specific countries in which they wish to claim patent rights. We'll talk about international patent practice in Chapter 28.

24.5. Literal Infringement

Before we go further into our discussion of infringement, it's important to make a few key distinctions in terminology. As previously discussed, a patent is made up of claims. The *claims* are the boundaries of an invention—they define the invention and give notice to the world about where the beginning and the end of each invention lies. Each claim is made up of elements, or limitations. In order to establish *literal infringement* of a patent claim, all *elements* of a claim must be found in the infringing activity.

Infringing on patent rights is very different from trespassing on real property. Entering or occupying any spot within the boundaries of real property will trespass on an owner's real property rights. It's not necessary for a trespasser to occupy the entire property to establish a trespass. Conversely, in patent law, the infringing activity must encompass each and every element of a claim in order to establish infringement. Anything less than practicing each and every element will not constitute infringement.

Thus, to avoid infringement, at least one element or limitation of a claim must be absent. On the other hand, the *addition* of an element or limitation does not negate infringement. Let's look at a ficticious example.

A claim for a cookie with raisins and chocolate chips might look like this:

The invention claimed is:

1. A cookie comprising:

a dough made from butter, sugar, eggs, flour, salt and vanilla,
said dough having raisins incorporated therein,
said dough having chocolate chips incorporated therein.

Notice that the claimed cookie is made up of several *limitations*, also referred to as *elements*. The limitations include the dough, the raisins and the chocolate chips. Remember, to establish infringement of a claim, each limitation must be practiced in the infringing item. Accordingly, the claimed cookie would be infringed by a cookie that incorporated dough, raisins, chocolate chips *and macadamia nuts*. After all, the macadamia nut cookie is still technically the claimed cookie, but with the addition of macadamia nuts. Adding an element, the macadamia nuts, does not negate the fact that the macadamia nut cookie practices the invention of the claimed cookie.

On the other hand, a cookie that incorporates only dough and chocolate chips may not infringe because it excludes a limitation—namely the raisins. Excluding an element or limitation negates infringement.

24.6. Claim Interpretation and Literal Infringement

Because the claims set out the boundaries of an invention and provide the basis of a patentee's rights, establishing a clear interpretation of those boundaries is an essential step in an infringement analysis. Accordingly, *claim interpretation*, or claim construction as it is sometimes referred to, is the first step to any infringement action. Because of the nature of patent claims, claim interpretation is complex process central to the determination of whether the claims of a patent have been infringed. In many instances, it requires an understanding of the technology underlying the invention in addition to the analysis of the claim language. In *Markman v. Westview Instruments, Inc,* 517 U.S.370 (1996), the Supreme Court held that the interpretation of the claims in a patent is a step for the court and not for the trier of fact, or a jury. This means that claim interpretation is a matter left for the judge in a case. Accordingly, claim interpretation takes place during a pretrial hearing known as a *Markman hearing*.

In *Markman v. Westview,* 517 U.S. 370 (1996) at issue was a patent for an "Inventory Control and Reporting System for Dry cleaning Stores." The patent was directed towards a system that monitors and reports the status, location, and movement of clothing within a dry cleaning establishment. In this case, the defendant used the patented system for the purposes of tracking an *inventory of receivables* rather than inventory of articles of clothing, as directed in the claimed invention. At issue was the meaning of the term *inventory* in the plaintiff's patent and whether the defendant's use of the patented system was encompassed by the claims in the plaintiff's patent. At trial, the jury interpreted the term *inventory* broadly and found that the claims were infringed by the defendant's activity. But the trial court disagreed, finding the jury's interpretation of the term "inventory" erroneously broad. On appeal, the Supreme Court held that for the purposes of uniformity among the courts, questions of claim construction are questions of law for a judge, not questions for a jury.

Claim interpretation requires a court to consider *intrinsic evidence* and *extrinsic evidence*. Intrinsic evidence is evidence found within the patent and includes, the claims themselves, the written description found in the specification, and the *prosecution history*. Hence, claim interpretation starts with a plain reading of the claims. As you recall from Chapter 23, the claims are interpreted in light of the written description found in the specification of the patent. It is for this reason, the written description must include an explanation of all the elements of a claim. Moreover, using the aforementioned lexicographer's rule, any definitions that a patentee has assigned to terms in the written description section of the application will be controlling during claim interpretation.

Intrinsic evidence also comes from the prosecution history. This includes Office actions from a PTO examiner and the responses to Office actions from an applicant. It is during this correspondence that the claims are shaped. Let's consider an examiner's rejection of certain elements in a claim. In response, an applicant may agree to limit the scope of the claim or amend it. This is clear evidence that the applicant intended to surrender that subject matter in an effort to make the application conform to the requirements of patentability. Accordingly, the prosecution history is given consideration in claim interpretation. After all, if a claim would have been rejected as being too broad, the applicant's offer to modify the element provides strong evidence of the true boundary of the claim. A patentee's monopoly must not extend beyond the boundaries as they were established during the PTO examination process.

During the process of claim interpretation, a court also looks to extrinsic evidence, or evidence outside the scope of the patent and prosecution history, such as a dictionary or even expert testimony in an effort to understand and interpret scientific principles that are a part of the claimed invention. The combination of both intrinsic and extrinsic evidence allows a court to fully interpret the meaning of terms in the patent. Once the step of claim interpretation has been satisfied, a determination of infringement can be made.

24.7. Doctrine of Equivalents

Infringement can also be found under the *doctrine of equivalents*. As we have just established, infringement requires a finding that all the elements of a claim are present in the infringing item or activity. However, in some instances, infringement can be established when an element of a claim is not literally copied, but is so close that it is deemed to be an *equivalent*. Under this doctrine, the general rule is that an element will be regarded as an equivalent if it performs "substantially the same function in substantially the same way to obtain the same result." This is the test for equivalency that the Supreme Court articulated in *Graver Tank & Mfg. Co., Inc. v. Linde AirPorducts Co.,* 339 U.S. 605 (1950). This well-established doctrine is intended to protect patentees from "unscrupulous copyists" who may make "unimportant and insubstantial changes and substitutions" that may avoid the literal meaning of the claims, but add nothing new to the invention. Hence, equivalency may be found where the patented claims are not exactly the same as the infringing activity.

Recall, *designing around,* the practice of creating something that functions similarly to a patented invention, but does not literally infringe. Designing and inventing around is a perfectly legal practice and is, in fact, encouraged so long as the resulting invention does not infringe on an existing patent. Those who invent around a patented invention benefit from knowing that there is certainty in the boundaries of the elements in a claim. For this reason, many critics claim that the doctrine of equivalent takes away that certainty, making activity that was not originally claimed by the inventor, part of the inventor's domain. Thus, courts endeavor to strike a balance between protecting patentees through the doctrine of equivalents and recognizing the benefits that a degree of certainty in the contours of patent claims provides to future inventors.

24.8. Indirect Infringement

There are instances in which it may be difficult or futile to bring legal action against an infringer. In some instances, it can be difficult to determine the identity of an infringer while in other instances an infringer may not have the resources to adequately compensate the patentee. Or still, the number of infringers is so great that bringing an action for liability against each is would prove inefficient. In these situations, a patentee may wish to bring an action against an individual that was involved in the infringement, but whose activity does not amount to direct infringement. In these cases, a patentee is usually looking for a *deep pocket* in order to be adequately compensated. After all, a suit for patent infringement is costly and time consuming and winning a judgment does not necessarily guarantee that the patentee will be paid.

Under certain circumstances, it is possible to bring an action based on *indirect infringement* against one who has either *contributed* to the actual infringement or *induced* the actual infringer to commit the infringement. These derivative actions are based on statutory provisions found in the patent act and allow patentees to bring suit against individuals that may have played a substantial role in an action of direct infringement. A finding of *inducement to infringe* can be found when a defendant took steps to encourage or instruct another to infringe. *Contributory infringement* can be found when a defendant supplies non-patented components of a patented invention knowing that the components will likely be used to infringe the plaintiff's patent and when the only use for the component is in connection with the patented subject matter. On the other hand, if the component has other non-infringing uses in addition to its use with the patented subject matter, the manufacture and supply of the component will not constitute contributory infringement.

Let's look at an example. U.S. Patent 4,641,645 is patent directed to a facemask that is molded or thermoformed to fit certain specifications giving the mask a superior fit. For purposes of demonstration, imagine that the material used to produce the mask is specially produced material constructed of several filtration layers including one layer that allows the mask to be molded according to the patent. If a supplier of the filtration material supplies the material to another who infringes the mask, the supplier of the filtration material may be liable under a theory of contributory infringement if it is proven that there are no other non-infringing uses for the filtration material. If, on the other hand, there are other applications for material that are non-infringing, the supplier of the material will likely not be found liable under a theory of contributory infringement.

Figure 24.2

United States Patent [19]

Tayebi

[11] **Patent Number:** **4,641,645**

[45] **Date of Patent:** **Feb. 10, 1987**

[54] **FACE MASK**

[75] Inventor: **Amad Tayebi,** Westford, Mass.

[73] Assignee: **New England Thermoplastics, Inc.,**
Lawrence, Mass.

[21] Appl. No.: **754,955**

[22] Filed: **Jul. 15, 1985**

[51] Int. Cl.⁴ A62B 7/00
[52] U.S. Cl. **128/206.19;** 128/206.24
[58] Field of Search 128/205.29, 206.12,
128/206.13, 206.19, 206.21, 206.24, 206.28,
207.11

[56] **References Cited**

U.S. PATENT DOCUMENTS

1,142,990	6/1915	Stern	128/206.16
2,344,669	3/1944	Barker et al.	128/206.15
2,787,264	4/1957	Thiebault et al.	128/206.19
3,220,409	11/1965	Liloia et al.	128/206.19
4,248,220	2/1981	White	128/206.19
4,319,567	3/1982	Magidson	128/206.19
4,384,577	5/1983	Huber et al.	128/206.19
4,454,881	6/1984	Huber et al.	128/206.15

FOREIGN PATENT DOCUMENTS

491273 2/1930 Fed. Rep. of
Germany 128/206.24

Primary Examiner—Henry J. Recla

Attorney, Agent, or Firm—Joseph E. Funk

[57] **ABSTRACT**

What is disclosed is a face mask formed from a porous sheet made of a plurality of fibers. The mask is formed into a generally cup shape shell that fits over the mouth and nose of the wearer and is held thereto by elastic straps attached to the mask that pass behind the head when the mask is worn. The mask filters breathed air passing through the mask. The border of the mask is more tightly compacted during forming. The mask of the present invention features rearwardly projecting portions located on either side of the nose bridge area of the mask parallel to and close to the border of the mask. The peak of the rearwardly projecting portions extend from the face mask in the direction of the face of the wearer of the mask to conform the portion of the mask close to its border to the contours of the face of the wearer between the bridge of the wearer's nose and the upper areas of their cheekbones. The more tightly compacted rearwardly projecting portions, rib elements and border cooperate to provide shape retention to the mask, and to provide a spring action that holds the mask firmly but comfortably to the face of the wearer even when they talk or change facial expression to prevent the passage of air between the mask and the face of the wearer.

1 Claim, 12 Drawing Figures

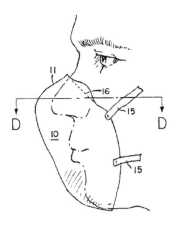

A prerequisite to establishing a case of indirect infringement is a finding of *direct* infringement. Absent a finding that one party directly infringed on a patentee's rights, infringement based on either contributory infringement or inducement to infringe will necessarily fail.

Chapter Summary

A patent affords inventors the right to exclude others from a patented invention. Joint inventors share an equal interest in a patent resulting from their collaboration. Joint inventors must contribute some conception or something inventive to the resulting invention in order to be credited as a joint inventor. Employee-inventors, in many cases, assign their rights to an employer at the beginning of the employment relationship. Without such an agreement, employers may still enjoy shop rights in an employee's invention.

Priority among inventors under the 1952 Act was determined through an interference proceeding. Priority under the AIA is established by being the first inventor to file an application with the PTO. When questions of derivation arise, under the AIA inventors must prove that the invention was not derived from another inventor.

A patent provides rights of a contractual nature between inventors and the government. The government provides the legal authority for inventors to enforce their rights while inventors agree to teach the public the innovation behind their invention.

Literal infringement is established when all the elements of a claim are practiced in the alleging infringing activity. The addition of an element does not avoid infringement while eliminating an element can avoid infringement. The first step in establishing infringement is claim interpretation. Claim interpretation is performed by a court rather than a jury. Courts use intrinsic and extrinsic evidence to determine the boundaries of the invention. Infringement can also be established through the doctrine of equivalents when one element of a claim is not literally copied but found to perform substantially the same function in substantially the same way producing the same result.

Infringement may also be established against those who do not directly infringe, but act in a way to induce others to infringe or contribute to infringement under certain circumstances. Here a finding of direct infringement must first be established before a finding of indirect infringement can be found.

Key Terms

Joint Inventors
Shop Rights
Bayh-Dole Act
Priority
Literal Infringement
Claim Interpretation
Intrinsic Evidence
Prosecution History
Extrinsic Evidence
Doctrine of Equivalents
Designing Around
Contributory Infringement
Inducement to Infringe

Review Questions

1. In general, who can be credited as an inventor?
2. What are the rights of joint inventors?
3. When can an employer enjoy shop rights?
4. Under the AIA, how is priority determined among inventors?
5. Describe the contractual relationship between the government and an inventor.
6. Explain why prosecution history is important in defining claims.
7. What is the difference between intrinsic and extrinsic evidence?
8. What is the *doctrine* of equivalents and why is it important in patent law?
9. Do you agree that the practice of designing around inventions should be encouraged?
10. What are some of the reasons a patentee might bring a suit based on indirect infringement?

Web Links

1. The Court of Appeals for the Federal Circuit hears appeals for intellectual cases and other cases stemming from federal law. Many influential decisions have come from this court. The court's website posts audio recordings of oral arguments as heard before the court. See: http://www.cafc.uscourts.gov/oral-argument-recordings/search/audio.html.

Discussion Exercise

1. In *Graver Tank & Mfg. v. Linde Air Products*, the Court acknowledged the doctrine of equivalents as necessary to protect patentees from "unscrupulous copyists...." Do you believe the doctrine of equivalents is necessary to protect inventors? Do you think it is beneficial to future inventors?

Chapter 25

Defenses

"He who receives an idea from me, receives instruction himself without lessening mine; as he who lights his taper at mine, receives light without darkening me." —Thomas Jefferson, Letter to Isaac McPherson

Chapter Outline

Chapter Objectives

- Understand the concept of patent invalidity and that it can be alleged in many ways.
- Recognize that exhaustion limits a patentee's rights over patented articles once the items are sold.
- Grasp that repair of a patented item is permissible while reconstruction is impermissible.
- Learn that patentees may not expand the scope of their patent protection through improper tying arraignments.
- Appreciate a patentee's duty of candor towards the PTO during the prosecution process and that material omissions or misrepresentations can render a patent unenforceable.
- Recognize that trade secret holders may have prior use rights even when a subsequent inventor patents the same innovation.

- Realize that the experimental use defense, while not abolished, excuses a limited scope of activity from infringement.

Although the protection afforded under patent law is robust, there are many defenses available to defendants that limit the rights of a patentee. For example, a defense strategy can focus on the invalidity of a patent or on various theories of non-infringement. Recall that in order to establish infringement, a patentee must demonstrate that *all the elements* of a claim were practiced by the defendant. Assuming that even one limitation of a claim was missing from the defendant's activities, infringement cannot be established. For this reason, many defendants attempt to prove that the accused activity is missing an element and thus, does not infringe the patent. In addition to the defense of non-infringement, there are many recognized defenses to patent infringement including affirmative defenses and invalidity.

25.1. Patent Invalidity

Obtaining a patent involves a rigorous prosecution process that examines whether a claimed invention meets the standards of patentability. If even one of the requirements of patentability is not met, the patent application will be denied. Often times, a defendant will attack the foundation of a patent alleging that the patent is invalid based on anything that would have precluded the invention from becoming patented. For example, if the invention lacked novelty, was obvious, lacked utility, was not fully disclosed or was outside the scope of patentable subject matter, the patent could be found invalid and thus unenforceable. After all, if the requirements of patentability are not present, a patent should never have issued and the invention should simply have remained as part of the public domain, free for anyone to practice. Indeed, in *Juicy Whip v. Orange Bang, supra*, the defendant alleged that the patentee's invention lacked utility and accordingly, should not have received a patent; in *State Street Bank v. Signature Financial Group, supra*, the defendant alleged that the subject matter of the invention at issue was outside the scope of patentable subject matter and therefore, was unpatentable; and in *KSR v. Teleflex, supra*, the defendant argued that the invention was obvious and therefore, unpatentable. In each of these cases, the defense went straight for the heart of the patent alleging *invalidity*. The logic underlying an invalidity defense is very simple; no patent—no infringement.

Prior to the passage of the AIA, failing to disclose the best mode for practicing an invention could result in patent invalidity. Under the AIA, although it is still required that a patentee disclose the best mode for practicing a claimed invention, failure to disclose the best mode is no longer a basis for invalidity. It is still too soon to know what effect this change will have on the disclosure of best mode. Patents issued before the enactment of the AIA will still be subject to the best mode defense.

25.2. Exhaustion

Patent law recognizes the doctrine of *exhaustion* as a limitation on a patentee's rights over an patented item once the item has been sold. A patentee is said to have exhausted the granted patent rights, making a lawful purchaser free to use, resell, discard, repair, or modify the patented item. Indeed, these activities that were once reserved only for the patentee are outside the scope of the patentee's rights under the exhaustion doctrine. As you may recall, this is conceptually similar to the first sale doctrine found in copyright law.

Recently, in *Bowman v. Monsanto*, 569 U.S. ___ (2013), the Supreme Court heard a case involving what a what is known as *self-replicating* technology. Monsanto, a large multinational seed corporation, developed and patented variations of soy bean seeds that are resistant to pesticides, specifically Round Up®. The technology allows a farmer to plant the seeds and spray pesticides on the soy bean plants thereby killing the weeds that encroach on the growing areas without affecting the soybean plants. A natural consequence of planting seeds is that second generation seeds are necessarily produced by the plant and contain the same genetic modifications that are found in the originally patented seeds. Thus, the new seeds contain all the properties of the patented Round Up Ready® seeds.

Monsanto requires all seed purchasers to sign an agreement that restricts the future use of the second generation seeds, specifically stating that farmers are prohibited from saving and planting future seeds. The agreement does, however, allow farmers to sell the second generation seeds to grain elevators which in turn sell the seed for use as animal feed. When Bowman, a farmer, purchased the seeds from a grain elevator, he planted them. The seeds, of course, self-replicated the following year and Bowman saved the second generation seeds, planting them the following year. Monsanto sued the farmer for patent infringement based on his unauthorized use of the second generation seeds.

The question in this case was whether the sale of the seed exhausted Monsanto's rights in the *second generation* seeds as purchased from the grain elevator. In a unanimous Supreme Court ruling, the Court held that the farmer's use of the replicated seeds was impermissible infringement and not protected under the exhaustion doctrine. The Court reasoned that the farmer could use or resell the seeds he purchased from the grain elevator. Indeed, the patentee's rights in selling and using the seeds were exhausted. However, when the planted seeds created second generation seeds that the farmer saved and replanted, the farmer was in fact *replicating* or *creating* a copy of a new item—the second generation seeds. Recall, exhaustion allows a purchaser to use, resell, discard, repair, or modify a lawfully purchased item. Exhaustion does not extend the right to create a new item on the template of the original.

25.3. Repair or Reconstruction

The repair-reconstruction doctrine allows the purchaser of a patented item to make repairs to the item as necessary, but only to a certain extent. *Repairs* that extend the useful life of a patented item are permissible while *reconstructing* a new article "on the template of the original" patented article goes beyond the scope of permissible repair. The question is: at what point are the defendant's actions permissible repair or impermissible *reconstruction*? Because patentable subject matter varies to such a great extent, there is difficulty in establishing a bright line rule delineating the difference between which activities are considered permissible repair and which cross the line to impermissible reconstruction.

Let's look at *Aro Manufacturing Co. v. Convertible Top Replacement Co.* 365 U.S. 336 (1961). The plaintiff's patent covered a convertible car's folding roof that was constructed using a metal frame and fabric covering which wore out more quickly than the metal frame. The patentee brought suit against the manufacturer of replacement fabric tops for contributory infringement stemming from the manufacture and supply of the replacement of the fabric tops. The Court held that the replacement of the fabric tops was not infringement, but rather permissible repair because the replacement of the fabric tops had merely extended the useful life of the car roof rather than constructing a new convertible roof on the template of the original roof.

In *Jazz Photo Corp. v International Trade Commission*, 264 F.3d 1094 (Fed. Cir.2001), Fuji Photo brought suit alleging that Jazz Photo Corporation had engaged in impermissible reconstruction of its single use disposable cameras by reconstructing the cameras after they had been used and the film developed.

Figure 25.1

United States Patent [19]

Mochida et al.

[11] Patent Number: 4,884,087

[45] Date of Patent: Nov. 28, 1989

[54] PHOTOGRAPHIC FILM PACKAGE AND METHOD OF MAKING THE SAME

[75] Inventors: Mitsuyoshi Mochida, Tokyo; Tokuo Maekawa, Kanagawa; Hisashi Takei, Kanagawa; Yasuo Matsumoto, Kanagawa; Hiroshi Ohmura, Tokyo; Shigeru Sugimoto, Kanagawa; Seimei Ushiro, Tokyo; Seiji Asano, Saitama; Toshio Yoshida, Ibaragi, all of Japan

[73] Assignee: Fuji Photo Film Co., Ltd., Kanagawa, Japan

[21] Appl. No.: 87,388

[22] Filed: Aug. 20, 1987

[30] Foreign Application Priority Data

Aug. 20, 1986	[JP]	Japan	61-126942[U]
Oct. 17, 1986	[JP]	Japan	61-246977
Oct. 17, 1986	[JP]	Japan	61-246978
Jan. 19, 1987	[JP]	Japan	62-5694[U]
Jan. 19, 1987	[JP]	Japan	62-5698[U]
Feb. 14, 1987	[JP]	Japan	62-32185

[51] Int. Cl.⁴ G03B 1/10; G03B 1/66; G03B 17/02; G03B 17/28

[52] U.S. Cl. 354/75; 354/202; 354/212; 354/217; 354/288

[58] Field of Search 354/75, 76, 202, 212, 354/217, 288

[56] References Cited

U.S. PATENT DOCUMENTS

2,557,297	6/1951	Lea	95/31
2,612,092	9/1952	Heyer et al.	354/76
2,933,027	4/1960	Hollingworth et al.	95/31
3,247,773	4/1966	Doblin et al.	95/31
3,511,153	5/1970	Steisslinger et al.	354/213
3,752,050	8/1973	Wolfe	354/213
3,896,467	7/1975	Hamada	354/204
3,906,535	9/1975	Takahama et al.	354/288
4,274,726	6/1981	Yoneyama et al.	364/212 X
4,397,535	8/1983	Harvey	354/212

4,687,311	8/1987	Malloy Desormeaux	354/217
4,707,096	11/1987	Lawther	354/217 X

FOREIGN PATENT DOCUMENTS

1100461	2/1961	Fed. Rep. of Germany .
1975027	12/1967	Fed. Rep. of Germany .
1979883	2/1968	Fed. Rep. of Germany .
1991324	3/1968	Fed. Rep. of Germany .
2026967	12/1971	Fed. Rep. of Germany .
2351891	4/1974	Fed. Rep. of Germany .
2156078	1/1975	Fed. Rep. of Germany .
3716812	11/1987	Fed. Rep. of Germany .
2048752	3/1971	France .
52-43303	10/1977	Japan .
6708486	3/1968	Netherlands .
607242	8/1948	United Kingdom .
1462353	1/1977	United Kingdom .
2138580	10/1984	United Kingdom .

Primary Examiner—Michael L. Gellner
Attorney, Agent, or Firm—Young & Thompson

[57] ABSTRACT

A lens-fitted photographic film package comprising a light-tight film casing having an exposure opening, a rolled film disposed on one side of the exposure opening in the light-tight casing, a removable light-tight container having a film winding spool therein disposed on the other side of the exposure opening in the light-tight film casing, and an externally operable film winding member for winding the rolled film around said film winding spool of the light-tight film container. The lens-fitted photographic film package is assembled by the steps of winding film withdrawn from a light-tight film container in a roll in a darkroom; loading the rolled film and the light-tight film container in separate respective receiving chambers formed in a main body section of the lens-fitted photographic film package; and fixing a back cover section to the main body section so as to assemble light-tightly the lens-fitted photographic film package.

15 Claims, 14 Drawing Sheets

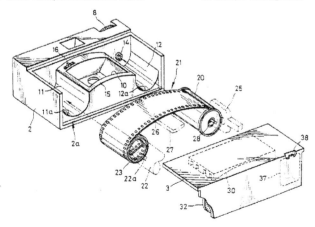

The allegations were based on a variety of activities including, removing the cardboard cover, cutting open the casing, inserting new film, resetting the film counter, replacing the battery for the flash, and applying a new cardboard cover. The defendants argued that those actions did not constitute a reconstruction of the cameras, but merely repair to extend the cameras' useful life. The court agreed holding that the defendant's actions were permissible repair and not an infringement of the patentee's rights. The court reasoned that replacing parts of a patented item that wear out more quickly than other parts is permissible in order to extend the article's useful life. After all, changing the batteries for a flash or replacing a film cartridge are clearly permissible activities when performed in connection with traditional, non-disposable cameras, even when a camera is patented or has patented components.

25.4. Patent Misuse

In some instances the defense focuses on the actions of the patentee. This is the case when a defendant raises the defense of *patent misuse*. A charge of patent misuse alleges that the patentee improperly used the market power conferred by the patent. A common situation involves impermissible *patent tying* in which a patentee requires that as a prerequisite to licensing the patented subject matter, a licensee must agree to license or purchase another product in addition to the patented item, thereby expanding the monopoly beyond the patented invention.

In *Morton Salt Co.v. G.S. Suppiger Co.*, 314 U.S. 488 (1942), the patentee manufactured and licensed a patented machine that deposited salt tablets used for canning. The patentee, however, required licensees to use its unpatented salt tablets in connection with its patented machine. In a suit for infringement, the defendant argued that the patentee's practice of tying the license for the patented machines to the sale of its unpatented salt tablets created a monopoly, restraining competition in an unpatented article, namely, the salt tablets. The Court found that the patentee had engaged in impermissible tying by using its patent monopoly to suppress competition in the salt tablets. Accordingly, the improper tying rendered the patentee's patent *unenforceable*.

25.5. Inequitable Conduct

Inequitable conduct is another affirmative defense that shifts the focus from the defendant's actions to the patentee's conduct. The crux of inequitable conduct alleges that the patentee acted inequitably in connection with the patent prosecution process. During the prosecution process, the applicant has a *duty of candor* and good faith towards the PTO. This duty requires that the applicant disclose all information that would be *material* to patentability. The duty of candor makes the patent process more effective when an examiner can rely on the information found in a patent application. Typically, the inventor-applicant has a depth of knowledge in the relevant field that may be greater than that of the examiner. Although the examiner must perform the necessary due diligence to prosecute an application, the process is more efficient when the examiner can rely on the veracity and completeness of the applicant's statements.

For this reason, the duty of candor is a crucial element in the prosecution process. Indeed, the effect of violating an applicant's duty toward the PTO is that the entire patent will be completely unenforceable. Because of the gravity of this result, a finding of inequitable conduct requires that the applicant acted intentionally and that the deception was material. Deception will be held to be material when, *but for* the deception, the patent would not have been granted. After all, an application that would have been denied, but for a material misrepresentation or a failure to disclose material facts, may not have been patentable subject matter and should have been left as part of the public domain.

25.6. Prior User Rights

Prior use addresses an issue that can arise when an inventor chooses to protect an invention as a trade secret rather than seeking patent protection. There are many reasons that an inventor may choose trade secret protection over patent protection, namely patent protection is finite, lasting for a maximum of 20 years from the date of filing while a trade secret can endure for much longer, or perhaps the relative ease of establishing trade secret protection may make pursuing trade secret protection preferable. What if a second inventor files a patent application on the same subject matter a first inventor has been practicing, but protecting as a trade secret? Can a trade secret holder preclude a subsequent inventor from patenting the very same invention? As we will see in Unit 6, independent creation by another inventor is permissible under trade secret law. Thus, a first inventor-trade secret holder would not have any recourse against a subsequent patentee. Can a subsequent patentee exclude a prior trade secret holder from practicing the invention although the trade secret holder preceded the patentee in time?

Under a new provision in the AIA, a trade secret holder may be permitted to invoke a defense based on prior use and continue practicing the trade secret alongside a subsequent patentee who obtains a patent on the same invention. To raise a defense based on prior use, a trade secret holder must have practiced the invention in good faith and have been using the invention *commercially* and *continuously* for at least one year before the effective filing date of the patent or the date on which the invention was made public. Moreover, a prior user must have come to the invention by independent creation and not derived from the subsequent patentee. This defense creates a safe harbor for inventors who decide to keep their innovation a trade secret rather than seek patent protection.

25.7. Experimental Use

Although the *experimental use* of patented subject matter is a recognized defense to infringement, there is a very limited scope of activity that falls within the ambit of permissible experimental use. The doctrine has been held to allow experimentation "to satisfy idle curiosity, or for strictly philosophical inquiry ... without ... commercial purpose." Accordingly, any activity that has even the slightest connection to a commercial purpose will not be permissible under this exception to infringement. Recently, the experimental use doctrine has been limited to the extent that it is no longer a practical defense. In *Madey v. Duke University*, 307 F.3d 1351 (Fed. Cir. 2002), the court found that even a University's use of a former professor's patented equipment was held outside the scope of experimental use. The court held that Duke University's use of the patented equipment furthered of its primary function as an educational institution and accordingly was not permissible experimental use.

Because the experimental use doctrine has become so limited, Congress has created legislation that provides a safe harbor provision for experimental activity by pharmaceutical companies in connection with the FDA approval of generic drugs. Experimentation performed in furtherance of FDA approval of generic drugs is permissible during the duration of a patent. The policy behind this safe harbor is that the process for FDA approval can be lengthy, potentially resulting in a significant delay before the public has access to the generic versions of patented drugs. Moreover, the monopoly period pharmaceutical companies enjoy would be extended during the wait for their competitors to go through the FDA approval process.

Chapter Summary

A defense based on invalidity challenges the foundation of a patent by alleging that the invention does not meet the standards of patentability. Such challenges can include, lack of novelty, obviousness, lack of utility, unpatentable subject matter or failure to dequately disclose the invention.

Exhaustion limits the rights of a patentee once a patented item is sold giving the owner of the patented item the right to use, sell, discard, repair or modify the patented item. Recently, in a case before the Supreme Court, it was established that a patentee's rights in self replicated technology are not necessarily exhausted in the second generation patented article. An extension of exhaustion involves the repair or reconstruction doctrine in which the purchaser of a patented article has the right to make repairs to the article in order to extend the useful life of the article, but may not reconstruct a new article of the template of the patented item.

Defendants can raise affirmative defenses to infringement that focus on the patentee's actions rather the defendant's. In a defense of patent misuse, defendants allege that a patentee misused the market power provided by a patent and unlawfully expanded the scope of patent rights. Patent tying is a common example of patent misuse. Here, a patentee requires that licensees purchase or license other products from the patentee as a prerequisite for a license in patented items. A defense based on inequitable conduct similarly looks at a patentee's actions alleging that the patentee made a material misrepresentation or material omission in connection with the patent prosecution process.

A defense of prior use allows a trade secret holder who has been practicing an invention commercially for a full year to continue practicing the invention alongside a subsequent patentee without being found liable for infringement.

The experimental use defense will not extend to any activity that is even slightly commercial in nature and is limited only to activity that is intended to satisfy an idle curiosity. Congress has created an exception to infringement that allows generic drug companies to experiment with patented drugs in connection with certain FDA required tests during the patent period.

Key Terms

Invalidity
Exhaustion
Repair
Reconstruction

Patent Misuse
Tying
Inequitable Conduct
Duty of Candor
Prior Use
Experimental Use

Review Questions

1. On what basis can a defendant assert a defense based on patent invalidity?
2. What activity can be excused under the theory of exhaustion?
3. Compare exhaustion under patent law with the first sale doctrine under copyright law.
4. Do you agree with the Court's holding in *Bowman v. Monsanto*?
5. Why do you think the repair of a patented item is permissible while the reconstruction of a patented item is not?
6. Why is the duty of candor important to the patent prosecution process?
7. Under the theory of inequitable conduct, what makes a misrepresentation or a failure to disclose *material*?
8. Under what circumstances can an inventor invoke a defense of prior use?
9. What type of activity is permissible under the experimental use defense?

Web Links

1. The Director's Forum posts a blog the PTO's leadership. This site focuses on a variety of intellectual property issues. See: http://www.uspto.gov/blog/.

Discussion Exercise

1. Courts have not articulated a bright line rule between permissible repair and impermissible reconstruction. Can you create a set of rules to guide the issue? Do you think the percentage of the parts that are repaired in a particular item should govern the line between repair and reconstruction? Should it matter whether some elements are more durable than others?

Chapter 26

Patent Remedies

"In America an inventor is honored, help is forthcoming, and the exercise of ingenuity, the application of science to the work of man, is there the shortest road to wealth." —Oscar Wilde, *Impressions of America*

Chapter Outline

26.1.   Legal Remedies
26.2.   Attorney Fees and Enhanced Damages
26.3.   Equitable Remedies

Chapter Objectives

- Distinguish between reasonable royalty and lost profits and the basis for calculating each.
- Recognize that patentees can seek attorney fees and treble damages in cases of willfulness.
- Understand the concept of injunctive relief.
- Explain the four requirements for a preliminary injunction.
- Appreciate the concept of a permanent injunction.

Patent law affords inventors a comprehensive set of rights for a relatively short duration. Accordingly, the remedies available under patent law are fashioned with an eye towards compensating patentees in light of this unique balance of rights. Upon a finding of infringement, a patentee can seek *equitable remedies* and *legal remedies*. An equitable remedy comes in the form of *injunctive relief* while a legal remedy comes in the form of *monetary compensation*. As applied, both are tailored to address the limited duration of patent rights and the robust set of rights afforded to patentees.

26.1. Legal Remedies

A plaintiff can seek *monetary damages*, sometimes known as *compensatory damages*, upon a finding of infringement. Compensatory damages are intended to make the patentee whole and can come in the form of *reasonable royalties* or *lost profits*. We'll examine each below. In either case, the patent statute provides that the damages awarded to a successful plaintiff should be *no less than a reasonable royalty*.

Damages that come in the form of reasonable royalties compensate a patentee as if the patentee and infringer had negotiated a licensing agreement and the patentee had received fees based on the infringing activity. A common approach to calculating a reasonable royalty is called the *willing licensor-willing licensee approach*. Here, the court attempts to determine the royalty rate that would have resulted from a hypothetical negotiation between the parties just *before* the infringement began, thus compensating the patentee as if the parties had entered a licensing arrangement prior to the infringement. Because a plaintiff-patentee and defendant are likely not on such terms at the close of an adversarial trial, to establish a reasonable royalty rate, a court will look to other factors including, royalties received by the patentee for the same patent as negotiated with other parties in addition to licensing fees paid for patents that are comparable to the patent at issue.

A patentee can also demand *lost profits*. To calculate lost profits, the patentee must prove several factors including, (1) the demand for the patentee's product, (2) the absence of non-infringing substitutes, (3) the patentee' capacity to have met the demand, and (4) proof of actual profits the patentee would have made, but for the infringer's activities. The totality of these factors provides an indication of the profits the patentee would have gained in the absence of the defendant's infringement. Notice that a lost profits calculation does not assume that the patentee would have necessarily had the same success that the defendant had. Instead, a patentee must prove to have had the capacity to achieve the same success through its own channels of marketing and manufacture.

In *BIC Leisure Products, Inc. v. Windsurfing International, Inc.*, 1 F.3d 1214, (1993) at issue was whether "but for" the infringement by the defendant, the patentee would have made the infringer's sales. In this case, the plaintiff manufactured and marketed its patented sailboards. At least fourteen competitors, including the defendant, sold similar sailboards with prices ranging from approximately $200 to $800. The patentee's board typically sold at the higher end of the price range while the defendant's board typically sold at the lower end of the price range. The difference between the plaintiff's and defendant's price point was approximately 60–80%. During the damages phase of the trial, the defendant introduced evidence that the entry level market for sailboards was "particularly sensitive to price disparities." Moreover, because several others in the market sold sailboards at price points closer to the defendant's, the defendant argued that patentee could not prove that it would have captured the share sales made by the defendant.

Indeed, under this set of facts, without the defendant in the market, it was unlikely that customers would have purchased the patentee's higher priced sailboards. Instead, it is likely that customers would have purchased sailboards from competitors in the price point closer to the defendant's. Accordingly, the patentee could not prove that "but for" the defendant's infringement the patentee would have realized the defendant's sales. Nevertheless, the patent statute requires that the patentee is entitled to receive no less than reasonable royalties based on the infringing activity. In this case, although the patentee would not be awarded lost profits on the sales made by the defendant, the patentee would still be entitled to reasonable royalties based on the defendant's sales.

26.2. Attorney Fees and Enhanced Damages

In some cases, a defendant's activity is found to justify the additional award of attorney's fees and *treble damages*. Treble damages are equal to triple the amount of compensatory damages. A court can award these enhanced damages in exceptional cases upon a finding of willfulness by a defendant. Where a defendant had reason to believe the patent was valid, but nevertheless continued the infringing activity, willfulness may be found. A patentee must prove that the defendant's actions were *reckless*, in other words, that despite an *objectively high likelihood* that the defendant's actions would constitute infringement of a valid patent, the defendant continued the infringing activity.

26.3. Equitable Remedies

In patent law, an injunction is a form of equitable relief that orders a defendant to stop practicing the invention. There are two types of injunctions that can be issued: a *preliminary injunction* or a *permanent injunction*. A preliminary injunction can be issued even before the parties have been to court and adjudicated the case on the merits. Patent litigation can take several years, sometimes upwards of five years. Because the term of a patent is only 20 years from the effective date of filing, the duration of litigation can last for a significant percentage of the duration of the patent. For this reason, there are situations in which a patentee can be granted a preliminary injunction.

Before a court will issue a preliminary injunction, the plaintiff must overcome several hurdles. As an initial matter, the burden of proof is on the plaintiff to prove that a preliminary injunction should be issued. After all, the patentee is asking the court to compel the defendant to stop the allegedly infringing activity before the plaintiff has proven that the infringed patent is valid or that the defendant's activity constitutes infringement that is not excused under any of the limitations discussed in Chapter 25. Accordingly, the plaintiff must present a strong preliminary case that convinces the court that: (1) the patentee has a reasonable likelihood of succeeding on the merits of the case, (2) that without the issuance of a preliminary injunction the patentee would suffer *irreparable harm*, (3) that the potential harm to the patentee if an injunction is not granted outweighs the potential harm to the defendant if an injunction is erroneously granted, and (4) that it is in the public interest to issue a preliminary injunction. Each of these standards must be met before a preliminary injunction will be issued. Let's look more closely at these requirements.

In order for a plaintiff to prove that there is a reasonable likelihood of success on the merits, the plaintiff must present evidence that convinces the court that the plaintiff has a good chance of prevailing when the case is tried—in other words, that the patentee has a valid patent and that the defendant's activity will amount to unexcused infringement. Next, in order to show irreparable harm, a plaintiff must show that there is no adequate remedy at law—meaning that money alone will not repair the damage that may result if the infringer is allowed to continue practicing the patent before the trial has come to an end. In most cases, money damages will compensate the patentee for losses stemming from infringement. However, in certain situations, money damages alone may not adequately compensate the patentee. Because the duration of a patent term is relatively short, patent holders have a limited window of time to exploit the monopoly the patent has granted. During the monopoly period, a patentee may benefit from the patent monopoly by building a strong customer base. In such instances, money damages alone may not remedy the harm caused by the defendant's infringement. Finally, a plaintiff must prove that it is in the public interest to issue a preliminary injunction. Under certain circumstances, although the plaintiff may show that a success at trial is likely, a court may be reluctant to issue an injunction when the public may be harmed by an injunction. Here, the court looks to whether there is some critical public interest that would be infringed by the grant of an infringement. In *Hybritech, Inc v. Abbott Laboratories*, 849 F.2d1446 (CAFC 1988), Hybritech sued Abbott Labs for infringement of Hybritech's patented cancer diagnostic and hepatitis diagnostic test kits. Here, the court found that it was in the public interest *not* to issue a preliminary injunction against the defendant, Abbott Labs. The court reasoned that the public interest was best served by the availability of the test kits and accordingly, did not enjoin Abbott Labs from continuing to produce the test kits during the trial period.

Finally, if a patentee has prevailed after a full trial, the court can issue a permanent injunction. This means the court will order the defendant to cease practicing the invention for the remainder of the patent period. After all, patent law gives the owner of a patent the right to exclude others and that is essentially the effect of an injunction.

Chapter Summary

Upon a finding of infringement, patentees can seek monetary damages or injunctive relief. Monetary damages are intended to compensate a patentee for a defendant's infringement and can come in the form of reasonable royalties or lost profits. A reasonable royalty rate is established by looking at similar licensing agreements to determine a royalty rate that would have been negotiated between a willing licensee and willing licensor. Lost profits require a patentee to prove that the patentee would have gained the profits made by the defendant if the defendant had not infringed. In cases of willful infringement, a patentee may be entitled to receive treble damages and attorney fees.

Patentees may also seek injunctive relief against a defendant. In certain cases, a court may order a preliminary injunction before the adjudication of the case. Here, a patentee must prove that the patentee has a reasonable likelihood of prevailing on the merits of the case, that the patentee will suffer irreparable harm without the issuance of an injunction, that the balance of the possible harm favors the patentee, and that an injunction is in the public interest. At the conclusion of the trial, a prevailing patentee may be awarded a permanent injunction, keeping the defendant from practicing the invention until the patent period expires.

Key Terms

Legal Remedies
Equitable Remedies
Monetary Damages
Compensatory Damages
Reasonable Royalty
Lost Profits
Treble Damages
Injunctive Relief
Preliminary Injunction
Irreparable Harm
Permanent Injunction

Review Questions

1. Explain the difference between injunctive relief and monetary relief.
2. What factors does a court look to when determining a reasonable royalty rate?
3. What must a patentee prove in order to be awarded lost profits?
4. When can a plaintiff be awarded attorney fees?
5. What are treble damages?
6. Why are preliminary injunctions sometimes necessary in patent cases?
7. Describe a scenario in which a patentee could suffer irreparable harm making a preliminary injunction necessary.
8. In what type of situation might a court find that it is not in the public interest to issue a preliminary injunction?
9. In patent law, when does a permanent injunction end?

Web Links

1. PatentlyO is a website dedicated to patent law and is always on the cutting edge of the latest issues concerning patent law. See: http://www.patent-lyo.com/ to read recent posts.

Discussion Exercise

1. A calculation of lost profits is based on several concrete factors a patentee must prove. Explain why *the absence of non-infringing substitutes* should be part of the evaluation. How can patentees prove they have the ability to meet market demand? What type of evidence would a patentee provide? On the other hand, what type of evidence would a defendant provide to prove that a patentee *does not* have the ability to meet market demand?

Chapter 27

Special Topics

" ... ingenuity should receive liberal encouragement."
—Thomas Jefferson

Chapter Outline

Chapter Objectives

- Recognize the concept of a non-practicing entity.
- Explain how the policy goal to incentivize inventors and the policy goal to benefit the public are in certain circumstances, in competition.
- Identify some of the issues that are raised against NPEs.
- Recognize the difficulty in defining an NPE.
- Identify some of the proposed solutions the problems posed by NPEs.
- Understand the concept of gene patenting.
- Recognize some of the issues surrounding gene patenting.
- Explain the reason that isolated genes are not patentable subject matter.

Innovation and technology move forward rapidly and our system of patent law has often struggled to keep pace. While legislation and the courts attempt to address new issues as they arise, often times, legislators and judges are not familiar with the science behind certain areas of invention. Accordingly, legal opinions and legislation may not always adequately address issues posed by changing technology.

Although the AIA produced sweeping changes aimed to address many issues in patent law, new questions of patentability arise with constantly changing technology. For instance, the Supreme Court recently tackled the question of gene patenting. For a time, it was believed that *isolated genes* could be patented. Nevertheless, the Court struck down a patent directed towards an isolated human gene. Another equally challenging issue has arisen from changes in the way businesses use patents. Entities that acquire patents for the sole purpose of enforcement have raised questions about patentee's rights. Here, the need for reform is complicated by the complexities of business models and the business practices found in different industries. Let's examine each of these issues in more detail.

27.1. Non-Practicing Entities

Recently, much attention has been given to *non-practicing entities* ("NPE") sometimes referred to as a *patent trolls* and more recently referred to as *patent assertion entities* ("PAE"). There is significant debate regarding the practices of NPEs and recently legislation has been proposed to address some of the problems stemming from the abusive practices of certain NPEs. The debate involves entities whose business model is to acquire patents for the sole purpose of enforcing patent rights without practicing the underlying inventions.

Before we go further into the debate, let's take a step back and review two important principles: the policy goal of patent law and the rights conferred upon an inventor. The policy goal behind patent law is to incentivize inventors in order to benefit the public. The public realizes a benefit on two levels: first, when an invention is practiced and made available to the public during the patent period and next, when the invention falls into the public domain and becomes a part of the basic tools of scientific and technological innovation. Moreover, the right afforded to inventors under patent law is the right to exclude others. Nothing more and nothing less. Notice, the right to exclude others does not come with a requirement that the inventor practice the patented invention. Indeed, there are many reasons an inventor might not practice a patented invention. In some cases, inventors cannot raise the capital needed to market and produce their invention. Still, there are other instances in which an inventor may put a patented invention aside while working towards achieving success in another area. In any of these situations, the inventor still enjoys the right to enforce the rights conferred under the patent. The right to exclude others is fundamental to patent law—even when the patent holder does not practice the invention.

The issue with NPEs is that, at times, these two principles seem to be at odds. We know that patent law incentivizes inventors for the purpose of benefitting the public. Yet NPEs seek to enforce their patent rights without necessarily conferring any benefit to the public until after the patent term expires. Let's look at some of the issues that have been raised by the litigation practices of NPEs.

Patent litigation is costly and time consuming, draining the resources of the litigants. Yet these costs are high regardless of whether the litigation is initiated by an NPE or by an individual inventor practicing the invention. The issue is that the litigation practices of NPEs has become extensive. NPEs frequently initiate litigation against numerous defendants in the same law suit, even where the root of the alleged infringement is unrelated among defendants. Moreover, NPEs have been criticized for using the high cost of litigation to extract settlements from end users. These tactics have come under fire as being an abusive extension of the patent system. Indeed, there are reports that the percentage of patent litigation initiated by NPEs is more than fifty percent of all patent litigation and that the overall cost to defendants is several billion dollars. Moreover, critics of NPEs often assert that the patents enforced by NPEs are weak patents. Yet even entities that practice a patented invention may enforce a weak patent.

One of the biggest challenges in addressing the issue of NPEs is defining an NPE. By virtue of its name, an NPE is an entity that owns a patent, but does not practice the invention. Yet not all NPEs follow the profile that has been painted by the critics. There are individual inventors or small corporate entities who cannot commercialize a patented invention because of the timing of their invention or because of a lack of financial capital. Many large corporations acquire portfolios of patents, sometimes referred to as *patent thickets*, in an effort to prevent competitors from designing around their patented technologies. In any of these instances, most would agree that the parties have the right to enforce their patents if infringed. Yet it may be difficult to differentiate the practices of these entities from the practices of the so-called *patent trolls*. Where the parties are so similarly situated in fundamental ways, it can be difficult to justify the denial of patent rights to some and not others.

Recently, there have been a variety of proposals aimed at addressing some of the abusive litigation practices of certain NPEs. Proposed solutions include giving more discretion to courts in awarding attorney fees to prevailing parties as a means for sanctioning plaintiffs, particularly in cases of abusive filings. Another proposal would require plaintiffs to file separate lawsuits for each defendant, rather than aggregating defendants into one suit, or requiring a damages evaluation *before* litigating the substantive allegations of a suit. As you recall, reasonable royalties or lost profits require patentees to prove compensatory damages using concrete calculations while in many cases, the pleaded damages are based on more speculative figures.

The issue of NPEs is one that will not easily be solved. A patentee's right to exclude others and patent law's policy goal of incentivizing inventors to benefit the public are both central to patent law and will both play a role in any resolution.

27.2. Patenting the Human Gene

In June, 2013 the Supreme Court decided *Association for Molecular Pathology v. Myriad Genetics*, 569 U.S. ____(2013), regarding the validity of patented genetic material. The question in this case was whether an isolated gene could be regard as a composition of matter and thus, patentable subject matter or was merely naturally occurring phenomena, falling outside the scope of patentable subject matter. As you recall, naturally occurring phenomena, or physical phenomena as it sometimes referred to, is excluded from patentable subject matter. In this case, Myriad Genetics discovered the precise location and sequence of two *human genes*. A mutation of these genes is correlated with a dramatically increased risk of developing breast or ovarian cancer. Once it was able to locate and isolate the genes, Myriad obtained several patents on the genetic material claiming an isolated DNA coding for the two genes. Using the patented genetic material, Myriad then developed and commercialized a process that can test for the existence of mutations in the gene and charged close to $4000 to those wishing to be tested for the existence of the gene.

When competing hospitals provided similar tests using the isolated genes, Myriad filed suit for infringement. Although, all the defendants settled agreeing to cease all testing activity, several patient groups and advocacy groups filed suit against Myriad claiming that the genes were simply a product of nature and not patentable subject matter. Myriad asserted that isolating the genetic material severs the chemical bonds, thereby creating a molecule that is not naturally occurring. Indeed, in the past the Court has confirmed that naturally occurring subject matter which is enhanced can be patentable. Specifically, when an invention claims subject matter that has markedly different characteristics than that which is found in nature, the resulting subject may be patent eligible. On the other hand, in this case, the Court found that merely separating the gene from its surrounding genetic material was not an inventive act and that Myriad did not create or alter the genetic material. Instead, it merely uncovered the location and genetic sequence of the gene making the resulting claimed invention nothing more than naturally occurring phenomena.

As discussed in Chapter 21, even groundbreaking and innovative discoveries do not alone satisfy the standards of patentability and similarly, extensive efforts are insufficient for establishing patentability. In this case, although Myriad's discovery is certainly a ground breaking and beneficial discovery, the result is simply a product of nature.

Patent law must "strike a balance between creating incentives to inventors and impeding the flow of information that may spur innovation." If valid, the patent would have given Myriad the exclusive right to isolate the genes. Historically, the scientific community has struggled with the notion of patenting human genes. Because patentees have the right to exclude others, granting patents on genetic material keeps crucial research tools in the hands of a few, potentially stifling future advancement as researchers would need to gain a license or permission to conduct research. Moreover, what if a patent owner simply refuses to grant licenses or permission to others in the medical community? Indeed, in this case, Myriad had filed suit and successfully precluded others from providing the genetic testing before the patent was invalidated. As we know, the right to exclude others is fundamental to patent law, but what about the need for medical progress. Affording patentees the right to prevent others from research and testing could come at a cost in the case of medical research. On the other hand, there is a strong belief that scientists should be rewarded for their work through patent protection. The incentives provided by the patent system promote innovation and accordingly patent law must seek to strike a balance by keeping the basic tools of scientific and technological work outside the scope of patentability while still providing incentives to innovate.

Chapter Summary

An NPE is an entity that enforces patent rights without practicing the underlying invention. Critics of NPEs object to the practice of obtaining patents for the sole purpose of the systematically enforcing the patents without any intention to practice the underlying invention. Because of the high costs associated with patent litigation, this practice is seen as a waste of corporate resources. The policy goal to incentivize inventor is at times in conflict with the policy goal of benefitting the public since the public does not realize a benefit when patents are merely enforced and not practiced. One of the biggest difficulties is defining NPEs in a way that is not overly inclusive. Several solutions have been proposed including, expanding a courts' ability to award attorney fees to a prevailing party or requiring a proof of damages hearing to take place before a full trial.

The Supreme Court recently took on the issue of the patentability of human genes. At issue was whether an isolated gene is within patentable subject matter or falls into the categorical exception that is physical phenomena. The patentee argued that because technological intervention is required to isolate or purify genetic material, the isolated genes fall into ambit of patentable subject matter. The Court rejected this argument ruling that an isolated human gene is simply a product of nature and outside the scope of patentable subject matter.

Key Terms

Non-Practicing Entity
Patent Troll
Patent Assertion Entity
Human Genes
Isolated Gene

Review Questions

1. How is the business model of an NPE at odds with the philosophical justification behind patent law?
2. What two factors make patent litigation costly?
3. What are the issues raised by NPEs?
4. How would requiring a patentee to initiate separate suits against several defendants rather than allowing the patentee to aggregate defendants have an effect on the issues raised by NPEs?
5. What do you see as a potential downside for expanding a court's ability to award attorney fees to prevailing parties?
6. What are some of the proposed solutions to the problems posed by NPEs?
7. What is an argument in support of patenting human genetic material?
8. What is an argument against patenting human genetic material?

Web Links

1. Many have weighed in on the issue of patenting human genes. The National Human Genome Research Institute provides detailed information and links. See: http://www.genome.gov/19016590.

Discussion Exercise

1. Finding the appropriate definition for NPEs is an important step in establishing an effective solution to the problems identified. How would you define an NPE for the purposes of proposing legislation aimed at curbing abusive litigation practices? What elements do you think are the most salient in defining NPEs?

Chapter 28

International Aspects of Patent Law

"You have to file in each country, you have to translate in each country, you have to sue in each country, and you have to pay renewal fees in each country. It's complete madness—very, very expensive."
—Sir James Dyson, inventor and entrepreneur

Chapter Outline

28.1.   The Paris Convention and the Patent Cooperation Treaty
28.2.   TRIPS

Chapter Objectives

- Appreciate the complexities of filing for patent protection abroad.
- Identify the challenges of enforcing patent rights abroad.
- Understand the nature of the Paris Convention and the Patent Cooperation treaty.
- Identify the goals of the TRIPS Agreement.
- Recognize the balance struck by the TRIPS Agreement.

The U.S. patent statute enumerates the activities that constitute infringement and notably, specifies that only activity occurring within the United States can establish infringement. The reach of U.S. patent laws does not extend beyond our nation's borders. Yet, in the last several decades, business has become increasingly more global, making the need for patentees to protect their interests overseas vital. Inventors must look at two issues when it comes to international patent practice: gaining patent protection abroad and addressing infringement that takes place overseas.

Of course, the complete harmonization of intellectual property laws through-out the world is an impossibility. Instead, over the last 150 years many inter-national treaties have been established in an effort to address the issue of enforcing intellectual property rights throughout the world. Let's take a look at some of the treaties that have emerged in this area. An important caveat is that in order to benefit from the rights found in a *treaty*, the country in which a patentee seeks to enforce the treaty's benefit, must be a member of that par-ticular treaty. In other words, countries are not required to adhere to the pa-rameters of a treaty without first agreeing to do so by becoming a *member* of the treaty. To this end, although the United States has had a long history of strong intellectual property rights, there are many developing countries that do not have the same history. Indeed, many developing countries have political conflicts and medical crises that take precedence over intellectual property con-cerns. Consequently, these countries have been slower to recognize intellec-tual property rights.

Let's look at the practice of gaining patent protection abroad. For patent protection in a particular county, patentees must look to the patent laws of each country in which patent protection is sought. For this reason, under-standing how to file a patent application in each country is vital. International patent practice can be an extremely complex matter because filing a patent ap-plication in one country may affect a patentee's ability to file in another coun-try. As you recall, novelty requires that a claimed invention is new compared to the prior art. Under many statutory schemes, prior art can include previ-ously filed patent applications. In this respect, a patentee can defeat novelty by his own patent application filed in another country. There are mainly two treaties which address this scenario: The *Paris Convention for the Protection of Industrial Property*, referred to as the Paris Convention, and the *Patent Co-operation Treaty*. Let's take a look at each.

28.1. The Paris Convention and Patent Cooperation Treaty

The Paris Convention was one of the first international treaties that ad-dressed the patent rights of inventors. A significant element of the Paris Con-vention is that the treaty affords patentees what is known as *national treatment*. National treatment requires that individual citizens of member countries re-ceive the same protection of intellectual property laws that a country offers its own citizens. The Paris Convention also provides that the filing date in a member country will be recognized for a period of time in other member countries giving applicants the benefit of an earlier filing date to establish priority. When it was signed in 1883, only 11 countries signed on as members. The treaty now has over 170 member countries.

The Patent Cooperation Treaty similarly addresses the issue of international patent filings by allowing a patentee to file an application, referred to as a *PCT application*, with a designated *Receiving Office* establishing an effective filing date to be recognized in other member countries. An applicant can then decide to pursue a patent application in a member country. Each country will prosecute the patent application for validity under its own set of patent laws, determining whether to accept or reject the application. Multinational corporations with a presence in many countries can greatly benefit from the advantages of PCT when seeking patent protection overseas.

28.2. TRIPS

Aside from issues arising from patent filings, enforcing patent rights overseas can also pose a challenge for inventors. How can a U.S. inventor enforce U.S. patent rights in a foreign country? Where would the inventor file suit? The U.S? The country in which the infringement takes place? As an initial matter, foreign nationals do not necessarily have to answer to a suit filed in the U.S. This is a matter of personal jurisdiction. Similarly, other nations will not enforce U.S. laws. Thus, infringement that takes place in a foreign country poses questions of enforceability. Many of these issues have been addressed by international agreement. One of the primary treaties providing the basis for the recognition intellectual property rights throughout the world is the *Agreement on Trade-Related Aspects of Intellectual Property Rights* ("TRIPS"). In addition to patent rights, TRIPS provides a means for the enforcement of other areas of intellectual property, including copyrights, trademarks, and geographic indicators. An objective of the TRIPS agreement is to establish minimum levels of intellectual property protection throughout the world among its member nations. TRIPS also provides procedures on how member countries should enforce intellectual property rights and settle disputes.

A situation in which TRIPS and the U.S. patent laws differ is where a patentee does not practice an invention, but attempts to assert patent rights against others. Under these circumstances TRIPS allows a country the option of granting a compulsory license to a competitor. Contrast this with the patent rights afforded under U.S. patent law where an inventor is simply given the right to exclude all others, regardless of whether the patentee practices the invention. The implication is that an inventor has the right to exclude others from practicing the invention without providing the public the benefit of the patented innovation. TRIPS takes a different approach awarding exclusive patent protection only where an inventor is practicing the invention. Under TRIPS, when a compulsory license is granted to a competitor, the patentee will be compensated for the use of the patented invention and the public has the benefit of the innovation. In this regard, TRIPS aims to strike a balance between benefiting the public and protecting the interests of inventors.

Chapter Summary

Because U.S. patent laws do not extend beyond the nation's borders, patentees must look to international treaties in order to establish patent protection internationally. When seeking to enforce patent rights abroad, patentees must look to the country's laws in which they wish to enforce patent rights. Several international treaties address the issues that can arise in international patent practice.

Filing for patent protection abroad raises the possibility that a patent application filed in one country can defeat patentability in another country. The Paris Convention and the Patent Cooperation Treaty provide patentees the ability to file for patent protection without necessarily defeating novelty in another country. The Paris Convention provides that the filing date in one member country will be recognized in other member countries for a period of time. The Patent Cooperation Treaty allows patentees to file a PCT application facilitating filing in multiple member countries.

TRIPS provides a means for patentees to enforce patent rights in member countries and establishes minimums for intellectual property protection. TRIPS allows governments the option of granting compulsory licenses in certain situations. Both the Paris Convention and TRIPS require that member countries afford patentees national treatment.

Key Terms

Treaty
Paris Convention
National Treatment

Patent Cooperation Treaty
TRIPS

Review Questions

1. Why must a patentee look to the patent laws in another country?
2. What is a prerequisite for enforcing the rights found in a treaty in a specific county?
3. Explain the complexity of filing for patent protection in several countries.
4. How does the Paris Convention address the difficulties associated with filing for protection in several countries?
5. Explain the meaning of national treatment under the Paris Convention and TRIPS.
6. What is the purpose of a PCT application?
7. Why is it difficult for patentees to enforce their patent rights abroad?
8. Under what circumstances does TRIPS allow the imposition of a compulsory license?

Web Links

1. The treaties discussed above are administered by two organizations. TRIPS is administered by the World Trade Organization. See: http://www.wto.org/ to find out more about TRIPS, including which countries are members of the treaty. The Paris Convention is administered by the World Intellectual Property Organization. See: http://www.wipo.int/portal/index.html.en to find out more about which countries are members of the Paris Convention.

Discussion Exercise

1. TRIPS allows for the imposition of compulsory licenses in certain instances. Do you agree with this notion? Under what circumstances do you think compulsory licenses should be allowed? Are there certain industries in which you think it is more or less appropriate to grant compulsory licenses? Do you think compulsory licenses would be a good addition to the U.S. system of patent laws? Why or why not?

Unit 6

Trade Secret Basics

Chapter 29

Introduction to Trade
Secret Law

"The problem with trade secrets is that they must be kept secret."
—James E. White

Chapter Outline

29.1.   A Short History of Trade Secret Law
29.2.   The Policy Goals of Trade Secret Law
29.3.   Trade Secret in Practice

Chapter Objectives

· Learn the history of trade secret protection under the law.
· Understand the policy considerations behind protecting trade secrets.
· Learn an overview of how trade secrets are used in business.

A *trade secret* is any information that can be used in the operation of a business or other enterprise and that is sufficiently valuable and secret to afford an actual or potential economic advantage over others. Restatement (Third) of Unfair Competition (1995). Classic examples of trade secrets include secret formulas, such as the recipe for Coca-Cola, and secret processes or devices that make manufacturing easier, cheaper, or faster somehow. Almost anything that enhances a business and that is secret from competitors may be protected as a trade secret, but trade secret protection is only available as long as the secret is maintained. An owner of a trade secret must take careful steps to protect it, or it may be lost without recourse.

29.1. A Short History of Trade Secret Law

There are conflicting opinions regarding the exact origins of trade secret law. One popular theory is that Roman law regarding the inappropriate extraction of confidential business information from slaves was the first legal embodiment of a right to maintain trade secrets. *Trade Secrets and the Roman Law*: The Acto Servi Corrupti, 30 Colum. L. Rev. 837 (1930). This idea is sharply contested by other scholars, who contend that, although certain Roman laws could theoretically be used to protect trade secrets, there is no evidence to suggest that they were ever used in that manner. Alan Watson, *Trade Secrets and Roman Law: The Myth Exploded*, 11 Tul. Eur. & Civ. L.F. 19, 19 (1996). Despite this controversy, it is clear that modern trade secret law began in England in the early 1800s and quickly spread to the United States.

Once in the United States, trade secret law developed rapidly as a common law cause of action. Each state developed its own, slightly unique, body of common law trade secret case law, which led to variations in the law on a state-by-state basis. These variations resulted in slightly different expectations in trade secret cases, depending on the state, which posed a problem for interstate business operations. Some states were perceived to offer a greater level of protection to trade secrets than others, and this uneven playing field was bad for interstate businesses who were concerned about having to manage business information differently in each state.

In 1923, the American Law Institute was created in order to promote the clarification and simplification of the common law in the United States. This is done primarily by drafting "Restatements of the Law" and model statutes or codes to incorporate what the American Law Institute believes is the best the common law of the country has to offer, while excluding the worst. In 1939, the American Law Institute released the Restatement (Second) of Torts, which provided a concise expounding of the common law of trade secrets of the time. The Restatement of Torts proved to have a lasting impact, as it became the standard trade secret reference of the century, and at least four states continue to rely on it today. Most states moved on, in or shortly after 1995, when the Restatement (Third) of Unfair Competition (1995) was released with updated trade secret material.

As of today, at least forty-seven states, Puerto Rico, the U.S. Virgin Islands, and the District of Columbia have adopted some form of the Uniform Trade Secrets Act ("UTSA"). The UTSA was released by the Uniform Law Commission in 1979, and amended in 1985. The Uniform Law Commission is a nonprofit organization of commissioners appointed from each state, Puerto Rico, the U.S. Virgin Islands, and the District of Columbia for the purpose of discussing areas of law in need of increased uniformity and drafting model acts accordingly. The UTSA was drafted to bring the same body of law regarding misappropriation of trade secrets to the entire country, if possible. The Prefatory Note of the UTSA provides an assessment of the state of trade secret law at the time of its initial release, and explains the need for change:

> A valid patent provides a legal monopoly for seventeen years in exchange for public disclosure of an invention. If, however, the courts ultimately decide that the Patent Office improperly issued a patent, an invention will have been disclosed to competitors with no corresponding benefit. In view of the substantial number of patents that are invalidated by the courts, many businesses now elect to protect commercially valuable information through reliance upon the state law of trade secret protection. *Kewanee Oil Co. v. Bicron Corp.*, 416 U.S. 470 (1974), which establishes that neither the Patent Clause of the United States Constitution nor the federal patent laws pre-empt state trade secret protection for patentable or unpatentable information, may well have increased the extent of this reliance.
>
> The recent decision in *Aronson v. Quick Point Pencil Co.*, 99 S.Ct. 1096, 201 USPQ 1 (1979) reaffirmed *Kewanee* and held that federal patent law is not a barrier to a contract in which someone agrees to pay a continuing royalty in exchange for the disclosure of trade secrets concerning a product.
>
> Notwithstanding the commercial importance of state trade secret law to interstate business, this law has not developed satisfactorily. In the first place, its development is uneven. Although there typically are a substantial number of reported decisions in states that are commercial centers, this is not the case in less populous and more agricultural jurisdictions. Secondly, even in states in which there has been significant litigation, there is undue uncertainty concerning the parameters of trade secret protection, and the appropriate remedies for misappropriation of a trade secret. One commentator observed:

"Under technological and economic pressures, industry continues to rely on trade secret protection despite the doubtful and confused status of both common law and statutory remedies. Clear, uniform trade secret protection is urgently needed...."

Comment, "Theft of Trade Secrets: The Need for a Statutory Solution", 120 U.Pa.L.Rev. 378, 380-81 (1971).

In spite of this need, the most widely accepted rules of trade secret law, §757 of the Restatement of Torts, were among the sections omitted from the Restatement of Torts, 2d (1978).

The Uniform Act codifies the basic principles of common law trade secret protection, preserving its essential distinctions from patent law. Under both the Act and common law principles, for example, more than one person can be entitled to trade secret protection with respect to the same information, and analysis involving the "reverse engineering" of a lawfully obtained product in order to discover a trade secret is permissible. *Compare* Uniform Act, Section 1(2) (misappropriation means acquisition of a trade secret by means that should be known to be improper and unauthorized disclosure or use of information that one should know is the trade secret of another) *with Miller v. Owens-Illinois, Inc.*, 187 USPQ 47, 48 (D.Md.1975) (alternative holding) (prior, independent discovery a complete defense to liability for misappropriation) *and Wesley-Jessen, Inc., v. Reynolds*, 182 USPQ 135, 144-45, (N.D.Ill.1974) (alternative holding) (unrestricted sale and lease of camera that could be reverse engineered in several days to reveal alleged trade secrets preclude relief for misappropriation).

For liability to exist under this Act, a Section 1(4) trade secret must exist and either a person's acquisition of the trade secret, disclosure of the trade secret to others, or use of the trade secret must be improper under Section 1(2). The mere copying of an unpatented item is not actionable.

Like traditional trade secret law, the Uniform Act contains general concepts. The contribution of the Uniform Act is substitution of unitary definitions of trade secret and trade secret misappropriation, and a single statute of limitations for the various property, quasi-contractual, and violation of fiduciary relationship theories of noncontractual liability utilized at common law. The Uniform Act also codifies the results of the better reasoned cases concerning the remedies for trade secret misappropriation.

29.2. The Policy Goals of Trade Secret Law

Trade secret law is unique in that it derives force from the common law of property, like other forms of intellectual property, but also from the common law of fiduciary relations. When a trade secret is improperly taken, the owner of the trade secret, like any owner of any property, has some rights to stop the taking and to recover the property, if possible. Society despises theft, and our laws reflect that notion. However, trade secret also involves trust. The essence of a trade secret is that it is, and must remain, a secret. Yet, in order to use a trade secret in a productive, efficient, and effective manner, it is almost always necessary to share that trade secret with others who will use it in the conduct of business. As long as the owner of the trade secret takes reasonable measures to protect the secrecy of the trade secret, and to secure the obligation of those trusted with the trade secret to keep it secret, then the law will generally enforce those obligations. The policy of trade secret law is therefore a combination of property policy, contract policy, and potentially the policy of fiduciary relations.

29.3. Trade Secret in Practice

Trade secrets serve as an alternative to patents in the United States. While there are a variety of advantages to each type of intellectual property involving inventions and novel processes, the basic choice for the creator of an invention or process may be between the relative certainty of patent protection and the potential for indefinite benefit of trade secret protection. In order to obtain a patent, the creator must disclose his invention or process to the world. If the patent application is rejected, the secrecy of the invention or process is lost and no protection is gained. If the application is granted, the disclosure still happens but solid protection is in place for a limited duration. This public disclosure and freedom to market the patented idea may bring new opportunities, but when the patent expires the protection expires with it and the monopoly on the idea is no more.

Trade secrets are potentially much more fragile than patents, and the danger with trade secrets is that the secret may be inadvertently released, or even stolen, at almost any time. The advantage is that a trade secret can last forever, along with the monopoly of the idea and the accompanying benefits. The temptation of indefinite protection leads many businesses to opt for trade secret protection for ideas that have lasting potential. Some industries that are particularly susceptible to reverse engineering will find much more use in patent protection, but for those industries where it is practical to conceal a process or formula or device from the world, trade secret protection is immensely valuable.

Chapter Summary

Trade secret law continues to evolve in the United States, but its basic elements are essentially the same as they have been since the 1800s. State laws change over time to better reflect improvements in trade secret law nationally and to enhance uniformity, which is desirable for business reasons. There is great value in trade secrets, which provide an economic advantage that competitors do not have and do not automatically receive after a predetermined time period, as is the case with patents. Although fragile, the potential for indefinite protection makes trade secret protection an extremely attractive option for many businesses.

Key Terms

Trade Secret

Review Questions

1. What type of information may properly be a trade secret?
2. What advantages do trade secrets have over patents?
3. What advantages do patents have over trade secrets?

Web Links

1. http://www.ali.org/—Website of the American Law Institute.
2. http://uniformlaws.org/—Website of the Uniform Laws Commission.

Discussion Exercises

1. What types of patentable ideas would not be well suited for protection with trade secret law?
2. In light of the potential for trade secret protection to last indefinitely, is the duration of utility patents reasonable?
3. Would longer utility patent lifespan cause more companies to apply for patents, which would result in the eventual transfer of the idea to the public domain, rather than relying on trade secret protection?

Chapter 30

Establishing and Protecting Trade Secret Status

"Keep it secret. Keep it safe."
—Gandalf, *The Lord of the Rings* by J.R.R. Tolkien

Chapter Outline

Chapter Objectives

- Learn how states regulate and protect trade secrets.
- Learn how trade secret owners must protect trade secrets.
- Understand the ways that a trade secret may be shared without losing secret status.

30.1. State Statutes and Common Law

As described above, each state has absorbed the English common law heritage of trade secret protection and has developed its own, somewhat unique body of state case law to interpret that common law. In order to make the country's trade secret laws more uniform as a whole, the Restatement (Second) of Torts, the Restatement (Third) of Unfair Competition, and the Uniform Trade Secrets Act have each been adopted, in whole or in part, in some form in every state. The lack of any one model code being uniformly and universally adopted still gives rise to variation in trade secret law across the country, but much less so than pure common law and case law would produce alone.

A trade secret is defined in essentially the same way under each of the model codes and under traditional common law principals:

> A trade secret may consist of any formula, pattern, device or compilation of information which is used in one's business, and which gives him an opportunity to obtain an advantage over competitors who do not know or use it. It may be a formula for a chemical compound, a process of manufacturing, treating or preserving materials, a pattern for a machine or other device, or a list of customers. It differs from other secret information in a business in that it is not simply information as to single or ephemeral events in the conduct of the business, as, for example, the amount or other terms of a secret bid for a contract or the salary of certain employees, or the security investments made or contemplated, or the date fixed for the announcement of a new policy or for bringing out a new model or the like. A trade secret is a process or device for continuous use in the operation of the business. Generally it relates to the production of goods, as, for example, a machine or formula for the production of an article. It may, however, relate to the sale of goods or to other operations in the business, such as a code for determining discounts, rebates or other concessions in a price list or catalogue, or a list of specialized customers, or a method of bookkeeping or other office management.

Restatement (Second) of Torts § 757 (1939), cmt. B (1965-79).

A trade secret is any information that can be used in the operation of a business or other enterprise and that is sufficiently valuable and secret to afford an actual or potential economic advantage over others. Restatement (Third) of Unfair Competition (1995).

"Trade secret" means information, including a formula, pattern, compilation, program, device, method, technique, or process that:

(i) Derives independent economic value, actual or potential, from not being generally known to, and not being readily ascertainable by proper means by, other persons who can obtain economic value from its disclosure or use, and

(ii) Is the subject of efforts that are reasonable under the circumstances to maintain its secrecy.

Uniform Trade Secrets Act (1985), § 1.

The United States is a party to the Agreement on Trade Related Aspects of Intellectual Property (TRIPS), which requires members to enact trade secret protection. Specifically, TRIPS requires that party nations provide a means for protecting information that is secret, commercially valuable because it is secret, and subject to reasonable steps to keep it secret. This requirement is satisfied by the same requirements and protections provided by state law in every state. Interestingly, there is no federal statute expressly providing a uniform civil law with federal remedies for trade secret misappropriation. This seems unusual, given the availability of strong and comprehensive federal laws for patent, trademark, and copyright protection.

It is possible to bring a federal civil claim under the Lanham Act's unfair competition provisions, typically by classifying misappropriation of trade secrets as a form of passing off, although this is not very common. It is also possible to use other federal laws with civil action provisions creatively to protect trade secrets, such as the civil provisions of the Racketeer Influenced & Corrupt Organizations Act, 18 U.S.C. § 1962 (2006), or the Computer Fraud and Abuse Act, 18 U.S.C. § 1030 (2012). These options exist, but it is clear that Congress is content with allowing the bulk of trade secret litigation to play out in state court, or at least under state statutes and common law.

Congress has provided criminal penalties for trade secret misappropriation, however, through the Economic Espionage Act of 1996, 18 U.S.C. 1831. It is also possible to use other criminal laws on the state and federal levels creatively to take advantage of available criminal penalties that were not necessarily intended for protecting trade secrets, but which have broad enough provisions to provide coverage.

30.2. Establishing Rights

Under state law, trade secrets rights arise automatically whenever a party has some form of secret, valuable information that meets the definitions above. Under the UTSA, which represents the law in almost all states, and reasonably mirrors the law in the states that have yet to adopt it, the first step is to create or obtain some form of information that "[d]erives independent economic value, actual or potential, from not being generally known to, and not being readily ascertainable by proper means by, other persons who can obtain economic value from its disclosure or use." The first part of this step is easy to assess. If the information a business has is also known to others in the industry or generally in the public, it is not a trade secret. The more people who know about the information in question, particularly in the format in which it is assembled, the less likely it is that the information may constitute a trade secret.

This does not mean that nobody else may know about the information, as discussed in detail below. The information may be shared, as needed, with employees or contractors, so long as reasonable steps are taken to protect the secrecy of the information. The information may even be licensed out to other businesses, as long as it is subject to thorough agreements to protect its secrecy. The "secret" in trade secret is a relative term. It is possible for multiple persons to each independently invent or discover a trade secret by legitimate means, and each will own the trade secret and have the rights to protect it and carefully disclose it, subject to the rights of the other owners. If multiple businesses in an industry each own the trade secret, they may still protect the trade secret against other businesses in that industry and may thereby continue to benefit. If, however, the trade secret becomes so commonly known in an industry that it loses its essential secrecy, then it may not be protected as a trade secret.

A trade secret must also not be readily ascertainable by others by proper means. This means that information that might be valuable in business, but that any competitor can obtain from a public resource or otherwise with little expenditure of time and effort and money is not a trade secret. For example, public vendor lists or pricing lists, basic contact information for customers that are obvious, public telephone directories, or a process or formula that is or was the subject of a patent may not be trade secrets because these are all types of information that are readily ascertainable by a competitor. Anything published in a trade journal, a reference book, or online is generally considered to be readily available and easily ascertainable.

However, vendor or customer lists that contain proprietary information, such as specific pricing levels, order preferences, and anticipated needs, may well constitute trade secrets. The same is true for undisclosed improvements to patented devices or processes, or even the fact that a particular business is using or not using a particular device or process. This last type of negative information may be valuable and protectable in many cases, such as when a competing business is trying to determine the most efficient way to manufacture a competing product or deciding which technology or products to research. If a competitor learns that a successful business has abandoned an established technology in favor of a new one, or that research into a new type of product has been abandoned as unprofitable, that information can greatly influence the competitor's business decisions and potentially save the competitor significant time and money.

The last part of the first step mentions "other persons who can obtain economic value from its disclosure or use." This language allows the legal recognition of a trade secret that may be readily ascertainable or even commonly known in one industry or segment of the population, but unknown in another. For example, a certain type of high-strength, corrosion-resistant clamp might be used in certain types of surgeries and may be commonly known in the medical industry, but not outside the medical industry as they are only marketed toward surgeons and hospitals. If a power washing service discovered these clamps and realized that they could be used on high-pressure power washing equipment to resolve a frequent industry problem with corroded clamps, the use of those clamps could be protected as a trade secret as long as their use was kept secret. The fact that the clamps would be readily available to other power washing businesses does not make the information about their suitability and use readily available.

Legitimate means of obtaining a trade secret include reverse engineering. Reverse engineering is simply examining and disassembling or deconstructing some device or process that is readily available on the market or to the public in order to understand how it works and how to duplicate it. Trade secrets are potentially vulnerable

The second step to establish a trade secret is to determine and maintain the secrecy of the information described above. If information is already disclosed or readily ascertainable, it cannot be a trade secret, subject to the example above where the trade secret may be a new use or application for information that was previously disclosed in another context. If the information has not been disclosed, then its secrecy must be maintained. Courts expect a reasonable business person to take steps that are reasonable under the circumstances to protect a trade secret. While telling nobody and keeping the secret information locked away at all times is ideal protection, courts understand that such a scenario is not practical for business purposes.

30.3. Corporate Policies

The maintenance of secrecy starts with limiting disclosure of the secret. As disclosure is ultimately the test for secrecy, the fewer people who know about the trade secret the better. Therefore, companies will often establish certain policies to limit disclosures of trade secrets on a need-to-know basis. Only those employees or agents who have a legitimate need to know the trade secret to perform their function properly should have access to the trade secret, and then only to the extent needed. This means that access, when possible, should be both limited with regard to the number of people that have any access, and the amount of access that each person has. If the trade secret may be divided up, as in the case of a process that may be performed in parts by different workers, then it may be reasonable to expect the trade secret owner to limit each worker's access to only that portion of the trade secret that she must perform. This is typically expected when the trade secret is a compilation of confidential business information, such as a detailed client database with order and pricing information. Each salesperson with access to the database should only have access to the information needed to serve his clients, and not all of the clients' information.

There is no set of required steps that a court will determine are always reasonable and always required to protect a trade secret, but many common steps are prudent in most situations. The greater the effort made to protect and maintain secrecy, the more likely a court will be to deem those efforts to be sufficient. However, courts will not require elaborate, unduly expensive, unduly burdensome, or heroic efforts to protect trade secrets. Reasonable measures under the circumstances are all the law requires. Courts may expect more security measures when the value of the trade secret at issue is very high. Some common measures to ensure the secrecy of trade secrets include:

1. Limiting access to trade secrets to only those who have a legitimate need to know the information, and limiting their access to only those parts of the information that they need to know, and only when they need access to perform their jobs. Allowing employees who only need partial access to have full access, or allowing employees to remotely access trade secrets or access them from home, for example, may not be appropriate.

2. The use of a safe or locked cabinets to store documents or electronic files containing the trade secret or revealing information about it when those documents or files are not in use. If these are paper documents, a simple locking filing cabinet may suffice. If these are electronic records stored on removable media, the same locking filing cabinet may suffice. If they are stored on a computer system, the room containing that system should be locked.

3. The use of unique passwords to access electronic trade secret files or systems. Passwords keep the information secure form unauthorized users, and unique passwords for each user allow the trade secret owner to keep

track of who has accessed the files.

4. The use of enclosed and secured spaces when the trade secret must be revealed for business use. If the trade secret or device, the room or area in which it is used should be off limits to others, including the public and employees with no legitimate need to know the trade secret. This may be enhanced in appropriate cases by a prohibition on photography in the area.

5. The labeling of confidential business information or trade secrets as such, in order to put employees, contractors, or others who might encounter them on notice that they contain sensitive information and should be treated accordingly.

6. The use of proper *non-disclosure agreements* and *confidentiality agreements* with key employees and licensees of the trade secret.

7. Other measures, such as alarm systems, security guards, encrypted file storage, only using electronic trade secret files on un-networked computers, using challenge tokens for remote access, requiring employees and contractors to wear identification and access badges, etc., are always helpful proof of reasonable efforts to maintain secrecy, but they are not typically required unless the trade secret is particularly valuable. Generally, trade secret protection is expected to be in proportion to the value of the trade secret, and reasonable businesses will take proportional measures to secure them, just as they would do with any other property of value.

30.4. Non-Disclosure and Confidentiality Agreements

When employees or contractors must have access to a trade secret in order to perform their duties, a reasonable trade secret owner will require the execution of carefully drafted non-disclosure and confidentiality agreements. These agreements will typically identify the trade secrets and confidential information that is sought to be protected, at least in general terms that are specific enough to identify the information without revealing its content or essence, and put the parties on notice that the information described is a trade secret that must be treated with the utmost confidentiality. These agreements bind the parties to maintain the confidentiality of the subject information and not to disclose that information to anyone not expressly authorized by the agreement. These agreements may specifically describe the permissible uses of the information, and any protective policies or practices employed and required by the trade secret owner.

In addition, these agreements may also stipulate what may happen in the event of a breach of the agreement. Common provisions include an agreement to litigate in a specific jurisdiction, an agreement to the specific body of law that will be applicable, an agreement that injunctive relief is warranted, and potentially an agreement that damages may be too hard to calculate accurately in the event of a breach so that a specific amount of liquidated damages may be awarded instead. These agreements may also contain provisions providing for an award of attorney's fees and costs in the event of a breach, event where the law would otherwise not award such damages.

These agreements might even contain provisions for the assignment of any inventions, ideas, trade secrets, improvements or other interests relating to the subject trade secret to the owner of the subject trade secret. Such assignment provisions are based on the possibility that an employee or contractor with access to the trade secret, and to the trade secret owner's tools, equipment, laboratories, research, and other resources, might create some new and valuable intellectual property during the course of his exposure to the trade secret. Permitting such an employee or contractor to keep the new idea for himself would, in theory, reward that person for work done or concepts created within the scope of his duties for the owner. In addition to this new interest, the trade secret owner must also prevent the incidental disclosure of his own trade secret during the course of an employee or contractor securing his new rights. For example, if a contractor were permitted to keep a new idea developed from work with the trade secret, and that contractor decided to patent the new idea, the application for that patent might necessarily include revealing information on the trade secret itself. This could potentially disclose and destroy the trade secret.

While the term of use of a trade secret in the context of employment or contracting, or even of licensing, will typically be expressly limited in duration, the obligations of non-disclosure and confidentiality are typically not. Those obligations will persist indefinitely, typically until such time as the underlying trade secrets and confidential information are in the public domain. The geographic scope of these agreements will also typically be worldwide.

30.5. Licensing

The same concerns arise in the context of trade secret licensing. Licensing itself does not destroy the secrecy of a trade secret, but the owner must take careful steps to prevent any unintended disclosures. Licenses will typically model other non-disclosure and confidentiality agreements, but the additional requirements that the licensee take the same steps within her company that the owner takes to protect against disclosures. A licensee may disclose the trade secret to her own employees and contractors, if permitted by the license, but only if those people are required to sign comprehensive non-disclosure and confidentiality agreements, and only under the same protective circumstances used in the owner's company.

Courts will treat disclosures caused by others pursuant to careless licensing in the same manner as careless conduct by the owner of the trade secret. The concept of "naked licensing" from trademark essentially applies to trade secret as well. A reasonable trade secret owner will not leave the management and protection of its trade secret up to its licensees, but will ensure that its licenses are strict and thorough. It will also be sure to police those licenses, perhaps by inspection of licensees' facilities, and certainly by litigation if necessary to resolve a breach of a license agreement that could cause an unauthorized disclosure of the trade secret.

Chapter Summary

The acquisition of trade secret rights is a relatively simple process. Much like copyright, trade secret protection applies automatically to any information that fits the straightforward definition under the law, for as long as its secrecy is maintained. The many creative ways that businesses use information, particularly in the digital age with electronic data mining and an endless stream of new data being created daily, give rise to a nearly endless variety of trade secret embodiments. Even unexpected information, such as the fact that a company is not using a certain technology, may constitute a valuable trade secret. The trouble with trade secrets though is the requirement that they be kept secret, which conflicts with the business requirement for limited disclosure to be productive. This constant tension makes trade secret law an interesting area of intellectual property law.

Key Terms

Non-Disclosure Agreement
Confidentiality Agreement

Review Questions

1. What type of information may constitute a trade secret?
2. How can a trade secret owner protect the secrecy of a trade secret?
3. Can trade secrets be licensed for use by others?

Web Links

1. jolt.law.harvard.edu/articles/pdf/v08/08HarvJLTech427.pdf—Christopher Pace, *The Case For A Federal Trade Secrets Act*, 8 Harvard Journal of Law and Technology 427 (1995).

Discussion Exercise

1. How can businesses protect their trade secrets from disclosure in litigation over alleged trade secret misappropriation? Must the trade secret be revealed in court to prove a claim of misappropriation? What if the defendant alleges that the information at issue is not properly the subject of trade secret protection? How can that issue be resolved without disclosing the trade secret? Can the jury in a trade secret trial use the information it learns during the trial for business purposes? What about the other parties in the case?

Chapter 31

Losing Trade Secret Status

"There are no secrets that time does not reveal." — Jean Racine

Chapter Outline

Chapter Objectives

- Learn the ways that trade secret protection may be lost, including through misappropriation and disclosure by the owner.
- Learn the various defenses to a claim of misappropriation.
- Understand how the doctrine of inevitable disclosure may impact trade secret cases.
- Understand how reverse engineering may be lawfully used to discover trade secrets.

31.1. Misappropriation and Defenses

A trade secret may be lost in many ways, some of which are legitimate in the eyes of the law and some of which are not. The common law and the Uniform Trade Secrets Act ("UTSA") generally share the same view regarding which means of acquiring trade secrets are improper. There is no all-inclusive list of the specific conduct that may be deemed *improper means*, but the UTSA provides the following:

> "'Improper means' includes theft, bribery, misrepresentation, breach or inducement of a breach of a duty to maintain secrecy, or espionage through electronic or other means."

Theft might involve a competitor or his agent breaking into a secured facility to steal a trade secret. Bribery might involve a competitor paying an executive or researcher with access to the trade secret to provide it to the competitor. Misrepresentation might involve the lie that one is subject to a non-disclosure and confidentiality agreement when that is not the case in order to gain unprotected access to the trade secret. Breach of a duty to maintain secrecy might involve a disgruntled employee giving the trade secret away to a competitor in violation of a non-disclosure and confidentiality agreement. Inducement of a breach of the duty to maintain secrecy might involve a competitor hiring away an employee with access to the trade secret and encouraging that employee to bring the trade secret with them. Espionage can involve a variety of tactics designed to obtain trade secrets, such as planting "double agent" employees in positions with access, bugging offices or telephones, or hacking into computer systems. Espionage can also include actions that are not ordinarily illegal or improper, such as using an airplane to fly over a competitor's new plant construction to determine its layout before walls and a roof can be built to protect it.

With regard to *misappropriation* of trade secrets, the UTSA defines it as follows:

> "Misappropriation" means:
> (i) acquisition of a trade secret of another by a person who knows or has reason to know that the trade secret was acquired by improper means; or
> (ii) disclosure or use of a trade secret of another without express or implied consent by a person who
> > (A) used improper means to acquire knowledge of the trade secret; or
> > (B) at the time of disclosure or use, knew or had reason to know that his knowledge of the trade secret was
> > > (I) derived from or through a person who had utilized improper means to acquire it;
> > > (II) acquired under circumstances giving rise to a duty to maintain its secrecy or limit its use; or

(III) derived from or through a person who owed a duty to the person seeking relief to maintain its secrecy or limit its use; or

(C) before a material change of his [or her] position, knew or had reason to know that it was a trade secret and that knowledge of it had been acquired by accident or mistake.

The UTSA, therefore, not only provides an action for misappropriation in the traditional cases of intentional acts of misappropriation, such as theft, bribery, and espionage, but also in cases where the person using the trade secret was not the initial bad actor but had knowledge of the improper means used to obtain the trade secret. The statutory provisions providing this protection mirror the common law equity considerations that would prevent such use. This situation is analogous to criminal laws prohibiting the receipt of stolen property. A bona fide purchaser may lawfully take possession of stolen goods, but a person may not accept them as gifts or even buy them at full market price if that person has knowledge that they were stolen. The same is true for trade secrets under the UTSA.

31.2. Disclosures

The UTSA's misappropriation provisions, above, covers both disclosures of trade secrets by those with a duty to maintain their secrecy, and the use of trade secrets with knowledge that someone improperly or accidentally disclosed them. Specifically, the UTSA prohibits "disclosure or use of a trade secret of another without express or implied consent by a person who [...] at the time of disclosure or use, knew or had reason to know that his knowledge of the trade secret was [...] derived from or through a person who owed a duty to the person seeking relief to maintain its secrecy or limit its use; or [...] before a material change of his [or her] position, knew or had reason to know that it was a trade secret and that knowledge of it had been acquired by accident or mistake."

Intentional disclosure of a trade secret without authorization is a form of misappropriation. Courts will offer protection to trade secret owners who act quickly to preserve the secrecy of a trade secret that was disclosed without authorization. A disgruntled employee might decide to leave the company and take trade secrets with him, despite the reasonable protections put in place by the owner of the trade secrets. In these cases, courts will allow actions for misappropriation against the employee and against any new employer that uses the disclosed trade secret.

Generally, a disclosure of a trade secret by its owner or her authorized employee or agent will destroy the secrecy of the trade secret and therefore destroy the trade secret itself. This can occur through intentional action, such as giving the trade secret to a competitor, publishing it in a trade publication, posting it on a company website, revealing it through product design or facility tours, displaying it in a public location, or by licensing it without proper use of non-disclosure and confidentiality agreements. Disclosure may also occur through unintentional action, such as a failure to take proper measures to ensure secrecy or through a mistake or accident.

Courts will generally provide protection to those trade secret owners who suffer a disclosure due to a good faith mistake or accident. An example might include the accidental release of trade secret material to a contractor who was not supposed to have access to that material, and who did not have a non-disclosure and confidentiality agreement covering that material. Courts expect that a trade secret owner will act very quickly to seek relief in court, and will take reasonable steps to obtain assurances of secrecy from the person who received the accidental disclosure.

However, courts will not provide protection on the basis of accidental or mistaken disclosure when the trade secret holder has failed to take reasonable steps to ensure the secrecy of the trade secret. If the company offers tours, and the tour guide mistakenly brings the tour group into an area containing secret designs or machinery, a court is unlikely to provide protection. It would probably be unreasonable to take such a risk, and the reasonable steps of locking that area and restricting visitor access would have maintained the secrecy of the trade secret. The same is likely true for advertisements of a product or process with images that inadvertently reveal a trade secret. Given the planned nature of such advertisements, a court is likely to find such a mistake to be glaring and a failure to take the reasonable step of reviewing those images before releasing them.

Finally, even when the court finds a legitimate mistake or accident to be the cause of a disclosure of a trade secret, the court will only prevent its use when the trade secret owner takes action before the good faith end user has knowledge or should know that the disclosure was due to a mistake or accident. This means that the court will prevent a competitor from benefiting from the disclosure if the owner of the trade secret promptly takes reasonable steps to maintain the secrecy of the trade secret, such as contacting competitors who were aware of the disclosure and informing them that it was an accident and then heading to court. However, if a disclosure is made under circumstances that do not put a competitor on notice that the disclosure was a mistake, and the competitor invests significant money and time into adopting the trade secret, a court is unlikely to prevent its use.

31.3. Defenses to Misappropriation

When a trade secret is alleged to have been misappropriated, there are a number of potential defenses to consider. Most defenses involve an attack on the trade secret itself, essentially trying to disprove a required element of the case against the defendant. As many cases of misappropriation involve fairly clear evidence that the defendant improperly obtained the information in question, the only viable strategy is to claim that what was taken was not a proper trade secret. The common defenses to misappropriation actions are listed and briefly explained below.

No Trade Secret

In this defense, the defendant simply attempts to attack the general trade secret status of the information in question. There can be no misappropriation if there is no trade secret to misappropriate, even if information was taken. A defendant might be successful with this defense if he can show that the information taken was publicly available, was known throughout the industry, was easily assembled or recreated with relatively little effort from easily accessible sources, or that it did not have competitive value.

Failure to Maintain Secrecy

A related defense is the claim that the plaintiff failed to maintain the secrecy of its trade secret. A trade secret is only entitled to protection as long as its owner takes reasonable steps to preserve its secrecy. A defendant might be successful with this defense if he can show that the information taken was publicly available, known throughout the industry, or had previously been disclosed by the owner. It will help if the owner routinely licenses the trade secret information, or discloses it to employees, without using proper non-disclosure and confidentiality agreements. However, even given less than ideal secrecy protection, a court is unlikely to let a defendant off the hook if the misappropriation occurred due to an intentional exploitation of poor security in order to steal a trade secret.

No Improper Means

Another defense to a claim of misappropriation is to disprove the allegation that the trade secret was taken through improper means. This might be due to a bona fide purchase of the trade secret from another person without any knowledge that the trade secret was misappropriated. This might also be due to an independent discovery or development of the trade secret. It is not unreasonable to assume the possibility that two similar, competing businesses in the same industry with the same interests in product and process development might simultaneously work on the same new idea and might discover or invent the same trade secret over time. The trade secret might also be legitimately obtained through a disclosure, as discussed above, or through reverse engineering, as discussed below.

Contract Defenses

If a claim of misappropriation arises under the terms of a noncompetition agreement or a non-disclosure or confidentiality agreement, then traditional contract law defenses may apply. Those defenses are numerous, but the basic defenses include a lack of consideration for the agreement, breach of the contract by the plaintiff, subsequent release of contractual duties, or waiver or modification of contract rights.

Statute of Limitations

Whether a claim of misappropriation arises under a contract theory, the common law of torts, or a specific statute such as the UTSA, a defendant may rely on the *statute of limitations* as a defense. A statute of limitations is a specific period of time within which a plaintiff must bring a cause of action in court, or that cause of action will be barred. The policy behind limiting the amount of time a plaintiff has to bring a cause of action is primarily based on consideration of fresh versus stale evidence and the desire of society to have legal and business matters settled so that people on 'all sides may move on without a perpetually lingering potential lawsuit. Naturally, as time passes, witnesses forget what happened and some move away or die. Testimonial evidence is therefore less reliable the longer it takes for a plaintiff to get to court, and documents and other physical evidence tend to get lost or damaged over time.

A potential defendant who might be sued at any time may have trouble obtaining credit or insurance, and while society strives to give a potential plaintiff ample time to file a lawsuit, there must be some reasonable limit of time after which the claim expires and allows the defendant to move on in peace. Under the UTSA, the statute of limitations for trade secret misappropriation is three years from the incident of misappropriation or the time the plaintiff learns or should have learned of the incident of misappropriation. The statute of limitations under the common law is generally three years for tort actions and six years for contract actions.

Laches

The defense of *laches* is an equitable defense. It is basically an argument about fairness that states that a plaintiff should not be allowed to delay in taking action against a plaintiff if that delay reasonably causes the defendant some type of real prejudice. The argument is similar to the concept of the statute of limitations, but may be used even when the statute of limitations has not yet expired. Basically, a defendant claims that the plaintiff knew that the defendant misappropriated a trade secret and then used that trade secret, and the plaintiff did nothing about it for a long time. During that time, the defendant may have invested significant time and money into developing a business around the trade secret. If the plaintiff is then allowed to bring a lawsuit for misappropriation, the defendant will be unfairly harmed.

Some commentators have criticized the defense of laches for being unnecessary, given the more formal statute of limitations. Indeed, no defendant could be duped into thinking that a plaintiff would not file a lawsuit if that defendant simply waited until the statute of limitations had run before investing time and money into the trade secret. It seems that laches almost rewards the most bold trade secret thieves for investing so heavily into an improperly obtained trade secret. However, the defense makes sense in situations where a plaintiff knowingly allows a defendant to conduct business with the trade secret solely to inflate the damages that the plaintiff hopes to obtain at trial.

Unclean Hands

The equitable doctrine of *unclean hands* may be used as a defense to a claim of misappropriation in cases where the plaintiff is engaged in some form of unfair, illegal, deceptive, or otherwise improper conduct with respect to the subject of the litigation. The logic of this defense is often summarized as "those who seek equity must act equitably." An example might involve a defendant alleged to have misappropriated a trade secret comprised of detailed customer information that is valuable and not available to competitors. The cause of action may arise under breach of a noncompetition and non-disclosure contract. The defendant might oppose an injunction request by arguing that the plaintiff is not entitled to such an equitable remedy due to the fact that the plaintiff was intentionally withholding and keeping a portion of the defendant's earned commissions on sales to those customers. In that situation, both the plaintiff and the defendant have acted wrongfully and breached their contract, and neither may be entitled to equitable remedies, such as an injunction, although both may still be able to recover damages.

31.4. Doctrine of Inevitable Disclosure

The *doctrine of inevitable disclosure* is a concept that a plaintiff may rely upon to prevent a person who has had access to the plaintiff's trade secrets from going into a competing business venture or going to work for a competitor. The idea is that, regardless of the potential good intentions of the person and the new employer, the knowledge the person has of the plaintiff's trade secrets would be disclosed eventually because the person would be in a position where he would need to use that knowledge to compete. If, for example, a chemist worked for company A making glue with a number of trade secret formulas, and then he left and went to work for company B as a glue chemist, he could not avoid relying on the knowledge he already has of company A's formulas in creating formulas for company B. He cannot simply forget those formulas, and even if he does not copy them exactly for company B, any new formulas he creates are likely to be derivative of company A's trade secrets.

This doctrine can apply equally when the trade secrets involved are sales and marketing strategies, customer information, business plans, and other executive information. If a sales manager leaves company A and works for a competitor, company B, in a similar position, she would have no choice but to rely on the confidential business information she already learned at company A. Even if she did not use that information directly for the benefit of company B, she would have to use it indirectly. For example, if she knew that company A was investing heavily in soliciting a particular customer, she might not advise company B on how to better solicit that customer, but she might instead advise company B to pick a different customer to solicit to avoid a direct competition with company A. The knowledge used to avoid such a direct battle with company A is still a trade secret and it still gives company B an advantage

CHAPTER THIRTY-ONE · LOSING TRADE SECRET STATUS   375

that other competitors do not have.

31.5. Reverse Engineering

Reverse engineering is the legitimate process of examining, analyzing, disassembling, and otherwise tinkering with a readily-available product or source of information in order to work backward and discover how it works, how it is made, or the underlying formulas or methods associated with its creation. Trade secrets may be freely discovered by reverse engineering, so long as the product or information source is obtained properly, such as by purchase of a product. Reverse engineering done in violation of a contract, such as a non-disclosure and confidentiality agreement, is not legitimate and constitutes a misappropriation of trade secrets if successful. Products that are susceptible to reverse engineering are often better protected by patent than by trade secret. Patent protection eliminates the threat of reverse engineering, while a trade secret can be obtained or destroyed by it.

Chapter Summary

There are many ways, both legitimate and illegitimate, by which a trade secret may be lost. Unlike the protection offered by patent, trade secret protection may be lost through intentional or even unintentional disclosures. The need to maintain secrecy is important, and is the major drawback of relying on trade secret protection instead of patent protection. However, when improper means are used to obtain a trade secret, the courts will permit an action for misappropriation to stop the offending use and disclosures of the trade secret and provide the plaintiff with damages. A defendant in a misappropriation case has a variety of defenses available, depending on the circumstances of the case.

Key Terms

Improper Means
Misappropriation
Statute of Limitations
Laches

Unclean Hands
Doctrine of Inevitable Disclosure

Review Questions

1. List three ways by which a person can legitimately obtain a trade secret.
2. List three ways of obtaining a trade secret that are considered "improper means."
3. What is the purpose of a statute of limitations?
4. What is the difference between a statute of limitations and laches?
5. What does the doctrine of unclean hands do?

Web Links

1. http://www.uniformlaws.org/shared/docs/trade%20secrets/utsa_final_85.pdf— Uniform trade Secrets Act.

Discussion Exercises

1. Describe a situation where an employee with access to trade secrets could work for a competing company without invoking the doctrine of inevitable disclosure.
2. Should a defendant in a misappropriation case be able to rely on the defense of laches even when a clear statute of limitations applies? Does that doctrine reward bold trade secret thieves?
3. If a person can observe a trade secret by flying over a competitor's construction site, should that be considered misappropriation? If the trade secret holder has put the trade secret on display in such a way that it can be viewed from a public location, such as from an airplane in public airspace, why should that trade secret be protected?

Chapter 32

Trade Secret Remedies

"There is no evil in the world without a remedy."
—Jacopo Sannazaro

Chapter Outline

32.1.   Non-Monetary Remedies
32.2.   Monetary Remedies
32.3.   Criminal Penalties

Chapter Objectives

- Learn what kinds of remedies are available in trade secret cases.
- Understand how injunctions may be used to prevent trade secret disclosure.
- Understand the differences between temporary restraining orders and types of injunctions.
- Learn about criminal penalties available in trade secret cases.

32.1. Non-Monetary Remedies

One of the biggest concerns in trade secret litigation is maintaining the secrecy of the trade secrets at issue in the case. When an employee leaves and takes trade secrets with him, the most immediate concern is to prevent the disclosure of the trade secret, or to mitigate any disclosures that may already have occurred. In order to protect the trade secret, the most commonly used tool is the *injunction*. As previously discussed, injunctions are flexible, versatile court orders that can be used to force a person to either do something or refrain from doing something. They are the perfect quick-response tool for trade secret cases.

When the owner of a trade secret discovers that the trade secret has been misappropriated and is in danger of being disclosed, that owner must take immediate action to protect the trade secret. If the owner delays in taking protective action, that delay can be held against him in court. Given that concern, and the risk of further disclosure, the owner may seek emergency equitable relief in court. Even before a lawsuit is served on the defendant, the court may grant the plaintiff emergency protection by hearing an argument about the case *ex parte*, or without the defendant present. The matter will not be resolved permanently without the defendant having a fair opportunity to be heard, but some judges will grant a *temporary restraining order* or TRO, which is a very short-term injunction that prevents the defendant from engaging in activity that would cause the trade secret to be disclosed. When the defendant is served with the complaint and accompanying materials in the case, he will also receive a copy of the TRO, which is typically only in effect for a few days until the date of the hearing on the plaintiff's motion for a preliminary injunction.

The next step in this process is a hearing in court on the plaintiff's motion for a *preliminary injunction*, which is similar to a TRO but lasts until the resolution of the case on the merits. A preliminary injunction hearing is often the most important part of a trade secret case, as the winner of the hearing may well be the winner in the case. When the judge decides whether or not to grant a preliminary injunction, she must weigh the risk of harm to the plaintiff if the injunction is not granted against the risk of harm to the defendant if the injunction is granted. She must also weigh the likelihood of success of the case on the merits. If she rules in favor of the plaintiff, she is effectively signaling that the plaintiff has a solid case. If she rules for the defendant, she is effectively signaling that the defendant has a strong defense and a good chance of defeating the claims at trial. Either way, trade secret cases, particularly cases arising from the alleged breach of non-compete agreements, often settle quickly after the judge rules on the plaintiff's motion for a preliminary injunction.

Later in the case, and often once a judgment has entered, a preliminary injunction may be converted into a *permanent injunction*, which may contain the same restrictions or different restrictions as the preliminary injunction, but which lasts indefinitely or for a specified duration that is typically much longer than a preliminary injunction. A permanent injunction will usually prohibit the defendant from using or disclosing the trade secrets at issue in the case, and may prohibit the defendant from competing or working for a competitor for a specified duration, as in non-compete agreement cases. A permanent injunction can always be modified later if circumstances change in such a way as to make the injunction unfair or unreasonable. That could be the case where an employee is prevented from working for a competitor in order to protect trade secrets, and then the trade secrets at issue are otherwise disclosed to the public. As there would be no more risk of disclosure in that case, it would not be equitable to maintain the injunction and the defendant would likely be successful in requesting that the injunction be dissolved.

As injunctions are extremely versatile, one may be used to impose any manner of protective restrictions on a party or to compel a party to do or refrain from doing anything. An example might be an injunction ordering a party to destroy documents or records that contain trade secrets, or to turn such materials over to another party in order to prevent their disclosure. The court may also order that a party, or a designated neutral, be allowed to periodically enter the premises or examine the records of another party to determine whether trade secrets are being used unlawfully.

Another form of equitable remedy that may be ordered in a trade secret case is an *accounting*. An accounting order may issue where the court determines there is a need for detailed information about a party's business activities, profits, or expenses. Such an order could be used to better calculate monetary damages, or to determine the scope of use or disclosure that a trade secret was subjected to in a given timeframe. While parties in litigation may resort to discovery tools to gain a lot of this same information, an order for an accounting may be more thorough than what can be easily gained through discovery, and the costs of the accounting may be charged against the defendant, which is a significant advantage over normal discovery techniques.

The model Trade Secrets Act provides as follows with regard to injunctions:

SECTION 2. INJUNCTIVE RELIEF.

(a) Actual or threatened misappropriation may be enjoined. Upon application to the court, an injunction shall be terminated when the trade secret has ceased to exist, but the injunction may be continued for an additional reasonable period of time in order to eliminate commercial advantage that otherwise would be derived from the misappropriation.

(b) In exceptional circumstances, an injunction may condition future use upon payment of a reasonable royalty for no longer than the period of time for which use could have been prohibited. Exceptional circumstances include, but are not limited to, a material and prejudicial change of position prior to acquiring knowledge or reason to know of misappropriation that renders a prohibitive injunction inequitable.

(c) In appropriate circumstances, affirmative acts to protect a trade secret may be compelled by court order.

COMMENT

Injunctions restraining future use and disclosure of misappropriated trade secrets frequently are sought. Although punitive perpetual injunctions have been granted, *e.g., Elcor Chemical Corp. v. Agri-Sul, Inc.,* 494 S.W.2d 204 (Tex.Civ.App.1973), Section 2(a) of this Act adopts the position of the trend of authority limiting the duration of injunctive relief to the extent of the temporal advantage over good faith competitors gained by a misappropriator. See, *e.g., K-2 Ski Co. v. Head Ski Co., Inc.,* 506 F.2d 471 (CA9, 1974) (maximum appropriate duration of both temporary and permanent injunctive relief is period of time it would have taken defendant to discover trade secrets lawfully through either independent development or reverse engineering of plaintiff's products).

The general principle of Section 2(a) and (b) is that an injunction should last for as long as is necessary, but no longer than is necessary, to eliminate the commercial advantage or "lead time" with respect to good faith competitors that a person has obtained through misappropriation. Subject to any additional period of restraint necessary to negate lead time, an injunction accordingly should terminate when a former trade secret becomes either generally known to good faith competitors or generally knowable to them because of the lawful availability of products that can be reverse engineered to reveal a trade secret.

For example, assume that A has a valuable trade secret of which B and C, the other industry members, are originally unaware. If B subsequently misappropriates the trade secret and is enjoined from use, but C later lawfully reverse engineers the trade secret, the injunction restraining B is subject to termination as soon as B's lead time has been dissipated. All of the persons who could derive economic value from use of the information are now aware of it, and there is no longer a trade secret under Section 1(4). It would be anti-competitive to continue to restrain B after any lead time that B had derived from misappropriation had been removed.

If a misappropriator either has not taken advantage of lead time or good faith competitors already have caught up with a misappropriator at the time that a case is decided, future disclosure and use of a former trade secret by a misappropriator will not damage a trade secret owner and no injunctive restraint of future disclosure and use is appropriate. See, *e.g., Northern Petrochemical Co. v. Tomlinson*, 484 F.2d 1057 (CA7, 1973) (affirming trial court's denial of preliminary injunction in part because an explosion at its plant prevented an alleged misappropriator from taking advantage of lead time); *Kubik, Inc. v. Hull*, 185 USPQ 391 (Mich.App.1974) (discoverability of trade secret by lawful reverse engineering made by injunctive relief punitive rather than compensatory).

Section 2(b) deals with a distinguishable the special situation in which future use by a misappropriator will damage a trade secret owner but an injunction against future use nevertheless is unreasonable under the particular inappropriate due to exceptional circumstances of a case. Exceptional circumstances include the existence of an overriding public interest which requires the denial of a prohibitory injunction against future damaging use and a person's reasonable reliance upon acquisition of a misappropriated trade secret in good faith and without reason to know of its prior misappropriation that would be prejudiced by a prohibitory injunction against future damaging use. *Republic Aviation Corp. v. Schenk*, 152 USPQ 830 (N.Y.Sup.Ct.1967) illustrates the public interest justification for withholding prohibitory injunctive relief. The court considered that enjoining a misappropriator from supplying the U.S. with an aircraft weapons control system would have endangered military personnel in Viet Nam. The prejudice to a good faith third party justification for withholding prohibitory injunctive relief can arise upon a trade secret owner's notification to a good faith third party that the third party has knowledge of a trade secret as a result of misappropriation by another. This notice suffices to make the third party a misappropriator thereafter under Section 1(2)(ii)(B)(I). In weighing an aggrieved person's interests and the interests of a third party who has relied in good faith upon his or her ability to utilize information, a court may conclude that restraining future use of the information by the third party is unwarranted. With respect to innocent acquirers of misappropriated trade secrets, Section 2(b) is consistent with the principle of 4 Restatement Torts (First) § 758(b) (1939), but rejects the Restatement's literal conferral of absolute immunity upon all third parties who have paid value in good faith for a trade secret misappropriated by another. The position taken by the Uniform Act is supported by *Forest Laboratories, Inc. v. Pillsbury Co.*, 452 F.2d 621 (CA7, 1971) in which a defendant's purchase of assets of a corporation to which a trade secret had been disclosed in confidence was not considered to confer immunity upon the defendant.

When Section 2(b) applies, a court is given has discretion to substitute an injunction conditioning future use upon payment of a reasonable royalty for an injunction prohibiting future use. Like all injunctive relief for misappropriation, a royalty order injunction is appropriate only if a misappropriator has obtained a competitive advantage through misappropriation and only for the duration of that competitive advantage. In some situations, typically those involving good faith acquirers of trade secrets misappropriated by others, a court may conclude that the same considerations that render a prohibitory injunction against future use inappropriate also render a royalty order injunction inappropriate. See, generally, *Prince Manufacturing, Inc. v. Automatic Partner, Inc.*, 198 USPQ 618 (N.J.Super.Ct.1976) (purchaser of misappropriator's assets from receiver after trade secret disclosed to public through sale of product not subject to liability for misappropriation).

A royalty order injunction under Section 2(b) should be distinguished from a reasonable royalty alternative measure of damages under Section 3(a). See the Comment to Section 3 for discussion of the differences in the remedies.

Section 2(c) authorizes mandatory injunctions requiring that a misappropriator return the fruits of misappropriation to an aggrieved person, *e.g.,* the return of stolen blueprints or the surrender of surreptitious photographs or recordings.

Where more than one person is entitled to trade secret protection with respect to the same information, only that one from whom misappropriation occurred is entitled to a remedy.

32.2. Monetary Remedies

While non-monetary remedies are most important to "stop the bleeding" in a trade secret case, monetary damages are what makes an injured plaintiff whole. Many trade secret cases arise from situations involving license agreements or non-compete agreements, and those documents may specific an amount of *liquidated damages,* that may be recovered in the event of a breach. Given how hard it is to accurately determine what the real damages are in a trade secret case, many parties will agree that a reasonable estimate of those damages, made in advance, will be awarded in the event of a breach. These are called liquidated damages, and they may be totally inaccurate in practice. As license agreements and non-compete agreements are most often drafted by the owner of a trade secret, the liquidated damages provisions are often inflated to benefit the owner in the event of a minor breach. Predicting actual damages in order to make a good faith liquidated damages provision is almost impossible, as the extent of the breach and the resulting harm are unknown.

The Trade Secret Act provides the following with respect to damages:

SECTION 3. DAMAGES.

(a) Except to the extent that a material and prejudicial change of position prior to acquiring knowledge or reason to know of misappropriation renders a monetary recovery inequitable, a complainant is entitled to recover damages for misappropriation. Damages can include both the actual loss caused by misappropriation and the unjust enrichment caused by misappropriation that is not taken into account in computing actual loss. In lieu of damages measured by any other methods, the damages caused by misappropriation may be measured by imposition of liability for a reasonable royalty for a misappropriator's unauthorized disclosure or use of a trade secret.

(b) If willful and malicious misappropriation exists, the court may award exemplary damages in an amount not exceeding twice any award made under subsection (a).

COMMENT

Like injunctive relief, a monetary recovery for trade secret misappropriation is appropriate only for the period in which information is entitled to protection as a trade secret, plus the additional period, if any, in which a misappropriator retains an advantage over good faith competitors because of misappropriation. Actual damage to a complainant and unjust benefit to a misappropriator are caused by misappropriation during this time alone. See *Conmar Products Corp. v. Universal Slide Fastener Co.*, 172 F.2d 150 (CA2, 1949) (no remedy for period subsequent to disclosure of trade secret by issued patent); *Carboline Co. v. Jarboe*, 454 S.W.2d 540 (Mo.1970) (recoverable monetary relief limited to period that it would have taken misappropriator to discover trade secret without misappropriation). A claim for actual damages and net profits can be combined with a claim for injunctive relief, but, if both claims are granted, the injunctive relief ordinarily will preclude a monetary award for a period in which the injunction is effective.

As long as there is no double counting, Section 3(a) adopts the principle of the recent cases allowing recovery of both a complainant's actual losses and a misappropriator's unjust benefit that are caused by misappropriation. *E.g., Tri-Tron International v. Velto*, 525 F.2d 432 (CA9, 1975) (complainant's loss and misappropriator's benefit can be combined). Because certain cases may have sanctioned double counting in a combined award of losses and unjust benefit, *e.g., Telex Corp. v. IBM Corp.*, 510 F.2d 894 (CA10, 1975) (per curiam), cert. dismissed, 423 U.S. 802 (1975) (IBM recovered rentals lost due to displacement by misappropriator's products without deduction for expenses saved by displacement; as a result of rough approximations adopted by the trial judge, IBM also may have recovered developmental costs saved by misappropriator through misappropriation with respect to the same customers), the Act adopts an express prohibition upon the counting of the same item as both a loss to a complainant and an unjust benefit to a misappropriator.

As an alternative to all other methods of measuring damages caused by a misappropriator's past conduct, a complainant can request that damages be based upon a demonstrably reasonable royalty for a misappropriator's unauthorized disclosure or use of a trade secret. In order to justify this alternative measure of damages, there must be competent evidence of the amount of a reasonable royalty.

The reasonable royalty alternative measure of damages for a misappropriator's past conduct under Section 3(a) is readily distinguishable from a Section 2(b) royalty order injunction, which conditions a misappropriator's future ability to use a trade secret upon payment of a reasonable royalty. A Section 2(b) royalty order injunction is appropriate only in exceptional circumstances; whereas a reasonable royalty measure of damages is a general option. Because Section 3(a) damages are awarded for a misappropriator's past conduct and a Section 2(b) royalty order injunction regulates a misappropriator's future conduct, both remedies cannot be awarded for the same conduct. If a royalty order injunction is appropriate because of a person's material and prejudicial change of position prior to having reason to know that a trade secret has been acquired from a misappropriator, damages, moreover, should not be awarded for past conduct that occurred prior to notice that a misappropriated trade secret has been acquired.

Monetary relief can be appropriate whether or not injunctive relief is granted under Section 2. If a person charged with misappropriation has acquired materially and prejudicially changed position in reliance upon knowledge of a trade secret acquired in good faith and without reason to know of its misappropriation by another, however, the same considerations that can justify denial of all injunctive relief also can justify denial of all monetary relief. See *Conmar Products Corp. v. Universal Slide Fastener Co.*, 172 F.2d 1950 (CA2, 1949) (no relief against new employer of employee subject to contractual obligation not to disclose former employer's trade secrets where new employer innocently had committed $40,000 to develop the trade secrets prior to notice of misappropriation).

If willful and malicious misappropriation is found to exist, Section 3(b) authorizes the court to award a complainant exemplary damages in addition to the actual recovery under Section 3(a) an amount not exceeding twice that recovery. This provision follows federal patent law in leaving discretionary trebling to the judge even though there may be a jury, *compare* 35 U.S.C. Section 284 (1976).

Whenever more than one person is entitled to trade secret protection with respect to the same information, only that one from whom misappropriation occurred is entitled to a remedy.

License agreements and non-compete agreements may also specify that the successful party in court shall recover her reasonable attorney's fees. Even where the applicable law would not provide such a remedy, most jurisdictions allow contracts to provide for it and it will be enforced. With regard to attorney's fees, the Trade Secret Act states as follows:

SECTION 4. ATTORNEY'S FEES.

If (i) a claim of misappropriation is made in bad faith, (ii) a motion to terminate an injunction is made or resisted in bad faith, or (iii) willful and malicious misappropriation exists, the court may award reasonable attorney's fees to the prevailing party.

COMMENT

Section 4 allows a court to award reasonable attorney fees to a prevailing party in specified circumstances as a deterrent to specious claims of misappropriation, to specious efforts by a misappropriator to terminate injunctive relief, and to willful and malicious misappropriation. In the latter situation, the court should take into consideration the extent to which a complainant will recover exemplary damages in determining whether additional attorney's fees should be awarded. Again, patent law is followed in allowing the judge to determine whether attorney's fees should be awarded even if there is a jury, *compare* 35 U.S.C. Section 285 (1976).

32.3. Criminal Penalties

Most trade secret cases are resolved through the civil litigation process, where rapid injunctions are available and where civil monetary damages will usually make a plaintiff whole again. In rarer instances, these cases may involve criminal prosecution. Given that many trade secret cases involve allegations of theft or fraud or both, it is unclear why so few of these cases involve criminal charges. As many trade secret cases arise from alleged breaches of confidentiality, nondisclosure, and non-compete agreements, perhaps there has been a historical bias toward resolving these cases as purely civil matters like basic breach of contract cases. The relevant federal criminal laws, described below, often seem like overkill or a stretch to fit the facts of what many describe as civil business disputes. Despite this, individual state statutes have evolved to provide criminal penalties in common trade secret misappropriation scenarios, and their use is on the rise. Particularly in blatant cases of trade secret theft, criminal penalties are becoming a major factor in trade secret protection.

Economic Espionage Act

The *Economic Espionage Act*, 18 U.S.C. §§ 1831–1839, makes trade secret theft or misappropriation a federal crime. This is probably the most relevant and direct federal statute regarding trade secret protection, as the other federal laws that offer criminal penalties are typically aimed at other broad types of crime and only protect trade secrets incidentally. The Economic Espionage Act provides criminal penalties for theft of trade secrets to benefit foreign powers under one section, and penalties for theft of trade secrets for domestic commercial or economic purposes under another section. The Act makes it clear that, although criminal penalties are available, it is not the intent of Congress to make every trade secrets case a criminal matter:

> The [Electronic Espionage Act] is not intended to criminalize every theft of trade secrets for which civil remedies may exist under state law. It was passed in recognition of the increasing importance of the

value of intellectual property in general, and trade secrets in particular to the economic well-being and security of the United States and to close a federal enforcement gap in this important area of law. Appropriate discretionary factors to be considered in deciding whether to initiate a prosecution under § 1831 or § 1832 include:

(a) the scope of the criminal activity, including evidence of involvement by a foreign government, foreign agent or foreign instrumentality;
(b) the degree of economic injury to the trade secret owner;
(c) the type of trade secret misappropriated;
(d) the effectiveness of available civil remedies; and
(e) the potential deterrent value of the prosecution.

The availability of a civil remedy should not be the only factor considered in evaluating the merits of a referral because the victim of a trade secret theft almost always has recourse to a civil action. The universal application of this factor would thus defeat the Congressional intent in passing the [Electronic Espionage Act].

The Electronic Espionage Act criminalizes trade secret misappropriation, conspiracy to misappropriate, and subsequent acquisition of misappropriated trade secrets, with knowledge or intent to benefit a foreign power. Penalties for violation include fines up to $500,000.00 per offense and imprisonment of up to fifteen years for individuals, and fines of up to $10,000,000.00 for organizations. The Act also criminalizes misappropriation of trade secrets in the context of interstate commerce with knowledge or intent that the misappropriation will injure the owner of the trade secret. Individual penalties include up to five years' imprisonment and organizations may face fines up to $5,000,000.00. The Act requires courts to order criminal forfeiture of any profits generated by the misappropriator, and to make orders as needed to protect the secrecy of the trade secrets involved.

Computer Fraud and Abuse Act and the Racketeer Influenced & Corrupt Organizations Act

The *Computer Fraud and Abuse Act*, 18 U.S.C. § 1030, and the *Racketeer Influenced & Corrupt Organizations Act*, 18 U.S.C. § 1962, both offer some criminal penalties applicable to trade secret cases. Unlike the Electronic Espionage Act, these acts are intended to protect against and punish a much broader array of crimes, and they offer trade secret protection incidentally. As a result of this incidental coverage, many courts are unwilling to entertain overreaching charges in garden variety trade secret cases where the heavy criminal penalties involved may seem grossly disproportionate to the activity at issue, especially where a civil injunction has effectively prevented any real hard to the trade secret owner.

The Computer Fraud and Abuse Act covers a very wide array of crimes committed using computers. Given how common computers are in business, and the high likelihood that a computer would be involved in any given trade secret case, either by accessing trade secrets on a computer, emailing those secrets, storing them on a computer, etc., the Act will apply in most cases, regardless of Congress' intent to limit the scope of application to a specific set of crimes. The Racketeer Influenced & Corrupt Organizations Act is similarly broad, as it was designed to prosecute organized criminals engaged in activity that would fall through loopholes in existing criminal laws. The intent to make this Act as broad as possible has led to its use in many unexpected and creative ways. As the penalties available are aimed at punishing dangerous organized criminals, they are often viewed as potentially excessive in common trade secret litigation. As a result, this Act is rarely used to prosecute trade secret offenders, especially where more specific and balanced state criminal laws are available.

Chapter Summary

There are a wide variety of remedies available for trade secret misappropriation. The appropriate choice will depend on the circumstances of each case, but the civil injunction is the primary tool to prevent disclosure and stop any offending activity. Injunctions are extremely flexible remedies, and they may be ordered almost immediately at the start of a case and they may be extended permanently once a case has been resolved on the merits. There are adequate civil damages available to make the plaintiff whole, and there are state and federal criminal statutes in place for blatant or particularly harmful or deliberate cases. The majority of criminal prosecutions proceed under individual state laws, which vary significantly from state to state, and state criminal enforcement of trade secret rights has become more prevalent in recent years.

Key Terms

Injunction
Ex Parte
Temporary Restraining Order

Preliminary Injunction
Permanent Injunction
Accounting
Liquidated Damages
Economic Espionage Act
Computer Fraud and Abuse Act
Racketeer Influenced & Corrupt Organizations Act

Review Questions

1. What is the difference between a temporary restraining order and a preliminary injunction?
2. Under what circumstances can a defendant have an injunction dissolved?
3. What is the purpose of liquidated damages?
4. What kinds of criminal penalties are available under the Electronic Espionage Act?

Web Links

1. http://tsi.brooklaw.edu/category/legal-basis-trade-secret-claims/economic-espionage-act—A collection of case summaries regarding trade secret protection under the Electronic Espionage Act.

Discussion Exercise

1. Why should there be any hesitation to bring criminal charges against defendants accused of trade secret theft? Why do we view committing trade secret theft differently than stealing a car or committing a burglary?

Chapter 33

International Aspects of Trade Secret Law

"No treaty is ever an impediment to a cheat."—Sophocles

Chapter Outline

Chapter Objectives

* Learn how the TRIPS Agreement protects trade secrets internationally.
* Understand the procedural and administrative requirements imposed by TRIPS.

The *Agreement on Trade Related Aspects of Intellectual Property Rights* (TRIPS) provides the backbone of international trade secret protection. While each member country may have significantly different laws and procedures for protecting trade secrets, TRIPS establishes certain minimal standards. National treatment, discussed previously, is key, but there are specific provisions under TRIPS for the protection and procedure to be used in cases of trade secret, or *"undisclosed information."*

33.1. Agreement on Trade Related Aspects of Intellectual Property Rights

The TRIPS Agreement requires undisclosed information, which are essentially trade secrets, to benefit from protection pursuant to Article 39. Protection applies to information that is secret, that has commercial value because it is secret, and that has been subject to reasonable steps to keep it secret. The Agreement does not require undisclosed information to be treated as a form of property, but it does require that a person lawfully in control of undisclosed information must have the possibility of preventing it from being disclosed to, acquired by, or used by others without his or her consent in a manner contrary to honest commercial practices. Such practices include breach of contract, breach of confidence and inducement to breach, as well as the acquisition of undisclosed information by third parties who knew, or were grossly negligent in failing to know, that such practices were involved in the acquisition.

The Agreement also contains provisions to protect undisclosed test data and other data required to be submitted to governments as a condition of approving pharmaceuticals or chemical products. Member governments must protect such data against unfair commercial use and protect it against disclosure, except where necessary to protect the public. The relevant provisions of the TRIPS Agreement pertaining to protection of trade secrets and administrative requirements follow.

Article 39

1. In the course of ensuring effective protection against unfair competition as provided in Article 10 of the Paris Convention (1967), Members shall protect undisclosed information in accordance with paragraph 2 and data submitted to governments or governmental agencies in accordance with paragraph 3.

2. Natural and legal persons shall have the possibility of preventing information lawfully within their control from being disclosed to, acquired by, or used by others without their consent in a manner contrary to honest commercial practices so long as such information:

(a) is secret in the sense that it is not, as a body or in the precise configuration and assembly of its components, generally known among or readily accessible to persons within the circles that normally deal with the kind of information in question;

(b) has commercial value because it is secret; and

(c) has been subject to reasonable steps under the circumstances, by the person lawfully in control of the information, to keep it secret.

3. Members, when requiring, as a condition of approving the marketing of pharmaceutical or of agricultural chemical products which utilize new chemical entities, the submission of undisclosed test or other data, the origination of which involves a considerable effort,

shall protect such data against unfair commercial use. In addition, Members shall protect such data against disclosure, except where necessary to protect the public, or unless steps are taken to ensure that the data are protected against unfair commercial use.

Article 41

1. Members shall ensure that enforcement procedures as specified in this Part are available under their law so as to permit effective action against any act of infringement of intellectual property rights covered by this Agreement, including expeditious remedies to prevent infringements and remedies which constitute a deterrent to further infringements. These procedures shall be applied in such a manner as to avoid the creation of barriers to legitimate trade and to provide for safeguards against their abuse.

2. Procedures concerning the enforcement of intellectual property rights shall be fair and equitable. They shall not be unnecessarily complicated or costly, or entail unreasonable time-limits or unwarranted delays.

3. Decisions on the merits of a case shall preferably be in writing and reasoned. They shall be made available at least to the parties to the proceeding without undue delay. Decisions on the merits of a case shall be based only on evidence in respect of which parties were offered the opportunity to be heard.

4. Parties to a proceeding shall have an opportunity for review by a judicial authority of final administrative decisions and, subject to jurisdictional provisions in a Member's law concerning the importance of a case, of at least the legal aspects of initial judicial decisions on the merits of a case. However, there shall be no obligation to provide an opportunity for review of acquittals in criminal cases.

5. It is understood that this Part does not create any obligation to put in place a judicial system for the enforcement of intellectual property rights distinct from that for the enforcement of law in general, nor does it affect the capacity of Members to enforce their law in general. Nothing in this Part creates any obligation with respect to the distribution of resources as between enforcement of intellectual property rights and the enforcement of law in general.

Article 42

Members shall make available to right holders civil judicial procedures concerning the enforcement of any intellectual property right covered by this Agreement. Defendants shall have the right to written notice which is timely and contains sufficient detail, including the basis of the claims. Parties shall be allowed to be represented by independent legal counsel, and procedures shall not impose overly burdensome requirements concerning mandatory personal appearances. All parties to such procedures shall be duly entitled to substantiate their claims and to present all relevant evidence. The procedure shall provide a means to identify and protect confidential information, unless this would be contrary to existing constitutional requirements.

Article 43

1. The judicial authorities shall have the authority, where a party has presented reasonably available evidence sufficient to support its claims and has specified evidence relevant to substantiation of its claims which lies in the control of the opposing party, to order that this evidence be produced by the opposing party, subject in appropriate cases to conditions which ensure the protection of confidential information.

2. In cases in which a party to a proceeding voluntarily and without good reason refuses access to, or otherwise does not provide necessary information within a reasonable period, or significantly impedes a procedure relating to an enforcement action, a Member may accord judicial authorities the authority to make preliminary and final determinations, affirmative or negative, on the basis of the information presented to them, including the complaint or the allegation presented by the party adversely affected by the denial of access to information, subject to providing the parties an opportunity to be heard on the allegations or evidence.

Article 44

1. The judicial authorities shall have the authority to order a party to desist from an infringement, *inter alia* to prevent the entry into the channels of commerce in their jurisdiction of imported goods that involve the infringement of an intellectual property right, immediately after customs clearance of such goods. Members are not obliged to

accord such authority in respect of protected subject matter acquired or ordered by a person prior to knowing or having reasonable grounds to know that dealing in such subject matter would entail the infringement of an intellectual property right.

2. Notwithstanding the other provisions of this Part and provided that the provisions of Part II specifically addressing use by governments, or by third parties authorized by a government, without the authorization of the right holder are complied with, Members may limit the remedies available against such use to payment of remuneration in accordance with subparagraph (h) of Article 31. In other cases, the remedies under this Part shall apply or, where these remedies are inconsistent with a Member's law, declaratory judgments and adequate compensation shall be available.

Article 45

1. The judicial authorities shall have the authority to order the infringer to pay the right holder damages adequate to compensate for the injury the right holder has suffered because of an infringement of that person's intellectual property right by an infringer who knowingly, or with reasonable grounds to know, engaged in infringing activity.

2. The judicial authorities shall also have the authority to order the infringer to pay the right holder expenses, which may include appropriate attorney's fees. In appropriate cases, Members may authorize the judicial authorities to order recovery of profits and/or payment of pre-established damages even where the infringer did not knowingly, or with reasonable grounds to know, engage in infringing activity.

Chapter Summary

International protection of trade secrets has garnered somewhat less attention than international protection of patents, trademarks, and copyrights. This makes sense historically, as each country has developed its own form of trade secret protection, and the essence of trade secret is the maintenance of secrecy, which results in less need for complex legislation than intellectual property that must be made public in order to gain benefit and protection. If a patented device is not protected internationally, for example, it would be extremely easy for a foreign competitor to view the detailed patent application and reproduce the device. Trade secrets, being secret, are inherently more resistant to this type of problem. However, the TRIPS Agreement recognizes that some level of international protection must be available where trade secrets have been unfairly disclosed or used in competition. The need for these protections has increased as technology has made it easier to share large amounts of information quickly and globally, and the international nature of industry has increased the opportunities for unscrupulous people to profit from unfairly using trade secrets abroad.

Key Terms

Agreement on Trade Related Aspects of Intellectual Property Rights
Undisclosed Information

Review Questions

1. What types of remedies are available for trade secret misappropriation pursuant to TRIPS?
2. How must governments protect test data they require for chemical or pharmaceutical applications?

Web Links

1. http://www.wto.org/english/docs_e/legal_e/27-trips_01_e.htm—A gateway to TRIPS information, including information on trade secret protection, hosted by the World Intellectual Property Organization.

Discussion Exercise

1. How does the definition of undisclosed information provided in Article 39 of the TRIPS Agreement differ from the definitions of trade secret provided earlier in this book?

About the Authors

Michael E. Jones is a professor and director of the Legal Studies Program at the University of Massachusetts Lowell. He is well recognized as an expert in copyright law issues for visual artists. Professor Jones authored the award-winning text, *Sports Law*, and co-edited with his wife, Christine, the art book, *Timeless: Photography of Rowland Scherman*. He also served as a trial court judge for more than twenty years, and is a professional fine artist who created images for the last three summer Olympic Games.

Walter J. Toomey teaches in the Legal Studies Program at the University of Massachusetts Lowell, where he serves as a full-time lecturer. His courses include Intellectual Property Law, Cyber Law, and Business Law. His private law practice has included business and employment matters, including trade secret management and litigation of trade secret disputes, software and IP licensing, and the drafting and litigation of noncompetition, non-solicitation and non-disclosure agreements.

M. Nancy Aiken is an adjunct professor in the Legal Studies Program at the University of Massachusetts Lowell where she teaches Intellectual Property Law, Real Estate Law, Introduction to Legal Concepts, and Immigration Law. In private practice, Nancy has represented and counseled clients in commercial matters involving intellectual property, corporate transactions and commercial real estate. She has also represented brokerage firms in securities litigation and arbitration. Nancy is barred in Massachusetts, New York, and North Carolina.

Michelle Bazin teaches in the Legal Studies Program at the University of Massachusetts Lowell where she serves as a full-time lecturer. She has practiced business and transactional law in Colorado, New York and Massachusetts. She has filed for trademark and trade name registration and protection for her business clients and provided advice on trademark and copyright law issues.

Index